Saving the Neighborhood

Saving the Neighborhood

Racially Restrictive Covenants, Law, and Social Norms

Richard R. W. Brooks
Carol M. Rose

Harvard University Press • Cambridge, Massachusetts, and London, England • 2013

Library of Congress Cataloging-in-Publication Data

Brooks, Richard Rexford Wayne.
Saving the neighborhood : racially restrictive covenants, law, and social norms / Richard Brooks and Carol Rose.
pages cm
Includes bibliographical references and index.
ISBN 978-0-674-07254-1
1. Real covenants—United States. 2. Discrimination in housing—Law and legislation—United States. I. Rose, Carol M., 1940– II. Title.
KF662.B76 2013
346.7304'36—dc23 2012034463

To Trudy Travers, a pioneer and game-changer;
and to the memory of two norm breakers,
with their own stubborn understandings of the American Dream,
Carl Hansberry and Raphael Urciolo;
and to the writer Rose Helper, wherever she may be,
whose measured prose still scorches the page.

Contents

Saving the Neighborhood

Introduction

Recalling Racialized Property

In the summer of 1986, an embarrassing fact came to light about conservative jurist William Rehnquist, then an associate justice on the U.S. Supreme Court. Rehnquist had been nominated by President Ronald Reagan to become chief justice of the Court, and during his confirmation hearings before the Senate Judiciary Committee, a routine background check unearthed a decades-old deed restriction on the Vermont summer house that Rehnquist had purchased in 1974. The restriction purported to exclude anyone of the "Hebrew race."

Another embarrassing deed restriction came to light as well, this one dating back to 1929, on a house that Rehnquist had purchased in Phoenix in 1961 and sold a few years later. The racial covenant on that house would have barred sale or rental by "any person not of the White or Caucasian race," a code phrase often used for African Americans and sometimes Asians. When Rehnquist's opponents hinted that these transactions showed the justice's insensitivity to racial issues, his conservative defenders dug up the information that Democratic Senator Joseph Biden (then a member of the Senate Judiciary Committee and later vice president in the Obama administration) as well as deceased President John F. Kennedy had also owned or lived in residences with racially restrictive covenants.[1]

Rehnquist himself claimed that he had not known about these old restrictions or had forgotten about them, and he promised to take steps to get rid of the restriction on his Vermont house, which he still owned.

He observed, though, that covenants of this sort could not be enforced and were thus, in his words, "meaningless."[2]

Rehnquist was right that these covenants no longer had any legal effect, and he was probably right that he had not thought much about them even if he knew of them when he bought the properties. By the 1980s, covenants of this sort seemed to most people to be at most a dimly recalled remnant of past prejudices. In Vermont, one of Rehnquist's Jewish neighbors was startled to find out about the antisemitic restriction, and wondered whether there was a similar restriction on her own property. But Rehnquist's experience suggested that the restrictions were not entirely meaningless. Though lacking any legal effect, old restrictions in the records had a feeble but persistent life of their own. They could still convey information and create inferences about owners and neighborhoods, however anachronistic those inferences might become at a later time. Political opponents could still use those inferences to demand an explanation—as they were to do at Rehnquist's confirmation, and as they were to do again over a decade later. In January 1999, on the occasion when Chief Justice Rehnquist was sworn in to preside at the impeachment trial of President Bill Clinton, *New York Times* columnist Bob Herbert reminded his readers that Rehnquist had purchased the two properties, racial restrictions and all.[3] But then, of course, so had many other prominent figures of all political stripes.

What are these racially restrictive covenants? Why have they continued to float up from time to time as singularly unpleasant ghosts of the past, especially now that no one seems to take them very seriously anymore? The short answer is that racially restrictive covenants were once a standard part of real estate transactions in the United States, and American recording practices make them quite difficult to eradicate, whether they are legal or not. The longer answer is the subject of this book, which will use the legal history of racially restrictive covenants—particularly as applied to African Americans, where persistent litigation has created a rich legal source—to explore the ways that racially restrictive covenants expressed social norms, and the ways that those social norms have related to legal norms, together facilitating patterns of residential racial segregation that long outlived these once technically legal devices.[4]

As a matter of legal history, racial covenants had a distinct arc. Developers of high-end urban residential areas began to use them regularly in the early years of the twentieth century. In the new urban subdivisions, racial covenants were only one part in the packages of deed restrictions that developers deployed to control such matters as construction styles and land uses. But in those early days, courts in the United States understood traditional property law to be quite chary of any private arrangements that purported to control land uses over long periods of time—and that chariness included racial covenants. Nevertheless, by the 1920s, the courts began to relax their earlier strictures about all kinds of residential restrictions, including the racial ones. Thereafter racially restrictive covenants spread through both newer subdivisions and older urban neighborhoods. Constitutional law seemed to offer no limitations, since real estate covenants were thought to be merely private arrangements, and hence not subject to the constitutional limitations on discrimination by governmental bodies.

This pattern of acceptance received an abrupt shock in 1948, when the U.S. Supreme Court decided the landmark case, *Shelley v. Kraemer*,[5] ruling that any court that enforced racial covenants violated the equal protection clause of the Fourteenth Amendment to the U.S. Constitution. Surprisingly, racial covenants of one sort and another continued to be written into title documents, until they were finally flatly outlawed by the Fair Housing Act of 1968. Even after that act, however, old racial covenants were still in the record books, and they appeared in title searches and deeds copied from earlier documents, as in Justice Rehnquist's case, however much they might be ignored by all concerned.

The historical arc of racially restrictive covenants—judicial suspicion, followed by relaxation, followed by the *Shelley* case and the denial of legal enforcement, followed by continuing but unenforceable covenants, followed by illegality, and followed finally by general but not complete indifference—suggests a unique topic for investigating the relationship between social norms and law. With that topic in mind, let us briefly reconsider this historical arc in the context of racial covenants that aimed to exclude African Americans.

Throughout the first half of the twentieth century and beyond, many white persons in urban areas in the United States preferred to avoid living near African Americans (with the telling exception of servants), and they preferred that their neighbors not sell or rent to African Americans either. This very strong set of preferences created both an internal and an external issue about the implicit rules that would govern their behavior. Internally, the white neighbors needed to control one another's sales and rentals. Externally, they needed to stave off entry by unwanted minorities.

White neighbors could and did use what we euphemistically call "informal" methods to exclude racial minorities, including anything from polite warnings through threats to physical violence. Indeed, the most cohesive working class white neighborhoods were less likely to use formal racial covenants at all to enforce segregation; in many instances, informal enforcement was more than sufficient. But not every white neighborhood was so willing to rely exclusively on threats and violence. In a sense, racial covenants were a formal legal substitute for the more vigorous and potentially vicious informal means used by more closely knit social groups. Like real estate covenants of all kinds, racial covenants were supposed to "run with the land," binding future owners as well as the original signatories; thus they were intended to have staying power for a neighborhood and to repel entry by unwanted new residents. We will argue that in addition, one of the chief functions of racial covenants was to provide a kind of formal normative node around which more loosely knit communities could organize their resistance to entry by other racial groups.

As we shall see in later chapters, covenants were only one of several legal devices that might have assisted the white neighbors in their resistance to minority encroachment. But for various reasons, the alternative legal devices all fell away by about 1920. What was left as a formal, legal route to enforce residential segregation was the use of racially restrictive covenants. These flourished in new subdivisions and urban neighborhoods in the next few decades, powerfully encouraged by real estate professionals, banking institutions, and an array of other institutions, including perhaps most importantly the New Deal's Federal Housing Administration.

But uneasiness about racial restrictions also grew in this period. The pressure came from four major sources. Foremost was the sheer expansion of minority populations in American cities during and after the First World War, and especially during the Second World War, when overcrowding and ghettoization became increasingly alarming. Second, a larger public opinion grew wary of racial restrictions in light of the Nazi and fascist actions in Europe, again especially during and after the Second World War, in which many minority citizens fought, and some died, in service to the United States. Third was the postwar emergence of the Cold War, during which the legal segregation of residential neighborhoods became a profound embarrassment for American foreign policy. Finally, and fanning the discontent produced by all the other factors, was a steady drumbeat of anticovenant litigation spearheaded by the National Association for the Advancement of Colored People (NAACP).

When *Shelley* was decided in 1948, the NAACP and others had high hopes that the denial of racial covenants' legal enforceability would usher in an era of residential integration. This did not occur. Instead, white flight became the new vehicle of segregation. What is more surprising, the *Shelley* case did not even put an end to the now-unenforceable racial covenants. The Federal Housing Administration, which since its inception had favored racial restrictions in home loans, insured homes in newly covenanted subdivisions for over a year after *Shelley.* Real estate professionals continued for a time to write racial covenants into new deeds, and they continued to refer to racial covenants when selling older covenanted properties.

Why did so little change with respect to covenants? One obvious reason is that white social norms against integration continued. White homeowners had long feared that their properties would lose market value if minorities moved into the neighborhood, and they continued to believe this—and to act on their belief—after the *Shelley* case. Given that set of beliefs, real estate professionals continued to reason that total real estate values would be higher if neighborhoods were segregated racially.

Some developers included racial covenants at least for a few years after *Shelley* because they thought that *Shelley* was so much of an outlier that the case soon would be overturned or sharply limited, and they might as well have racial covenants in place. Still other developers continued to write and copy racial restrictions, not because these restrictions were legally enforceable—and by 1953 a second covenant case in the Supreme Court made it clear that they would not be—but because covenants sent a signal to buyers about the racial preference of their neighbors.

This communicative function of racial covenants will be of special interest in this book. The fact that racial covenants continued to be written after *Shelley* suggests that even before that case, a major function of racial covenants was to allow white neighbors to identify themselves as allies in a preference for segregation and an intention to maintain it, and to signal the same to outsiders. Actual legal enforceability had never mattered as much as civil rights advocates thought. And hence *Shelley*'s denial of legal enforceability did not matter so much either. The case certainly weakened the larger imprimatur on covenants, but it left intact covenants' ability to create among all the relevant parties a common knowledge of the local racial attitudes. Even though the courts would not recognize racial covenants after 1948, these documents could still bolster neighborhoods' sense of the rightness of whiteness, and they could send a message to would-be interlopers. Congress implicitly recognized the power of signals when it outlawed overt information about residential segregation—implicitly including information about covenants—in the Fair Housing Act of 1968.

THE CAST OF CHARACTERS

With that overall story in mind, let us identify some of the features that will be of most interest in this book.

Property claims. The tale of racially restrictive covenants is profoundly a story about property. One way in which property permeates this story is the ever-present mantra of property values. Probably the most consistent reason that people give for wishing to exclude unwanted outsiders is that the outsiders will exert downward pressure on the value of the insiders' homes. As other authors have pointed out, this position is akin to the NIMBY syndrome—the "Not in My Back Yard" attitude that creates pressure to place unwanted land uses somewhere else. Moreover, by referring to property values, individuals can mask their own prejudices: "it's not me, it's the market." On the other hand, their market assessment, sadly enough, has been correct often enough to mean that a concern for property values is not simply a makeweight but rather a powerful motivator, particularly in the case of the many persons for whom the home is the chief asset.[6]

Property permeates the restrictive covenant story in another and less obvious way as well. Property's most fundamental characteristic has often been said to be the right to exclude, a right that serves as a platform for an owner's use, investment, and trade. Through covenants, along with other signals of segregation, white neighbors attempted to establish a form of *collective* ownership, asserting that they informally "owned" the neighborhood as a whole, to the exclusion of nonwhite persons. Insiders were expected to understand and do their parts in maintaining this group property, but outsiders were supposed to get the message too. In the 1920s, '30s, and '40s, racially restrictive covenants were the one legally acceptable means to enforce this scheme of inside-group property. Racial covenants had the advantages that go with formality—written documentation, public recording, legal jargon—all of which would be effective in cajoling the insiders, but just as important, in warning off the outsiders who might be thinking of moving to the neighborhood.

Property law. Legal status gives property claims an especially long reach, both in space and in time. Through legal record systems, owners can effectively tell the world at large of their claims, and they can make their wishes effective on others far into the future—much further, for example, than contracts, which generally only affect the parties immediately involved in any given agreement and are largely unknown to the rest of the world.

Racially restrictive covenants enjoyed the reach and staying power that formal property law provides. But their formal legal status also meant that they were subject to the limits and logic of formal property law. In several ways, those limits and logic should have been distinctly unfriendly to racial restrictions. For example, group property has not fared well in traditional American property law, among other reasons because of the burdens that group property imposes on individual owners and the impediments it causes to new owners and uses. There are exceptions in traditional property law, and a considerable part of the brief legal history of racial covenants revolved around the question of whether those covenants could form a legal exception or not.[7]

But in addition, formal property law is generally hostile to constraints on *who* can own and use property, as opposed to the *uses* that owners or occupants can make. Constraints on land uses can solve problems of spillovers from individual property use, or what economists call externalities (e.g., loud noise or noxious fumes)—activities that affect other people without taking them into account. It smacks of rank prejudice, however, to block certain kinds of *persons* from owning or renting, for no reason other than their personal characteristics. This issue should have been particularly prominent to jurists in the early twentieth century, when many people continued to believe that property ownership would be the vehicle by which former slaves and their descendants would improve their status and become full participants in the larger community.

It is something of a puzzle, then, why courts were willing to allow racial residential restrictions through the property device of covenants running with the land. Although the opportunity was largely bypassed in the first few decades of the twentieth century, formal property law's policing capacity might have been deployed with considerably more bite to curb some of the most egregiously discriminatory forms of residential segregation, especially through covenants. Some scholars and judges seemed to be growing aware of this curbing potential by the 1940s, and we suspect that even if *Shelley* had not been decided on constitutional grounds, courts increasingly would have used traditional property law principles to invalidate racial covenants. The larger point is that formal legal status entailed higher-level limitations on property claims, and thus legality carried risks as well as advantages for white neighbors.

Neighborhoods. As mentioned above, tightly cohesive, less well-to-do neighborhoods often did without racial covenants. These neighborhoods operated through their own norms of exclusion, and they did their own enforcing. The same was true of all-white smaller communities that dotted the countryside, the so-called sundown towns where no black person was supposed to allow the sun to set upon him or her.[8] Racial covenants, on the other hand, seem to have been a by-product of less stable demographics and perhaps a kind of civility, albeit clearly a limited one. At the outset, racial covenants were adopted in more affluent new developments and subdivisions, but throughout their existence, these covenants were most widely used in white neighborhoods where the neighbors were reasonably well off but did not necessarily have particularly strong internal norms among themselves. This more fluid character of covenanted neighborhoods also meant that these neighborhoods were likely to be weaker on enforcement. Going to court is costly both in time and money, and less cohesive neighbors may well have weaker internal leadership for norm enforcement.

Norm entrepreneurs. Some institutions, like the National Association of Real Estate Boards and its local branches, along with the Federal Housing Administration, actively promoted racially restrictive covenants. In Chicago, a city whose history we will observe more closely, venerable institutions like the University of Chicago and the Newberry Library for a time also participated in racial covenants to control the surrounding neighborhoods. In the city of origin of the *Shelley* case, the St. Louis Real Estate Exchange made itself a party to covenants in order to ensure enforcement, largely to protect interior neighborhoods that were buffered by the areas bordering on expanding minority populations. Other persons and organizations were largely norm followers; developers might have no particular interest in segregation, but they wanted to sell houses at the best prices they could get, and many developers thought that housing sales hinged on racial exclusion. But norm followers also reinforced the view that property values depended on segregation.[9]

Norm breakers. Norm breakers are particularly interesting in this tale. Among the most important were organizations representing other normative communities, notably the NAACP, which continually challenged the legality of racial covenants. The nation's major African American newspaper, the *Chicago Defender,* was another strong voice against racial restrictions, deploring their presence and applauding their violation. Some norm breakers were individuals ostensibly driven by idealism, like the black entrepreneur Carl Hansberry, who set off an integration controversy—and imposed considerable hardship on his family—by moving into a residence in a covenanted Chicago neighborhood. Perhaps most poignant were the handful of communities of urban white and black residents who tried, largely unsuccessfully, to stave off real estate interests and to form stable integrated neighborhoods.

Needless to say, most of these norm breakers, from a different perspective, were norm entrepreneurs in a different cause. But an interesting if more ambiguous subset of norm breakers were the individuals motivated by economic opportunity, notably the "panic peddling" or "blockbusting" real estate developers who continually sought weak spots in white neighborhoods, so as to be able to make money by buying cheap from white persons and selling high to minorities. These norm breakers were widely reviled for inflaming racial prejudice, but they had a few defenders as well among minority commentators.

Larger communities. Racial restrictions came under increasing fire as the early twentieth century moved toward its middle decades. The impact of European fascism, the alliances of Jewish and African American organizations, the military service of minorities during the Second World War, the propaganda aspects of the Cold War—all contributed to a climate in which formalized and legal residential segregation seemed increasingly unacceptable. This gradual attitudinal shift gave further encouragement to the norm breakers and raised doubts about the legality of covenants from the perspective of higher principles of law, notably constitutional law, but also—a point not often noted—formal property law itself.

NORMS AND "GAMES"

Since our larger interest in this project is to explore the relationships between informal social norms and legal norms, it is appropriate to take up the topic of norms more specifically. There has been much interest in social norms in legal literature in the last two decades, much of it laudatory to informal norms in close-knit communities, and to the ways in which such communities can order their affairs without formal law.[10]

Our project, however, illustrates that not all social norms are attractive problem-solving mechanisms; some may be odious indeed. This is not a new point. Other scholars have pointed out that criminal groups can also be close-knit communities—with particularly predatory norms. Our project, however, also illustrates another point: that whatever may be the case in close-knit communities, legal devices may be extremely important as signals and focal points for assisting less close-knit communities to organize themselves, whether their projects are laudable or dismaying.

Formal and informal norms. What we mean by norms is a set of preferences that are accompanied by enforcement, whether formal or informal, stringent or mild. For example, as a preference, I might prefer that you not smoke. As a norm, not only do I prefer that you not smoke, but together with some of your other friends, I tease you for smoking; we all wrinkle our noses at the smell of your clothing, and we insist that you go outdoors to smoke. Meanwhile, you, seeking our approbation, comply if you can, in response to these various informal means of enforcement.[11]

In this example, antismoking is an informal norm of the group, enforceable informally even against those who would like to smoke but who also respect the group. On the other hand, there may also be a formal norm against smoking, even a legal norm, for example a rule against smoking in a public building. This would express a formally enforceable preference for nonsmoking, expressive of the views of a larger community.

A formal norm could assist our smaller group in maintaining our own norm informally. This would not be simply because we could call the building supervisor to enforce the rule. We might indeed be able to do so—after all, residents in big city apartments call the superintendent to tell neighbors to turn down the sound system. But we might not want to do so within an informal group of associates, where standing on our formal rights might seem unfriendly and might undermine group solidarity.

Nevertheless, the formal rule would be an asset because it would reinforce our views of the right thing to do as well as our sense of entitlement; we could remind the nonconformist of the rule, and the reminder alone might suggest that antismoking was not just our idiosyncratic wish but rather a more widely held social value. It is in that sense that formal norms might act as focal points or signals for informal enforcement.[12] Moreover, our logic is that this coordinating function of formal norms should be particularly important for groups that are not well organized and do not have tight and strong communication systems among themselves. The formal rules enable members of such groups to understand their mutual preferences and to coordinate their informal enforcement efforts.

Turning to racially restrictive covenants, these covenants represented a set of formal legal devices, and one of our chief questions is the following: during the period when both constitutional and property law permitted the creation and enforcement of covenants, what did covenants do for the neighbors who deployed them? They were *not* of much use to strongly cohesive neighborhoods, which did not need them in order to understand one another's views and to initiate and coordinate enforcement. But it seems clear that covenants did act in some ways to reinforce informal social norms in more loose-knit communities.

Loose knittedness, so to speak, was an important feature of many communities with racially restrictive covenants. In the case of covenants initiated by developers, the case is clear: there was no community at all prior to the development. There, the developers wrote the racial restrictions that informed new entrants about the behavior and attitudes that would be expected, and that also informed the disfavored would-be purchasers that they were not welcome.

In older urban neighborhoods, where racial covenants emerged after the fact from agreements among the existing neighbors themselves, the case for loose knittedness is somewhat more ambiguous. But the greatest covenant activity appears to have been in middle-class neighborhoods, many of which lacked several characteristics that support close knittedness in the such classic examples as western ranching communities or Maine fishing folk[13]—or rural sundown towns, for that matter. Those close communities often have well-defined physical locations; their residents have lived there for long periods, even generations; they work in the same occupations and many worship in the same churches; many too are related and they observe one another's activities closely; and they are susceptible to informal pressures from one another (e.g., gossip). Some urban neighborhoods indeed share these characteristics. But many do not: neighborhood boundaries are often porous; residents are at least moderately mobile; they work in different occupations and worship at different churches (if at all); and they do not have many relatives nearby and may not know a great deal about one another, much less gossip about one another.

As we shall see, in the neighborhoods that adopted covenants after they were already settled, the residents often acted when it seemed that some were about to defect. Difficulties plagued both the initiation process for these later-adopted racial covenants and their maintenance, and outside organizations were often centrally important both to orchestrate covenant campaigns and to enforce the covenants. Those factors suggest that the neighborhoods that later adopted covenants were generally of a type that needed a boost to maintain their segregated character—unlike the sundown towns and the tight, longstanding, working-class white neighborhoods that did not bother with covenants at all.

In all the neighborhoods covered by covenants—both the new subdivisions and the older, later-adopting areas—the covenants themselves appear to have been more significant as expressive focal points than as legal enforcement devices. One gets this impression from the judicial materials about racial covenants. While racial covenants were widespread in the United States during the first half of the twentieth century, only a handful of states developed a significant group of cases about them; one would have expected more if more people had taken them to court more regularly. To a considerable degree, covenants seem to have operated silently, sending signals both to insiders and to outsiders about who was and who was not wanted.

Moreover, when the signals were not enough, enforcement through the courts was not simply a free good for the conforming enforcers—just as harassment and violence were not free goods in more close-knit communities. It seems clear that at some times, none of the neighbors wanted to bother to undertake a lawsuit or pursue a legal threat very far. On the other hand, informal harassment—while also "expensive" for the enforcers—was significantly cheaper for at least some of them, even in some middle-class neighborhoods. Some of Carl Hansberry's white neighbors in Chicago challenged him in court, but some of them also vandalized his property and harassed his children, tactics that might have been more effective against a less hard-headed man.

Of course, if things seemed hopeless for the white homeowners, they might simply sell and move out, but that move put even more pressure on the remaining neighbors and covenanted neighborhoods. Perhaps that was why in some instances, the collapse of segregation in one white neighborhood frightened and galvanized others, whose owners feared a drop in their property values all the more. In fact, *legal* enforcement of racial covenants may have been most important to the norm-entrepreneurial institutions, which were likely to have reasons of their own for wanting to enforce covenants when some white neighbors wavered. For example, as mentioned above, the St. Louis Real Estate Exchange attempted to encourage and enforce covenants in buffer neighborhoods, so as to protect other neighborhoods that were further away from minority expansion. But to a very considerable degree, once racial transition was underway, covenant enforcement could be contrary to the interests of the covenanted neighborhood itself, whose departing residents had few potential purchasers aside from minority members.

"Games." One way to understand the complex relationships among neighbors in covenanted communities, and between the neighbors and the outsiders whom they hoped to keep out, is to map their situations onto some simple "game" matrices that attempt to capture the strategies that people take in various social situations. All these game matrices are now familiar in legal literature, but it is worth noting that no real-life condition is likely to map perfectly onto any given game; all make simplifying assumptions about self-interest that are clearly unrealistic about the complicated motivations that drive individual human beings. Hence we will refer to the stylized interactions depicted by these games only metaphorically. But with that understanding, we think that understanding these games can be a fruitful way to explore some broad-brush similarities in the ways people behaved with respect to covenants, and the ways that many of us behave in other situations.

There are three common game-theoretic interactions that are particularly relevant to racially restrictive covenants, bearing the conventional names of "Stag Hunt," "Prisoner's Dilemma," and "Hawk/Dove." Because these games may not be known to all our readers, we will spend a few paragraphs explaining them.

Stag Hunt is also known as an "Assurance Game," but the more colorful name derives from an example in Jean-Jacques Rousseau's *Discourse on Inequality.* Rousseau described a situation in which two (or more) persons, or, we might say, players, can do best by cooperating on a large task and sharing the proceeds (hunting a stag); but if one doubts the other will cooperate, he or she may defect from the common project and chase a smaller reward that one person can pursue alone (a hare). What each player needs is assurance that the other is going to cooperate to take the larger prize—hence the alternative name. There are two obvious equilibria in this game—that is, strategies from which neither party will move, given the strategy of the other: one where both parties cooperate to hunt the stag (producing the largest joint payoff); and a second where, lacking assurances, each individually hunts a hare (for a lesser payoff). One can often recognize a Stag Hunt situation when one hears admonitions like "we can all pull together on this," or "let's make sure we are all on board."

Less benign but closely related to Stag Hunt is the Prisoner's Dilemma, or simply PD, which has a quite similar structure, but a critical difference. Although, again, the highest *joint* payoff in a PD game comes where both parties cooperate, in this game the *individual* payoff is always greater when not cooperating. Indeed, the most profitable move is to defect while the other cooperates—and the least profitable move is to cooperate while the other party defects. This situation drives both parties away from cooperation toward mutual defection, where the joint payoff is lowest. The narrative version of Prisoner's Dilemma is rather confusing, but its multiparty variation, often called the Tragedy of the Commons, is more intuitive: each shepherd does best when he lets his sheep eat the grass that others have preserved; he does least well when he restrains his sheep while the others munch away what he has left. Without some common governance scheme, the shepherds all end up in the noncooperative box, with all the sheep eating the grass down to unregenerating nubbins. That is to say, without some constraint on the players, there is only one equilibrium in PD or Tragedy of the Commons, and it is not a good one for their collective well-being. One may be able to identify a PD situation when people warn one another with statements like "we all have to give up something for the common good," or "if we get too greedy, we're going to ruin the whole thing."

Finally, Hawk/Dove: this represents a game in which the best joint outcome involves parties who take opposite strategies: the dove defers to the hawk in order to avoid a wasteful fight. As with Stag Hunt, Hawk/Dove represents a problem of coordination, but here the parties need to coordinate on opposite strategies. As a fundamental matter, people need to know which role to play; if both play dove, resources will go unused, but if both play hawk, the same resources may be squandered in a struggle. Hawk/Dove situations may be recognizable when people say, "sorry, there's not enough room," or alternatively, "okay, I'll wait and you can go first."

Earlier it was mentioned that neighborhoods with racially restrictive covenants faced two kinds of problems for maintaining segregation: the first problem was controlling insiders, in order to restrain the existing neighbors from selling or renting to nonwhites; and the second problem was keeping outsiders away. In at least a crude way, these problems map onto the three games just described, and racial covenants played a role in solving them.

One might see the white neighbors as participants in a Stag Hunt or Assurance Game, where their most highly valued solution was to continue living together as a white community, but where, without assurance, some individuals might sell out to minority buyers. The role of racial covenants would then be that of reassurance and coordination, informing each of the white neighbors of the preferences, expectations, and commitments of the others, and presumably allowing them to coordinate their actions.

On the other hand, in the volatile circumstances where the white residents thought the neighborhood was already inexorably on the verge of "changing" (to minority occupancy), the Stag Hunt could turn into a Prisoner's Dilemma. Here the best option of each individual white owner might be move out quickly and to sell to a minority purchaser (since other whites would presumably not want to buy), and to do so before the other neighbors joined the bandwagon, flooded the sales, and depressed the prices. Under these panicky circumstances, covenants could play both an assurance role and threat of enforcement: not only did they remind the white owners of their mutual commitments, but the covenants represented potential punishment for defection. We want to stress that this punishment did not have to go all the way to formal legal enforcement. Punishment might take the form of the owner's own pangs of guilt ("I have to keep my word"), or the next-door neighbor's refusal to babysit on Saturday, or a vaguely threatening visitation by the neighborhood improvement association. Covenants in these circumstances not only reminded the neighbors of their commitments, but to some degree also kept them in line.[14]

Aside from assuring and policing one another, white neighbors had another and closely related problem in maintaining segregation: warning off and keeping out unwanted minorities. Here too one can see the neighbors' situation falling into the structure of a game, namely a Hawk/Dove game. Property in general has sometimes been analogized to a Hawk/Dove game, in which the owner plays hawk and the nonowners play dove, deferring to owners.[15] The name, Hawk/Dove, rings oddly and rather inappropriately for most of the things we consider property; property generally requires respect and civility more than the undertone of intimidation and fear implicit in the relationship between hawks and doves. But in the case of the white neighbors' assertion of informal group property rights over an entire neighborhood, the Hawk/Dove analogy seems quite apt. It was advantageous to the white neighbors to intimidate any minority members who might be thinking of moving in, and to threaten anyone who might act as an ally of new entrants. The sundown towns did this with signs on the roads coming into town; other close-knit neighborhoods did it with a brick through a window.

But covenants could play this intimidating role too, albeit behind a facade of legal civility. As public records, racial covenants were available to be perused by any outsider who was considering a real estate transaction. Moreover, because covenants were legal documents in the public records offices, they relieved the white neighbors from having to engage in the rougher forms of intimidation that would inform minority members that they should stay away. The neighbors could simply refer to the covenants, or indeed let the covenants speak for themselves—a relatively genteel version of common knowledge. These features were selling points for norm-entrepreneurial institutions when initiating subdivision covenants or organizing post-hoc covenant drives; racial covenants supposedly kept the neighborhood "safe" without resorting to overt violence.[16] Covenants undoubtedly often did perform this work by signaling neighborhood intentions and threats to outsiders; it takes unusual tenacity to move to a place where one knows one is not wanted, and where one knows there may be trouble, legal and otherwise. And even when a buyer was willing, home insurers, banks and other lenders no doubt appreciated the risks signaled by these covenants, and were correspondingly less willing.

We shall have occasion to refer to these games and variations on them in these and other situations, but for the moment, these three games should suffice: Stag Hunt (or Assurance) with respect to insiders' assuring one another; PD with respect to insiders' difficulties in controlling other insiders' sales or rentals; and Hawk/Dove with respect to signaling and warning outsiders.

Readers may be relieved to know, however, that we do not intend to beat them over the head with game theoretical considerations on a regular basis. Instead, while we will use the game theory tropes from time to time to clarify certain strategic considerations, the plan of the book will be largely chronological; we will follow the arc of racially restrictive covenants themselves over time, using different historical events and situations to illustrate the way that various actors adopted and deployed these legal devices to solve what they regarded as problems of defending their property. We will follow that arc as well to illustrate the legal strengths and weaknesses of racial covenants, particularly when both property law and constitutional law changed course; the first change took the direction of greater tolerance of race covenants, and then in the later change, those same legal regimes moved toward rejecting covenants. We will take the position that the primary function of racial covenants was to signal neighborhood intent, both to the neighbors themselves and to those who would be rejected; and we will argue that their legal status was of particular importance where neighborhood cohesion was not entirely certain—in the loose-knit as opposed to the close-knit neighborhoods.[17]

Covenants were signals that continued to have a sting even after they were merely voluntary and no longer legally enforceable. Oddly enough, they have continued to dog American real estate even now, when they are simply illegal and widely regarded as embarrassments. As a fitting coda on the covenant story, then, we will recount the efforts that some state lawmakers are now making to help residents get rid of these unwelcome reminders of the past.

Justice Rehnquist did not have the assistance of any such new statute. He removed the racial covenant from his Vermont house's deed by selling it for one dollar to his attorney, who then sold it back with a new deed. The new deed removed the offending covenant. But the new deed still referred to "the prior deed" and "all prior deeds" for a more complete description of all claims against the property. That old covenant is lurking in their midst.[18]

2 Before Covenants

Before the turn of the twentieth century, free persons of color seldom faced formal legal measures that excluded them from particular residential areas. All the same, informal norms of racial exclusion were old indeed, particularly with respect to African Americans, the citizens who would become the chief targets of legal exclusion. According to historian Leon Litwak, as early as the 1790s, a minister in Salem, Massachusetts, made a complaint that would echo across the centuries: that the presence of a "Negro hut" would injure the neighborhood, drive out the respectable folk, and drive down property values. Litwak described a second incident from a few decades later that would echo even more ominously across the years: "When a Boston Negro schoolmistress thought of moving to a better neighborhood, the inhabitants of the block . . . resolved either to eject her or to destroy the house."[1]

As we shall see, violence, real or threatened, has played a significant role in the racial segregation of American residential areas, giving off an especially sharp—if not legal—signal of the claim that white neighborhoods "belonged" to the white residents, to the exclusion of minorities. But it took some time before white claims to own the neighborhoods moved beyond informal measures ranging from disapproval to threats and violence, and jelled into the legal form of racially restrictive covenants. In this chapter, we give a very brief account of some of the social, demographic, and legal changes that preceded racial residential covenants through the later nineteenth and early twentieth century. We go on to describe some other early but misfired attempts at legalizing neighborhood segregation—ultimately leaving racially restrictive covenants as the dominating legal tactic for this dubious purpose.

AN UNEASY LEGACY

When racial restrictions did take legal form in the early twentieth century, they were largely associated with urban and suburban areas. But in earlier decades, few African Americans lived in cities and towns. In those years, most were slaves, living in the southern countryside as an especially low-status servile work force. The limited numbers of free African Americans did live in towns and cities, where a few became well-to-do but most slipped into poorer neighborhoods—often appallingly shoddy and overcrowded shantytowns with names like Cincinnati's "Little Africa" or Boston's "New Guinea," to mention only the more polite appellations. Southern white visitors to the North gloated over the dreadful conditions in these urban enclaves, and they felt themselves all the more justified in keeping black people enslaved.[2]

Before the Civil War, free African Americans often mingled with the poorer white residents of city neighborhoods. One was New York's infamously squalid Five Points area in lower Manhattan, where African Americans rubbed shoulders with—and were ultimately replaced by—immigrants from Ireland, Germany, and Eastern Europe. And to be sure as well, in that exotic and scandalous hotbed of racial mixing, New Orleans, white gentlemen contracted to support and live with their black mistresses at least part of the time, while elsewhere in the Deep South, white residents were quite indulgent when a handful of their freed kissing cousins from across the color line grew wealthy and moved into town.[3]

Indeed, one might speculate that in the antebellum period, urban whites in the lower South were more relaxed than their border state and Northern counterparts about physical proximity across the races, precisely because the social distance between the races was cavernous. Even those black persons who became well-to-do had to depend on white relatives and patrons, and as such they were unthreatening to the existing social order.[4] Nevertheless, aside from the poorest urban areas in both North and South, most respectable white townsfolk in the pre-

Civil War era were by no means well-disposed to residential integration with the free members of minority populations. It was something of an omen that many antislavery Northerners, including Abraham Lincoln himself for a considerable time, argued that the slaves should be freed, but thereafter they should go "back" to Africa or to some other foreign location, any of which would be totally unknown to the prospective new residents.[5]

As to the South specifically, the Civil War wrought great change in the later nineteenth century, but also a partial reinstatement and reconfiguration of some of the social and economic conditions that had existed there during times of slavery. The iconic and unfulfilled symbol of African American economic independence—forty acres and a mule—continued to speak to agricultural aspirations of a predominantly rural black population. But of course neither the forty acres nor the mule ever materialized. Historians have recounted how the former slaves—after 1865 formally free through the Thirteenth Amendment to the Constitution—faced a white planter class stung by defeat but determined to reassert control over black labor.

When Southern legislatures passed laws that would have effectively reversed much of the work of emancipation, Northern Congressmen reacted sharply, among other things forcing the Southern states to accept two more "Reconstruction" amendments—in 1868 the Fourteenth that required equal protection of the laws, and a few years later (1870) the Fifteenth that forbade racial limitations on the right to vote. But historians have also recounted how northern public opinion gradually shifted away from continuing efforts to protect the freed slaves from their former masters. Federal troops left the old Confederacy in 1877, and Reconstruction turned into "Redemption" as southern whites deployed violence and intimidation—well-known and well-organized drives of beatings, cross-burnings, and lynchings—to drive black citizens out of political office and effectively disenfranchise the black population.[6]

By the later decades of the nineteenth century, newly "redeemed" all-white southern state legislatures had reintroduced legal versions of semi-servile labor in the countryside. Alabama became notorious for laws that prescribed criminal penalties for farm laborers' breaches of contract. Not only was the threat of imprisonment intimidating in itself, but jail gave the prisoners little choice between forced labor in a system of prisoner leasing, or renewed contracts with their old employers "through the jailhouse bars," now enhanced with additional debt for payment of fines. One of Alabama's measures made it a criminal offense for a farm laborer or sharecropper to take an advance from one planter and then accept employment from another before repaying. This measure was overturned by a federal court in 1903 as peonage—that is, the imposition of criminal penalties for nonpayment of a debt; as such, the court ruled it a form of involuntary servitude in violation of the Thirteenth Amendment. The legal challenge sufficed only to make Alabama's labor law morph into a substitute form of peonage, ultimately overturned by the U.S. Supreme Court in *Bailey v. Alabama* in 1910. Despite *Bailey*, however, African Americans in the rural South still faced many oppressive legal and extralegal constraints on their choices for work. Pervasive black economic depression and political disenfranchisement lasted for decades more into the twentieth century.[7]

One might note that in their efforts to dominate an African American populace that strongly wished to assert its own autonomy, the southern white planter class had to cope with some of the same types of strategic problems that would play out later—although generally with less resort to violence—in the cities and suburbs in the context of race-based residential restrictions. Without in any way understating the cruelty of these interactions, one can observe the consistency of the planters' strategies with the games outlined in the introductory chapter. Planters had first to take the hawk role vis-à-vis the black laborers whom they wished to force into dove roles; and second, they had to play hawk again to drive off outside recruiters who saw an opportunity for arbitrage, and who might entice black workers to emigrate for higher wages. Third, and perhaps most interestingly, they faced a Prisoner's Dilemma game among themselves: they had to discipline themselves in order to prevent any individual planter from offering marginally higher wages to hire away other planters' laborers—a move that would unravel their hoped-for collective cartel over African American labor.

For all three of these tasks, white landowners used informal means—agreements among themselves along with violence and threats to the black population, to outside recruiters, and even to defectors among themselves. But they also used laws. For the first task, intimidating the black labor force, they used not only variations on Alabama's labor and debt legislation but also expansive definitions of petty crimes like vagrancy, adultery, and disorderly behavior. For the second task, dealing with outside emigrant labor recruiters, they imposed insuperable legal burdens on "enticement" of rural labor. For the third problem—curtailing competition among themselves—the same laws that controlled African American labor contracts also restrained the white landowners from "stealing" labor from one another.[8]

None of these measures succeeded in crushing black labor autonomy entirely. Indeed, as legal analyst Jennifer Roback observed, the very fact that the planters turned to legislation suggests that the white landowners lacked complete solidarity in their efforts to overawe the African American population. It was a straw in the wind that although white planters sharply resisted land sales to black farmers, threatening violence to any of their own number who did sell, at least some African Americans were able to buy their own farm plots throughout the Reconstruction era. Someone had to be selling them that land.[9]

Moreover, when white landowners turned to law to supplement social norms, they found that legal norms had a logic of their own. At least to some limited degree, this normative logic acted as a constraint on the planters' projects; constitutional challenges under the Thirteenth Amendment curtailed the most egregious of the white landowners' labor laws—that is, the criminalization of breaches of labor contracts. But the white southerners' experience also demonstrated the limitations of these higher-level legal norms. Aside from outright peonage, other laws limiting black labor independence remained in force, including the anti-enticement statutes, the vagrancy laws and other petty criminal offenses, and the use of convict labor. And of course informal and illegal violence and threats remained as powerful constraints.

The later history of racially restrictive covenants in urban areas would show some similar patterns: the turn to legal norms to supplement informal enforcement of neighborhood segregation; the subsequent policing of lower-level legal norms by higher levels of the law; the cat-and-mouse game to find new legal devices that could pass uncensored by higher-level legal norms; and to some degree, the well-known but problematic recourse to violence.

But first, African Americans had to move to the cities. By the end of the century, a stream of African Americans indeed began to abandon the southern countryside for the cities and towns, pushed not only by the oppressive labor conditions and violence that racked the rural South, but even more by the later nineteenth century's severe agricultural economic depression. In town, there might be less threat of physical intimidation. In town, there might be jobs that were less backbreaking and more remunerative, and perhaps too there might be more chances to own valuable property of one's own. In town there might even be a whiff of political influence, even if not fully equal citizenship. In short, town conditions might offer improvement, though certainly not an ideal life.[10]

But it was in town that African Americans began to face issues of segregation, including residential segregation.

URBANIZATION AND EXCLUSION: THE MOVE TO JIM CROW

Much has been written of the Great Migration beginning a few years after 1900, when so many black persons and their families left the rural South for the cities of the North and West. Those decades-long African American migrations to cities like Chicago and Detroit were to emerge sometime after the turn of the twentieth century, especially when the First World War and the newly emergent automobile industry opened up a seemingly endless cornucopia of job opportunities. But the exodus from the rural South began several years earlier, as rural African Americans found urban destinations both in the South and the North. Southern cities like Atlanta, Nashville, and Raleigh saw large increases in black residents in the post–Civil War era. Washington, D.C., became a particularly attractive destination for African American migration; the federal city promised the possibility of employment not only in the professions and trades, but also after 1883 in a civil service that was committed to some version of equal treatment. New York's African American population grew from under 24,000 to 60,000 during the years between 1890 and 1900, and then expanded to over 90,000 by 1910, causing black people to spill out of their overcrowded midtown neighborhoods and into the as yet largely white streets of Harlem.[11]

The larger picture in this era, however, was that of a general increase in urbanization, both black and white, fed in part by immigration from other countries. While New York's black population increased mightily, the overall percentages of black and white did not change much. Philadelphia had much the same story: the black population of about 20,000 in 1890 had tripled by 1900 and quadrupled—to over 80,000—by 1910, but African Americans still retained about the same percentage of the city's population. In Maryland, Baltimore's black population increased by 47 percent between 1880 and 1900, from 54,000 to 79,000, while the city's white population increased even more—by 54 percent. Similarly, in fast-growing Kansas City, Missouri, the black population remained in the vicinity of 10 percent of the total for decades, even while multiplying in numbers over three times between 1870 and 1890, from under 4,000 to well over 13,000—and then rising to between 23,000 and 24,000 by 1910. Significantly, Kansas City's black residents had been dispersed through the city at the outset of these decades, but with the city's growth residential segregation also increased.[12]

Indeed, it was in the urban areas that white efforts to establish residential segregation would emerge with special force. Turn-of-the-century European sociological thinkers pointed out—with some *Angst*—that larger urban areas were more socially fluid than smaller or more rural areas. People did not know each other so well in the larger cities, and presumably longstanding local hierarchical relationships were less obvious and less engraved in the personal knowledge of all the individuals involved. Members of the lower-status groups might venture to get "uppity" or "disrespectful," even though doing so could put them at risk of terrible violence even in the cities, as was to be shown in the southern urban lynchings in the early twentieth century.[13]

The relative plasticity of urban life meant that race-conscious white residents in the towns differed from their rural counterparts in at least one significant way: they could not count on a clearly understood social distance or set of social norms to separate themselves from the members of a different race that they disdained. Residence in town could blur or even obliterate the face-to-face contacts, the long intertwined personal histories that bolstered hierarchy in the country. What was left was physical distance: where social hierarchy grew hazy, physical separation could take on much greater significance. When an African American family wanted to move next door in the later nineteenth century, white townsfolk still did not like it, just as they had not liked it in earlier decades. But by the turn of the twentieth century, there were many more of those urban African Americans, and some of them might well want to escape the now overcrowded "Little Africas" or "Pigtowns"; furthermore, some might just have the means to move to the more attractive block next door—unless they could be contained.[14]

Why should they be contained, particularly if they had the means to buy a house in a middle-class neighborhood? In part, it was because of the *anomie* of city living: where people did not have detailed information about other people, race could act as an easy rule of thumb for a variety of imperceptible traits—even if it meant lumping the well-established black professional together with the unschooled black farm-hand from the South. Decades later, in extensive interviews in Chicago, Rose Helper found that the same shorthand calculations still applied in white neighborhoods.[15]

And how were these unwelcome persons to be contained? Informal intimidation was still an effective way to establish permanent white "ownership" of the neighborhood. But the impersonal urban setting may well have also undermined the necessary social solidarity even among white neighbors, making it difficult for them to establish and enforce social norms of exclusion. Under those circumstances, legal methods were comparatively more attractive. Those methods included racially restrictive covenants, although, as we shall see shortly, it could hardly have been predicted in 1900 that racial covenants would soon become the major legal route to enforce residential segregation.

It is notable that around 1900, white Americans, especially in the South and border states, were turning to the law for physical separation by race in a whole range of interactions, and not just in housing. This was the era when Jim Crow legislation emerged, separating the races legally throughout a spectrum of common spaces, both public and commercial. Trains, like urban areas, brought strangers together, and perhaps it is not surprising that transportation facilities were among the first to be segregated by law—over the objections of the railroad companies, which had to pay more to buy separate cars for the different classes of passengers. As several historians have pointed out, however, separation by race on the railroads covered over a variety of other sources of conflict among rail passengers, notably gender and class differences; race was a simple if inaccurate surrogate category that now eclipsed the others.[16]

Legal segregation on trains got an early test in the courts. The basis of the challenge was one of the constitutional amendments that had followed the Civil War: the Fourteenth, which prohibited states from denying the "due process of law" and "equal protection of the law" to any of their denizens. The challenge to segregation failed in the notorious case of *Plessy v. Ferguson* (1896). Here the U.S. Supreme Court allowed states to require the segregation of the races in public transportation, so long as the two sets of facilities were "equal but separate," a phrase that was soon to be transposed into "separate but equal" as the doctrine was applied to more and more public facilities in the South and other states nearby.[17]

Plessy's majority operated on a certain understanding of what *rights* are all about. It is an understanding that now seems almost incomprehensibly archaic, but at the time it was not unusual. In this older view, rights can be divided into three types: civil, political, and social. Civil rights were related to the natural rights that a person brought with him (and to a limited extent, her) into civil society in the first place. Those natural rights most prominently included the right to acquire and own property: while a person gave up the natural right of self-defense when entering civil society, he or she received in return the right to civil protection of his or her property. Things that one does with one's property—buying, selling, contracting—were among the other civil rights, the bedrock entitlements that one receives as a part of one's participation in civil society.[18]

Political rights were quite different—important, to be sure, but in this traditional understanding, the word *right* was something of a misnomer, since political rights were more properly designated privileges rather than rights. They had to be earned or deserved, and political bodies could set criteria for their exercise—criteria such as the ability to read, or to pay a certain amount in taxes. While these criteria could not unfairly exclude any given individual—including black citizens—theoretically they could be valid if they were applied evenhandedly.[19]

Notice that in this typology of rights, the prudent exercise of civil rights—contracting and property ownership—could bring about the reward of political rights. Husbanding one's property should lead to the wealth, independence, and respectability from which political participatory rights would flow. As we shall see, this idea seems to have influenced the early twentieth-century American courts' understandings about the legality of various measures undertaken to prevent African Americans from dealing with their property.

A third category, *social* rights, were not really rights at all. On this view, whether your neighbor likes you or not is purely an individual matter between you and your neighbor, and not a proper subject for legal intervention—which would be ineffective anyway—and certainly not for constitutional second-guessing. State legislatures, on the *Plessy* analysis, were free to pass legislation to protect health, safety, and morals, and if this legislation impinged only on social matters, the Supreme Court would be loathe to touch it. Why? Because social relations engaged no genuine issues of rights.[20]

In the wake of *Plessy*, southern states and communities segregated public facilities of all kinds—public schools, hospitals, parks, among others. Private owners got in on the act as well: hotels and restaurants refused service to African Americans; movie theaters relegated African Americans to the balcony spaces, and individuals gave legacies to parks or schools for the use of white persons only.[21]

The South was not alone in this pattern; a Chicago-area cemetery, for example, changed its policies to white only in 1907, and thereafter the officers refused to sell a burial plot to a black man for his deceased wife's body, even though the remains of four of his children had already been buried there. It was not that the cemetery managers had any animus against the black race, they averred, but simply that their white customers objected much too strenuously to having African American bodies nearby—an observation, incidentally, that suggests one way that social norms can work, where a social preference influences even those who might not share those preferences themselves. The Illinois Supreme Court refused to disrupt the cemetery's action, ruling that it was not covered by the Illinois law that required equal treatment in public accommodations. But at least Illinois *had* a public accommodations equality law, narrowly though it might be read—unlike the southern states that positively required separation of the races.[22]

The federal government took note of *Plessy* too: President Woodrow Wilson, newly elected in 1912, had a Princeton pedigree, a generally progressive agenda, and a debt to the newly founded NAACP, which had supported his candidacy after his promises of fair treatment. But he was a Virginian by birth, and he acquiesced in the plans of segregationists in Congress and the bureaucracy, who themselves must have been dismayed at the magnetic force that Washington, D.C., then exercised on southern blacks. With some vague comments on the goal of decreasing tensions in the civil service, Wilson cut back on patronage to black officials and permitted the most segregationist federal agencies to downgrade black employment at the same time that they segregated work spaces, cafeterias, and restrooms.[23]

All these segregationist moves roiled the black intellectual community. Older leaders like Booker T. Washington had urged separate development for black people, but the bitter pill of enforced separation enhanced the reputation of the new and more outspoken NAACP, whose leaders were determined to fight segregation laws, and who energetically and to some degree successfully protested Wilson's betrayal.[24]

Many years later, at the dawn of a new struggle over civil rights in the 1950s, the humorist Harry Golden observed that all the segregation laws stemming from this earlier era seemed to involve black people *sitting down* with whites—in school, in restaurants, on the job, in parks, and presumably in cemeteries at the end of life. His tongue-in-cheek solution to the great integration struggles of the day, therefore, was what he called the Golden Vertical Negro Plan: lawmakers should simply require everyone to stand up in schools, theaters, buses, and all other facilities, and all objections to integration would evaporate.[25] This was not quite the case, however. The utterly charming Delaney sisters, well over one hundred years old when they published their memoirs in 1993, had been children in Raleigh, North Carolina, when the Jim Crow laws fell down around their heads in the wake of *Plessy.* Among their more dismaying memories of childhood, they recalled the sudden introduction of segregated water fountains in the parks.[26] One does not sit down to drink at a water fountain; one merely bends over. Verticality, or at least standing up, would not have been a complete answer to the integration issue after all.

On the other hand, Golden had a point. Segregation laws in very large measure were about the maintenance of physical distance from those regarded as social unequals, and the concern was greatest when space was to be shared over some period of time—the implication of sitting down together. Then too, sitting down together implies a kind of equality and a blurring of class and status lines—the perfect hot button to accelerate the racial fears of status-anxious white urbanites. With the possible exception of burial sites, no kind of sitting down together seems more permanent than a residence. Even the word *reside* derives from the Latin *sedere,* to sit. No wonder, then, that even though residential segregation was by no means the only area in which white Americans were thinking about separating themselves physically from blacks at the turn of the twentieth century, it came high on the priority list.

The question was how to do it. For a time, there were quite a number of ways to do it, but all of them were a bit iffy. As we shall see, they were iffy because residential property was after all *property,* and property ownership has had a special role in American jurisprudence, perhaps at no time more than at the turn of the twentieth century. Even in that era of *Plessy,* disrupting people's rights to buy and own property—*any* people's property rights, including those of black men and women—had implications for constitutional equality that distinguished property from other rights.

Not that white Americans failed to try. For white people in town, the issue had shifted away from the preoccupation of their rural brethren, that is, asserting white group ownership and control over the labor of African Americans. In town, the issue was rather white group ownership of the *neighborhood,* to the exclusion of any potential black entrants—certainly an enterprise that smacked more of exclusion and less of domination, but still one with dramatic and far-reaching consequences. Obviously, extralegal informal means were available to enforce neighborhood segregation. Violence could and did range from petty harassment to threats, and then to arson, riot, and homicide—all serving as escalating signals of exclusionary social norms. But when both white and black populations were moving to cities—where social hierarchies between black and white blurred, and where white residents might not know even their white neighbors well—not only was the drive to exclusion greater, but the underlying "social capital" was weaker for violent exclusion.[27]

Hence white city residents' turn to legal routes to neighborhood segregation was itself a part of the general pattern of urbanization. Before they hit upon racial covenants that "ran with the land," white city denizens tried unsuccessfully to use two other major legal methods to separate their own homes from what they saw as the perils of African American and other minority neighbors. One of these methods derives from the common law of nuisance, the other from zoning legislation. As we shall see in the next sections, nuisance law never got a great deal of traction as a vehicle for racial residential exclusion; but zoning seemed much more promising for the purpose, probably even more promising than restrictive covenants—until racial zoning fell afoul of a rather surprising constitutional decision.

RESIDENTIAL RACIAL EXCLUSION THROUGH THE COMMON LAW: RACE AS NUISANCE

Nuisance law must have occurred to segregationists very early, since it was a well-established and well-known legal category in the early years of the twentieth century, one that attracted the attention of several authors in that great age of legal treatise writing.[28] Nuisance law was and continues to be a private remedy for persons whose neighbors overreach the bounds of normal activity on their property. Every man's home may be his castle, but nuisance law requires him to pay some attention to the owner of the castle next door. The basic gist of nuisance law is that you may use your property as you please, so long as you do not harm others or preclude them from enjoying their property just as you do.

What it means to "harm" the neighbor has always been rather vague. The usual subjects of nuisance suits are often rather airy—noise, fumes, smoke, and other such things that cross the boundary through the air. Pollution can be a nuisance too, either through the air or the water, even though the sources of pollution might not always be easy to find. Repeated instances of drunkenness and lewd behavior are candidates too. But you need not worry about a nuisance suit from your neighbor whose ears quiver with horror when you hit a B-flat instead of an A on your harmonica, for example, because nuisance law is not really about the harms suffered by those with unusually sensitive ears (or noses either, for that matter). On the hand, if you amplify your harmonica to play a string of B-flats at rock-concert level at three o'clock in the morning, your neighbor may well have a case. Nuisance law generally allows you to use your property "reasonably," that is to say, pretty much the way other people do in the vicinity. Your neighbor should be expecting that kind of behavior anyway, and nuisance law will generally not say he was harmed by it.

Was it a nuisance to white neighbors for minority group members to move in next door? Some property owners clearly thought so. Those old and repeated complaints that African American neighbors brought down the property values "sound in nuisance," as the lawyers say, because it counts toward a nuisance claim if your neighbor's activities diminish the value of your property. And there is no question but that some turn-of-the-century courts were sympathetic to the claim that African Americans in the vicinity would cause discomfort to white people and devalue their property.

An earlier section of this chapter mentioned a cemetery case, and another case about a cemetery—this one from Kentucky in 1907—yielded a particularly striking example of one court's view of racial attitudes. When the body of a dog was buried in a plot in Louisville's main white cemetery, the owner of an adjacent plot sued the owners of the dog's plot, as well as the cemetery itself, to require that the dog be removed. The court ruled in favor of the complaining plot owner, but not before pointedly comparing the burial of a dog to the burial of an African American, and noting that the latter would almost completely destroy the value of a plot for white persons. If a "non-Caucasian" human burial aroused such distaste, the court observed, a dog would do so all the more. The court noted that in the case both of the dog and the hypothetical black person, white people's attitudes might well result from an "unreasoned prejudice" rather than any physical nuisance, but given their contractual relationship with the cemetery, they nevertheless were entitled to have their prejudices safeguarded by the cemetery management.[29]

Despite judicial musings like this—quite shocking to a modern reader—nineteenth- and early twentieth-century nuisance law never did serve racial exclusion in any systematic pattern, and segregationists never really tried to use nuisance law in anything more than a half-hearted way. Even the Kentucky cemetery case, for all its appalling comparison of a black person's body to a dog's, would not have regarded the burial as a physical nuisance, actionable independently of the plot owner's contractual relationship with the cemetery. Much earlier, some cases from the antebellum south had raised the nuisance flag about race. For example, one early nineteenth-century case in Washington, D.C., allowed a fine against a liquor establishment as a "common nuisance" because the business attracted crowds of "negroes and slaves," ostensibly noisy and boisterous ones, who apparently compounded their transgressions by committing them on the Sabbath.[30] But in a case like that, repeated occurrences of noise and carrying-on would have counted as a nuisance all by themselves, no matter who the customers might have been. A Georgia case in 1858, shortly before the outbreak of the Civil War, described as a "nuisance" the presence of newly freed African Americans, presumably because they might give their enslaved compatriots some dangerous ideas about freedom for themselves.[31] But cases like this, though still in the books, were not only far in the past; they were also far too closely linked to the law of slavery to survive with any authority after the Civil War and the Thirteenth Amendment.

In the later nineteenth century, probably the best-known case in which an owner tried to use nuisance law for racial exclusion was *Falloon v. Schilling*, a Kansas case of 1883.[32] The plaintiff in the case had refused to sell his property to a neighboring owner, and he complained that the neighbor was retaliating, harassing him and creating a nuisance by renting the adjacent property to "worthless negroes." But the Kansas Supreme Court categorically rejected the idea that any person could be a nuisance simply because of his or her race. This decision was cited favorably in *Joyce on Nuisance*, one of the major nuisance treatises of the day, and over the next decades, other state courts took the same position, including courts in southern and border states.[33]

This pattern was consistent: in 1903, when a Kentucky town's governing board denied a building permit for an African American church, the state supreme court overturned the action, saying that the town council could not declare something a nuisance that was not.[34] In 1918, the Maryland Supreme Court held that the construction of residences for African Americans could not "of itself" be counted as a public nuisance—that is, one that like a so-called common nuisance is normally addressed by public officials.[35] But private white complainants certainly got the message as well. Even though they certainly mentioned race in nuisance suits, they generally raised additional factors such as noise or overcrowding; or alternatively, they based their claims on contractual arrangements, real or implied, that supposedly excluded residential racial mixing.[36]

It may well be, of course, that the courts gave a tacit plus factor to nuisance claims that included a racial element, or it may just be that the parties thought the courts would do so. Well into the twentieth century, parties continued to insert racial overtones into their nuisance claims, along with the standard counts of noise, fumes, traffic, and liquor. Some courts seemed to respond, others did not. A Tennessee court in 1917 agreed that a saloon was a nuisance after a protracted discussion not simply of its noise but also of its African American clientele;[37] but another Tennessee court four decades later flatly rejected a plaintiff's claim that he should get damages because his neighbors sold their house to a black family.[38] In none of these cases was race alone enough to get a nuisance claim off the ground. As Ernst Freund's magisterial and much-cited treatise on governmental authority had stated back in 1904, there could be no nuisance liability for a "natural condition not in any way traceable to positive human action." Unless there were some purportedly noxious *activity* to set the wheels rolling, the neighbor's race alone simply would not count as a legally cognizable nuisance.[39]

THE POTENTIAL OF ZONING

For the proponents of racial segregation, the newly invented regulatory device of zoning must have seemed much more promising than nuisance law, even though zoning too would soon go up in smoke as a legal basis for residential racial exclusion. Nuisance actions have a distinct disadvantage when some harmful activity affects larger areas: a specific property owner or set of owners must bring the action, even though other property owners may also feel the damage. But who will be the one to sue? As in so many Prisoner's Dilemma scenarios, all the neighbors have an incentive to free ride on the efforts of someone else.

This very common collective action problem can easily result in under-enforcement against nuisance activities. In a more modern context, for example, the collective action problem explains why many scholars and activists think that nuisance law cannot sufficiently rein in broad environmental harms, and why environmentalists call for regulation instead of or in addition to nuisance law. In a perverse way, racial zoning regulation would have had similar payoffs for the white neighbors who thought that nearby minority residents would damage their property values. Unlike nuisance actions, zoning could treat areas as whole neighborhoods instead of operating property by property. Even better from a segregationist perspective, racial zoning would place the cost of enforcement on the public at large.[40]

Zoning as a general form of land use control came to the United States by way of Germany, where this type of regulation had been in use since the 1890s. In the United States, the zoning concept came along just as a number of Progressive-era trends created a favorable climate for ratcheting up public planning and control of urban growth. Chicago was a central location for all this, with its astonishingly rapid growth and its experience with rebuilding after the devastating 1871 fire. The dazzling Chicago World's Fair in 1893 invigorated the idea that cities could and should be developed according to rational plans. So did the fair's intellectual follow-up in the early twentieth century, the "City Beautiful" movement that engaged some of the same architects who worked out the World's Fair's "White City," notably Chicago architect Daniel Burnham.[41]

Ideas of urban zoning thus arrived just in time: zoning could be enlisted as the practical means to meet the demand for rationally controlled urban growth. New York took a leading role in the move from planning to zoning. From the city's early planning efforts in 1911 to the comprehensive zoning ordinance of 1916, the dominating idea was that a city plan would come first, and then zones would be drawn up to carry out the plan. Here as elsewhere, both the general plan and the zoning scheme would give public officials the opportunity to guide otherwise haphazard land uses toward a mosaic of mutually harmonious locations.[42]

As it turned out over a longer run, many cities tended to be satisfied with zoning ordinances that served considerably more mundane goals: preserving a preexisting status quo in already-developed areas, and defending the single family home from the "lower" uses of multiple dwellings, commerce, and manufacturing, in that descending order. Over time, a derivative function would also emerge: zoning could enhance the powers (and sometimes the purses) of the local regulators who could grant exemptions from theoretically fixed but practically quite elastic zones.[43]

But at the turn of the century, the zoning idea was fresh and new and full of promise. Zoning plans generally simplified the more ambitious City Beautiful ideas, collapsing them into two basic principles: first, that land uses could be graded on a hierarchy from higher to lower; and second, that the higher land uses could be protected from the lower by physically separating them. By our own times, land use thinking has long since abandoned this "Euclidean" zoning model—so nicknamed for the landmark Supreme Court case that upheld zoning in Euclid, Ohio, in 1926—and has adopted a much greater tolerance for and even promotion of mixed uses. Not so, however, in the early days of American zoning, when separation seemed the appropriate way to deal with land uses then thought incompatible.[44]

The early-twentieth-century developments in land use regulation were not ostensibly focused on race, and it is hard to say that there was anything inherently racist about early zoning ideas. But race (and class) considerations were in the air, and certainly there was little to keep anyone from appropriating those early zoning ideas for racist purposes.[45] Indeed, a striking aspect of the Euclidean model is the ease with which its main elements could dovetail with the segregationist legislation of the day. Zoning's combination of *hierarchy*—albeit a disguised hierarchy—together with a protective *physical separation,* formed a pattern that resonated with the post-*Plessy* institutions that called themselves separate but equal. For those substantial segments of the urban white population who saw black people's presence as incompatible with good order, racial zoning was a natural.

Zoning of any kind, however, was a municipal matter, and municipal regulations faced some fairly longstanding legal obstacles. In the decades after the Civil War, many people came to regard city governments as hotbeds of corruption, and much state law became quite hostile to municipal initiatives. One much-noted constraint was the so-called Dillon's Rule, named for the author of the 1872 treatise in which the rule first appeared: municipal corporations could only legislate on subjects specifically delegated to them by state legislatures and/or essential to their stated purposes.[46] Nevertheless, as cities grew, a number of them passed ordinances that pushed the limits of Dillon's

Rule. Many adopted legislation that permitted locally unwanted land uses to be placed only in specified parts of the cities. Livery stables and animal-butchering facilities were among the major targets, with all their odors, noise, and flies. These businesses' owners objected when cities pushed their enterprises to the outskirts of town, and armed with Dillon's Rule, some attacked the municipal regulations as overreaching. But cities successfully defended their control measures on grounds of public health and safety, a longstanding legal justification for regulatory interference with the decisions of private property owners.[47]

In any event, the foul smells and loud sounds of these kinds of land uses put them in a category not far removed from traditional public nuisances—nuisances that, roughly speaking, affected everyone or large numbers of people—which local authorities had long had the power to abate. Around the same time that they shunted slaughterhouses to the outskirts, some cities began to regulate physical structures, especially the so-called tenements that housed immigrants and other low-income laborers. The goal here was not exactly to abate nuisances of a traditional sort, but rather to ensure that these dwellings provided some minimum of air, light, and sanitation to the residents. As with the slaughterhouses and livery stables, however, the justification was public health and safety, and commentators expended many pages on the diseases and disabilities that could be avoided by requiring better housing for the urban poor.[48]

By the early 1900s, and perhaps inspired by the Chicago World's Fair, cities had taken a further step on the regulatory road; they had begun to regulate such matters as the height and setback of structures. The justification here was harder to supply, since the courts still rejected regulation for what they called merely aesthetic purposes. The judicial view was that aesthetic regulation would lack standards, simply passing governing authority over to the public's subjective likes and dislikes—not enough reason, in the contemporary judicial account, to impede a man from using his property as he pleased.[49]

Hence when the City Beautiful movement itself drew attention to the "look" of the urban form, it emphasized urban design in a way that could have led to trouble in the courts. But municipalities defended the new building regulations too on traditional grounds of public health and safety. Were height restrictions simply a matter of taste, of the city's appearance? Certainly not. If a building were too tall, the problem was not just that the neighbors hated it, or that it blocked the sunlight they had previously enjoyed. No, the city lawyers argued, the problem was that taller buildings might present a greater danger if they should catch fire and their walls fall on the neighboring properties. In years to come, this public safety rationale was to cover a multitude of what might seem to have been primarily aesthetic regulations. How to justify billboard regulation? Why, it was fire protection and crime control too: robbers might hide behind billboards and jump out on unsuspecting residents.[50]

The larger point is that by the twentieth century's second decade, the earlier hostility to municipal regulation had weakened at least with respect to land use regulation, and courts were not so stringently guarding the subjects and justifications for municipal regulation. The lynchpin of municipal land use authority is what we now think of as zoning—that is, separating incompatible uses from one another across an entire municipality—and large-scale zoning duly arrived in 1916, when New York passed the nation's first major comprehensive zoning ordinance.[51]

THE LEGAL DEMISE OF RACIAL ZONING

Racial segregation was a part of the overall zoning picture, and, in fact, racial zoning chronologically preceded general land use zoning. Racial zoning may have come along early simply because urban white majorities were particularly anxious to separate themselves along racial lines. But there was another reason as well: zoning along racial lines might have seemed to present even fewer legal problems than other kinds of zoning. Race, after all, brought up the perennial and closely related issues of property values and violence. In the early twentieth century, perhaps even more than a century before, racial mixing could trigger people's fears about loss of property value, and those fears in turn could trigger unrest, disruption, and fights.

In Baltimore as in other cities in the post–Civil War era, African Americans had no specific quarter but rather generally lived in poorer neighborhoods together with a mix of other lower-income residents. But toward the end of the nineteenth century and into the twentieth, as more African Americans arrived and crowded into increasingly ghettoized slums, some of the black middle-class families began to move into nicer neighborhoods—and were then followed by less well-to-do black families. White homeowners were aghast. They protested vigorously, and some threw stones. In response to these disturbances, Baltimore's city council passed the first racial zoning ordinance in 1910, effectively adding a legal sanction to an emergent large-scale social norm of racial exclusion, ostensibly in the hope that the legal sanction could allay self-help violence.[52]

Several other cities quickly followed, particularly in the South and lower Midwest; among them were such cities as Norfolk, Richmond, Atlanta, Birmingham, Dallas, and Winston-Salem. Other racial zoning copycats included two cities from which we will hear more shortly: Louisville, Kentucky, and St. Louis, Missouri, the former with respect to zoning and the latter with respect to private restrictive covenants.[53]

The rationale for these ordinances was certainly not that they reflected mere aesthetic considerations or public tastes. Subjective reasons like that could have been the kiss of death in the property-conscious courts of the day. Nor was the rationale that racially drawn zones suppressed a nuisance—few public officials were willing to say openly that African American families constituted a nuisance per se. Instead, the ordinances were justified in large measure as a matter of public welfare and safety: the separation of the races, it was said, would help to preserve property values and to prevent racial tensions and ultimately violence.[54]

When one pushes on the property-values or antiviolence rationales, however, they fall back rather close to the aesthetic rationale, and to the nonrational social tastes that roused the suspicions of contemporary courts about aesthetic regulation. If you move next door, my property values will fall. Why? Because no one likes you or wants to live next to you. As to violence, perhaps I threaten to start throwing bricks if you move in. Why? Because I hate you, or even if I don't hate you, I know that other people do and your presence will make my property values plummet. All this is to say, if it is not enough to ground a regulation directly on subjective social desires and hates, it is at least somewhat disingenuous to ground a regulation on the threat of property losses or violence, when both emerged from the same kind of subjective social desires and hates.

Still, violence especially is a serious public matter whatever the cause, and it certainly must have seemed so at the time, given the increasing rumble of racial conflicts in the cities. When Baltimore passed its first racial zoning ordinance, New York had already had a major race riot in 1900, Atlanta in 1906, and Springfield, Illinois, in 1908. Black prizefighter Jack Johnson's victory over the "Great White Hope," Jim Jeffries, had set off numerous racial incidents in 1910, and other serious disturbances were to follow in the coming years.[55] *Plessy v. Ferguson* had permitted racial segregation for health, safety, and welfare purposes on trains; why not do the same where racial mixing set off such violent forms of protest? Instead of trying to deal with violence after the fact, why not aid white people to cordon off areas for their exclusive use, so long as other racial groups had the same opportunity? Would not separate enclaves for the different races allow all to enjoy safer and hence more valuable property? Legal norms, it seemed, could replace violence as an enforcer of social norms of separation, and all would be better off.

Aside from the violence-prevention rationale, a particularly disingenuous feature of these ordinances was their ostensible race neutrality, a stance presumably taken to satisfy *Plessy*'s separate-but-equal doctrine. Baltimore's ordinance provided that members of any given racial group could move only to those streets where their racial group already constituted a majority. Thus when blacks moved away from white majority streets, only whites could replace them, and, by parallel reasoning, only blacks could replace any white persons who left black-majority streets. Over time, presumably, every street would come to be occupied only by particular racial groups.[56]

This all looked neutral on paper—blacks would have their streets, whites would have theirs, and each group would enjoy a collective property right, legally enforced, in separate neighborhoods that would presumably be safer for all. A moment's reflection, however, reveals that this ordinance would severely curtail the quantity of real estate open to the minority groups who were then migrating to the cities. The members of any expanding minority would be unable to settle in any block on which they had not yet established numerical dominance. Thus at a time when large numbers of African Americans had begun to move to the cities where only a few had lived before, they would have had to squeeze into the relatively few blocks open to them, the "Little Africas" where their racial group had already become dominant.

Had ordinances of this sort been upheld, cities in the United States might have come to look very different than they do today—perhaps like those of South Africa in the apartheid era, where Africans could only settle in shantytowns on the outskirts; or perhaps like those of Latin America, where the relatively well-to-do live in the city center and the poor live outside in rings of ill-served barrios, where such basic urban services as water and sewers lines do not reach. As dismal as the racial divide was to become in many American metropolitan areas—a divide that to a large extent remains—at least minority members had the option of moving into an existing urban area, with its accompanying infrastructure. In the United States, it was the better-off white population who left the cities, and who had to build new schools, streets, and sewers for themselves in the suburbs and exurbs.

Perhaps it was a sign of things to come that the Baltimore ordinance ran into some rough sailing in the Maryland courts. The first two versions of the ordinance were invalidated, seemingly on technical grounds but with echoes of property rights concerns.[57] The supreme courts of two other states, North Carolina and Georgia, may have been located even farther south geographically, but they were more straightforward legally: they invalidated Winston-Salem's and Atlanta's racial zoning ordinances, respectively, as impermissible intrusions on property rights.[58] Even in these southern courts, concerns over individual property effectively reined in the attempt to use the legal norm of zoning to reinforce white social preferences for a segregated kind of group property.

Meanwhile, in 1914, Louisville, Kentucky, had passed an ordinance that mimicked Baltimore's initial 1910 ordinance, and it was in that guise that racial zoning reached the U.S. Supreme Court. The Louisville ordinance, like Baltimore's before it, exemplified the theoretical facial neutrality—and practical racist character—of these early ordinances. It too channeled new residents to streets where their race already constituted a majority. But the NAACP, established in 1909 and fresh from its run-ins with the new Wilson administration over the latter's segregationist policies, led the challenge to the ordinance. The organization adopted a pattern that would characterize much of its later litigation strategy: it found a test case that would let the organization showcase the issues that were of most importance to it. Indeed, in this case, the NAACP closely orchestrated the litigation, identifying both a white seller and a black buyer who disliked the ordinance. The resulting case, *Buchanan v. Warley* (1917), was set with a reverse twist: the black buyer averred that he did not have to go through with the purchase of the seller's property because of the racial zoning ordinance, whereas the white seller was the one to attack the ordinance as unconstitutional.[59]

Buchanan gave the NAACP one of its early and important victories. It was one of the Court's few departures from "separate but equal" in the early twentieth century, and the right to property was an important element in that departure. The Court relied on the Fourteenth Amendment to invalidate Louisville's ordinance, but the railroad case, *Plessy v. Ferguson,* had also been a Fourteenth Amendment case, and it had nevertheless upheld segregation in public facilities. In distinguishing the zoning case from *Plessy,* the Supreme Court—like the courts of North Carolina and Georgia beforehand—emphasized most heavily the point that racial zoning impeded a person's ability to own and dispose of substantial tangible property. Indeed, the Court seemed far less concerned about the Fourteenth Amendment's equal protection clauses than it was about the amendment's due process aspects—that is, the amendment's constraints on the ability of a state or municipality to pass such an ordinance at all, consistently with the federal requirement that states afford their residents "due process of law."[60]

The Court's thinking in this respect harkened back to a line of cases that had begun roughly in 1900, where it had interpreted the amendment's due process clause to include certain substantive restraints on the states, most notably on their ability to limit individual freedom of contract. These older "substantive due process" cases invalidated what were then important new social reforms like wage and hour regulations, and more modern jurisprudential thinking has subjected those cases to much criticism. In these cases, the early-twentieth-century Court seemed to reflect a doctrinaire conservatism and judicial interventionism that disrupted the legislative process of reform, especially in economic matters.[61] But to give the devil his due, the Court's concern for economic liberties had worn a considerably more attractive face in an earlier decision defending Chinese laundries against hostile local legislation, and it once again wore that face in *Buchanan,* where substantive due process served the African American complainants well.[62]

To be sure, solicitude for economic liberties was already rather old-fashioned even in 1917, as governments geared up for the massively increased economic intervention of the World War I years. Concerns about economic rights harked back to the later decades of the nineteenth century, tracking the trio of civil, political, and social rights discussed in connection with the *Plessy* case, a trio that informed much of the earlier era's thinking about rights generally. Within that division of rights, the right to acquire and dispose of property would certainly have fallen under the rubric of basic civil rights. The Court in *Buchanan* was by no means yet ready to relinquish this idea.

It was consistent with the traditional understanding of rights that for many years, the acquisition and disposition of property had been widely seen as a route to full civic participation by African Americans. As slaves, black men and women generally had been unable to own and dispose of their own property, and thus they had been unable to better their situations except by permission of a complaisant master. But as free people, and as people who enjoyed the *civil* right of property ownership, those former slaves could enter the cycle of earning, saving, and investing, and they could work their way into all the privileges of *political* rights—or so it was thought, no doubt rather optimistically, as we might now think in hindsight. But whatever hindsight may say now, racial zoning, as exemplified in the Louisville ordinance, would have disrupted this hoped-for cycle by operation of law, keeping otherwise willing buyers of residential properties from using the property in the most natural and suitable way—a matter that incidentally also disrupted the expectations of willing sellers of such property.[63]

Once one thinks of the right to acquire and dispose of property as this very basic right, and as the foundation upon which other rights might be built, laws that separated drinking fountains or trolley seats must have seemed relatively trivial matters. What really mattered to advancement was the right to own and dispose of one's property.[64] Thus perhaps it was not so surprising that according to the Supreme Court's rather old-fashioned views in *Buchanan,* governments' police powers could not stretch so far as to curtail access to property on a racial basis. The lawyers working with the NAACP were very much aware of the relevant substantive due process arguments, and in arguing *Buchanan,* they steered the Court's attention in this direction even while stressing issues of equality.[65]

In a contribution to a 1998 symposium on *Buchanan v. Warley,* David E. Bernstein, a modern conservative legal scholar, argued forcefully that the Court's embrace of traditionalism was exactly what advanced the cause of racial justice in *Buchanan*—by contrast to the adherents of the then-prevalent Progressive political movement, who in Bernstein's exceedingly chary view were often susceptible to the era's pseudo-scientific theories of race. Louisville had argued in favor of its ordinance on three grounds: that it maintained racial purity, that it maintained property values, and that it reduced friction between the races and thus the chances for violence. Bernstein discussed at length the legal scholarship of the time, and, depressingly enough, many of the commentaries before and after the *Buchanan* decision did support racial zoning, agreeing with one or more of Louisville's arguments, often on what seemed to be Progressive grounds.[66]

The racial purity argument was no doubt the least progressive, though some racial zoning proponents did make that argument, referring to contemporary "scientific" theories about the differences among the races. In *Buchanan,* however, the Court summarily cut off this justification, observing that the Louisville ordinance made an exemption to permit black *servants* to live in white blocks (and of course it also provided an exemption for white servants to live in black blocks, just to dot the i's and cross the t's of the equality issue). Given the notorious historical patterns of sexual imposition on servants, racial purity must have seemed at best far-fetched as a rationale. However, the second rationale, that of maintaining property values, attracted a number of adherents, who described racial zoning as an important element in the maintenance of well-to-do neighborhoods. Meanwhile other commentators focused on the third rationale, the public interest in avoiding racial violence.[67]

Property values and violence were related in ways not always mentioned in polite legal literature. Violence obviously could decrease property values, simply by destroying property. But given the widespread white preference for segregation, the causality could also work in the opposite direction: looming racial encroachment could threaten a neighborhood's property values, and that threat could make some residents more likely to engage in violence, as they took norm enforcement into their own hands while their quieter neighbors supported them.[68]

The Supreme Court itself acknowledged but rejected all of Louisville's arguments, including that of preventing racially motivated violence, and in so doing the justices illustrated how strongly they believed in the importance of property ownership. They certainly must have been aware that violence was a live issue; the race riots in East St. Louis, Missouri, had broken out in early July 1917, falling squarely between *Buchanan*'s oral arguments in April and the Court's actual decision date in November. But the worst implications of racial violence were yet to come. Two years later, in the summer of 1919, horrific race riots racked the city of Chicago, leaving behind thirty-eight persons dead along with tremendous loss of property. By the time these events shocked the nation, of course, the *Buchanan* case had already dispatched the Baltimorean zoning plan as a means of separating the races.[69]

This is not to say that *Buchanan* made municipalities give up on racial zoning altogether. They did not. For well over a decade, city councils continued to enforce racial zoning ordinances, attempting to tweak the Baltimore/Louisville formula in such a way as to slip past *Buchanan*'s strictures. Pursuant to a Louisiana statute of 1924, New Orleans passed an ordinance that forbade a black person from moving into a white neighborhood (and vice versa) *without the consent of the neighbors*. Richmond, Virginia, tried a somewhat different ploy. After Virginia's supreme court ruled that *Buchanan* invalidated a racial zoning ordinance very similar to Richmond's, the city cleverly revamped its racial zoning ordinance: it turned to the state's 1924 antimiscegenation law, and it prohibited anyone from moving onto a block where the majority of residences were occupied by persons *whom they were prohibited from marrying*.[70]

The U.S. Supreme Court made short work of these two evasions, in both cases citing *Buchanan* and ruling *per curiam* that the ordinances were unconstitutional. But still some cities kept trying: Atlanta gave up on fancy schemes to steer residents into blocks where they would join a majority of their own race. Instead, the city simply created zones, reserving some for white people, others for blacks. Oklahoma City dropped all pretense of evading *Buchanan*, and in 1934 it passed an ordinance much like the original Baltimore/Louisville racial zoning—until halted by Oklahoma's own supreme court.[71]

Thanks to these die-hard efforts, it is not entirely accurate to say that the *Buchanan* decision stopped racial zoning. Just as Alabama's legislatures had evaded federal peonage decisions with ever-shifting variations to give white planters control over black labor, so did southern cities and towns continually tweak the *Buchanan* decision, coming up with one new version of racial zoning after another, in order to help white neighborhoods hold on to their racial composition. These variations on the zoning theme were a drain on the slender litigation resources of the NAACP for years. But the pattern of judicial rulings, both in the federal and the state courts, clearly illustrated that those local laws could not last forever.[72]

This fact considerably narrowed the options for those who had hoped to use the law to maintain residential racial segregation, and to permit white urban residents to claim an exclusive racial group property in their neighborhoods. Nuisance, based on the general rights and obligations of property, had never gotten off the ground as a means to keep out unwanted minorities. Without some specific agreement by owners, courts simply would not allow this kind of intrusion on the rights of property. *Buchanan* hung a guillotine over the second major option, racial zoning; the courts thought that these public ordinances too were an undue intrusion on private property rights.

After *Buchanan,* it seemed, the only legal route that remained open to enforce residential segregation was through private agreements among owners—that is to say, racially restrictive covenants that were agreed upon by the property owners themselves, and that would somehow run with the land to bind future purchasers as well. But the covenant route too led across some potential minefields, both from constitutional law and, even more, from the law of property. The next two chapters illustrate how proponents created racial covenants while they dodged those legal obstacles, at least for a considerable time.

3 The Big Guns Silenced

How Racial Covenants Overcame Major Objections from Constitutional Law, Property Law, and Corporations Law

When the Supreme Court invalidated racial zoning in *Buchanan v. Warley* in 1917, it illustrated the vulnerability of legal devices to higher-level legal norms. Violence might still have been an option to keep a neighborhood segregated, but not everyone was willing to use violence or capable of doing so. Hence it is no surprise that the legal status of covenants would begin to generate much attention after the *Buchanan* decision ruled out racial zoning, and after the Chicago riots of 1919 gave a special urgency to issues of violence between the races. Racially restrictive covenants were the only legal method left for enforcing segregation against minority expansion in the cities.

But just how legal *were* they? In the early years of the twentieth century, racial covenants faced several potential obstacles at a higher level of the law. This chapter takes up the three legal issues that seemed to loom largest as potential problems for racial covenants, and that were actually litigated over the first several decades of the twentieth century. The first of these issues was constitutional, deriving from the objection that racial covenants violated the Fourteenth Amendment. The second was based on property law principles that limited "restraints on alienation." The third was the issue whether the corporate form might negate racial restrictions because corporations had no race. Until *Shelley v. Kraemer* in 1948, defenders of racial covenants managed to overcome all three obstacles, and this chapter explains how. The next chapter takes up some legal issues that were more specific to covenants and explains how they too were evaded, but with some consequences for the forms that racial covenants acquired.

THE REAL ESTATE BACKGROUND: COVENANTS IN THE SCHEME OF PRIVATE LAND USE PLANNING

One very important thing to remember about covenants on real property is that most covenants have never had anything to do with race. In the United States, as we shall see at greater length in Chapters 4 and 5, developers began to use restrictive covenants extensively in the early years of the twentieth century in order to establish and maintain the kinds of neighborhoods they wanted to create. At that time and continuing to the present day, most restrictive covenants have not been about race but rather about other things altogether—lot size, building type, noise limitations, land uses deemed appropriate and inappropriate, and so forth.[1]

Unless a property owner has a great deal of space and wants no neighbors—a somewhat limited set of persons, even in the age of robber barons[2]—the value of her residence area will be affected by neighboring uses. Not surprisingly, different owners have different preferences about the kinds of neighboring uses they like. Restrictive covenants allow owners to tailor their control over neighboring uses, and because these restrictions are ostensibly private and consensual, they can do so in considerably greater detail than would be possible through publicly imposed constraints like zoning. Even more than public regulations, residential restrictive covenants allow home buyers to pick and choose among packages of limitations, knowing that the limitations will stick with the properties even when some of the neighbors sell.[3]

Many covenants focus on negative externalities, offering home buyers lasting protections against land uses that are not so noxious as to amount to legal nuisances, but that the neighbors would still rather not have in the vicinity. These covenants might limit street parking, for example, or they might prohibit plastic elves, pink flamingos, and garish paint colors. Beyond those negative limitations, covenants might require property owners to undertake certain positive obligations that exceed their general civic duties, such as keeping the hedges clipped below five feet, submitting building plans to an architectural board, or paying dues to the community association for internal street maintenance, tennis court and pool upkeep, or other common charges.

Modern housing developments make extensive use of covenants, and indeed these covenants form the legal basis for modern condominiums and other privately planned communities. In the past, however, it was not always clear that covenants could intrude so far into the prerogatives of property owners, and part of the story of this book concerns the legal changes that allowed these intrusions to occur. If anything, the restrictive covenants of our own times are considerably more elaborate and *dirigiste* than most of those in existence one hundred years ago. While their strictures often give rise to a certain amount of griping among the residents—why can't I park my car on the street overnight? what do you mean I can't paint my house purple?—the usual answer is, you knew what you were getting into, or at least you should have known. Even if you did not make the deal yourself, you bought a house whose restrictions "run with the land," and they bind you too. That level of stability over time, with obligations passing from past owners to new ones, is what makes covenants valuable for a neighborhood.

Developers of residential areas began to make extensive use of these covenants running with the land, or deed restrictions, at about the same time that urbanites started to think seriously about zoning. The private residential real estate covenants of the early twentieth century shared with early zoning the impulse to create and maintain a City Beautiful. Covenants too aimed at establishing attractive and appealing neighborhoods that were free of activities and structures that might annoy the participating neighbors and disturb their peace and aesthetic enjoyment of the area.[4]

But from a relatively early date, many private real estate plans included racial exclusion as one element among the many others.[5] That is to say, racial exclusivity was one of the things that was supposed to make a well-to-do neighborhood attractive. One gets a whiff of this attitude in a Michigan case, *Kathan v. Stevenson,* that was not brought and decided until 1943, but where the central issue was the meaning of subdivision deed restrictions that had been drawn up in 1912. On the basis of these older restrictions, one subdivision resident objected when an African American couple moved into the neighborhood, and this resident was not fazed by the fact that the documents said nothing explicit about race. They did not have to, he argued. He referred to the subdivision's 1912 advertising, which had announced that the development would have a "high-class" character. All one had to do was to note this stated purpose, he argued, and put it together with the covenants' extensive building restrictions, to see that the expense would have excluded "colored" persons from purchasing. Taking these elements together, according to the complaining homeowner, one should be able to infer that the restrictions also implicitly prohibited any future occupancy by nonwhite persons.[6]

The homeowner lost the case in *Kathen,* but his argument speaks volumes about the links that some owners drew between racial exclusiveness and residential "niceness." One can envision white owners like this as participants in the assurance game or Stag Hunt described in the Chapter 1: the first preference of all would be to remain together in an all-white neighborhood; but if some faltered and sold or rented to the dreaded non-Caucasians, the others would do the same, departing from the so-called high-class neighborhood and arriving at a less desirable location, in an outcome akin to a bank run.[7] The hope of the white homeowners in *Kathen* was that ambiguous language like "high class" would be enough to convince a court that they had a legally binding assurance against minority entrance. Perhaps it would have been enough in an earlier decade, but by the 1940s it was not. What was well-established in the early 1940s, however, was that there were no major legal obstacles to *explicit* racial covenants, even if a court would not automatically assume that "high class" meant exclusively white, as the *Kathen* complainant hoped.

On the other hand, the legal acceptability of racial covenants in the early 1940s had been nowhere near so clear forty years earlier. When developers first began to use deed restrictions to put together "high-class" neighborhoods, there were a number of questions whether any deed restrictions at all could work legally; and even if they could, there was a subset of questions specifically about whether racial segregation could be incorporated into otherwise valid schemes of deed restrictions. Some of those questions came from constitutional law.

CONSTITUTIONAL DOUBTS AND THEIR RESOLUTION

Before *Shelley v. Kraemer* in 1948, one of the first of the very few successful constitutional challenges to racially restrictive covenants occurred in a lower federal court in California in 1891, in the case *Gandolfo v. Hartman*. Indeed, if *Gandolfo* had been taken seriously, it would have made covenants seem distinctly unpromising as a legal device for excluding undesired races from residential areas. The real estate covenant in *Gandolfo* was a relatively primitive affair, a one-lot restriction prohibiting occupancy by "Chinamen." The judge refused to enforce this restriction, citing the post–Civil War Fourteenth Amendment, according to which no state may deny to any person the equal protection of the laws. The *Gandolfo* judge tossed off the observation that it would be an unduly narrow reading of the Fourteenth Amendment "to hold that, while state and municipal legislatures are forbidden to discriminate against the Chinese in their legislation, a citizen of the state may lawfully do so by contract, which the courts may enforce." As an alternative ground for this decision, the court then went on to cite the treaty between the United States and China, which required equal treatment to Chinese residents in this country.[8]

Gandolfo's treaty discussion was not what gave the case an afterlife, but rather the remarks about the Fourteenth Amendment. Even today, it is widely thought that in constitutional-law matters, courts should distinguish between "state action," which applies to governmental bodies, and the "private" actions that deal with such matters as contracts and torts. Even though these so-called private matters might be enforced in court, judicial enforcement does not normally turn them into state action. Instead, they represent a kind of private law—that is, legal relations created by acts of individual persons, as opposed to the more authoritative relationships that take place between governments and citizens. But *Gandolfo*'s offhand conflation of the two would have brought racial covenants into the rubric of state action, which then would have made them subject to the Fourteenth Amendment's limitations on discriminatory state actions.[9]

After the NAACP's victory in *Buchanan v. Warley*, the *Gandolfo* opinion seemed to open a route to extend *Buchanan*'s prohibition of racial zoning to the ostensibly private segregation created by racial covenants. Thus when civil rights lawyers challenged racially restrictive covenants in the 1920s and later, they seized upon *Gandolfo*'s analogy between official legislation on the one hand, and judicial enforcement of private contracts on the other. Over the decades to come, NAACP-supported lawyers would repeat that equation like a mantra in their attacks on racial covenants: judicial enforcement of private agreements, they said, citing *Gandolfo,* was tantamount to legislation by a public body. *Buchanan* had made it clear that public bodies could not enact and enforce racial zoning without violating civil rights; how could the courts enforce the private racial "zoning" that was created by developers and homeowners? Covenants were the same thing as legislation, the NAACP lawyers argued, and that thing was state action.

But until the *Shelley* case decades later, this was a losing argument. It may have been that with their thin resources further stretched by fighting the ever-morphing racial zoning of various municipalities, the NAACP lawyers turned automatically to *Buchanan* to deal with covenants and had little time to go beyond the *Gandolfo* gloss. Or it may have been that they were trying to build on a popular view that there was something unconstitutional about racial covenants. In a 1927 treatise, the prominent Chicago real estate lawyer Nathan MacChesney (of whom we will hear more in Chapter 6) scoffed at the home buyer who "frequently . . . has a doubt" about racial restrictions on the ground that the Constitution's Civil War amendments "somehow" forbade them. MacChesney sharply dismissed this notion with a quick primer on the Fourteenth and Fifteenth Amendments, but his very vehemence suggests that he was fending off a view that he had encountered a number of times.[10]

MacChesney was right, however, that the *Gandolfo* view was not shared in other courtrooms. Through the first forty-plus years of the twentieth century, courts hearing the argument either distinguished *Gandolfo* or ignored it altogether. Those that mentioned *Gandolfo* treated it with only faintly disguised disdain, saying that the case had simply been wrong in likening contractual relations to state action, since the former were private actions and not subject to the Fourteenth Amendment's constraints on state action. Alternatively, they said, *Gandolfo* rested on the Chinese-American treaty that specially protected persons of Chinese origin. By 1944, a lower court in California would refer to Gandolfo as a "stray."[11]

For decades, then, *Gandolfo*'s constitutional position on state action presented no great impediment to racially restrictive covenants. The NAACP's great victory against racial zoning in *Buchanan v. Warley* had not changed this picture, and no one in the legal world except the NAACP thought that it had. In Michigan and Missouri, the home states of the two challenges that would be decided in *Shelley v. Kraemer* several decades later, each of the highest state courts took an important early case on racially restrictive covenants. But each of these high state courts upheld the restrictions, all but ignoring any analogies to zoning from *Buchanan*. Instead, the two opinions both asserted that restrictive covenants were private actions, unaffected by any equal protection limitations on state action. From that point of view, *Buchanan*'s prohibition on racial zoning was simply irrelevant. Zoning was a public matter—state action—whereas racially restrictive covenants were private.[12]

In their defense, these courts' views were not entirely foreign to modern thinking about constitutional law. Prior to the 1948 *Shelley* case, which did expand the concept of state action to racial covenants, a progressive if conventional legal analysis might well have taken the following form: "Racially restrictive covenants reflect a deplorable prejudice that is clearly forbidden to public bodies and officials, but the Fourteenth Amendment nevertheless has no bearing on *private* discrimination. While we may find private discrimination morally repellant, it is not necessarily illegal." Upon reflection, even modern civil libertarians might concede that there are some plausible reasons for the persistence of this conventional analysis. However frail and contested the divide between public and private in theory, the distinction assures a space for personal decisions, letting people do things as private actors that would be off limits to public actors—for example, giving preference to one's friends or family in contracts, or contributing to particular religious organizations, or excluding unwanted political solicitors from one's property. None of those activities would be legitimate for public officials, but we generally think that it is understandable that individuals might want to engage in them. Moreover, we generally think that however much we might dislike any given individual's choices, it is important that individuals—including ourselves—continue to have these choices, and that they be legally enforceable. As we shall see in later chapters, it was *Shelley's* disruption of this conventional public/private distinction that proved to be especially difficult to cabin.

Until that case, however, the most important constitutional case of all mirrored the conventional view that racial covenants were private instruments and thus nothing like public zoning. That case was *Corrigan v. Buckley*, a 1926 decision of the U.S. Supreme Court. The case grew out of some racially restrictive covenants in the District of Columbia, a city that had been an especially strong magnet for African Americans in the previous decades. In *Corrigan*, the Court paid no attention when the NAACP lawyers cited *Buchanan*, and instead maintained that no alleged constitutional violation gave it jurisdiction to hear the case. According to the Court, none of the claimed constitutional bases to strike down racially restrictive covenants—the Fifth, Thirteenth, or Fourteenth Amendments—"prohibited private individuals from entering into contracts respecting the control and disposition of their own property."[13] If anything, *Buchanan* might have even seemed to work against the NAACP's attacks on racially restrictive covenants, because a central feature of the *Buchanan* decision was the Court's effort to insulate private property owners' decisions from undue governmental intrusion.

In fact, there were some issues about *Corrigan* that made it less authoritative than it appeared to be. One technical matter was that *Corrigan*'s remarks on the Fourteenth Amendment were what lawyers call "dicta," judicial observations on an issue that is not before the court and hence are not authoritative as precedent. The Court's comments on the Fourteenth Amendment were dicta in this Washington case because that amendment limits the states, but it does not apply to the District of Columbia, which is a federal city and not an independent state. But this was a nicety that lawyers largely ignored in later years. What they noticed instead was that the *Corrigan* opinion seemed to put the Supreme Court's imprimatur on the distinction between public racial zoning on the one hand, and the seemingly private agreements of racially restrictive covenants on the other. The former were invalid after *Buchanan*, but the latter were valid according to an array of state judicial decisions and now a major federal one. Within a decade after

Buchanan's dismantling of racial zoning, it seemed increasingly clear that any legal constraints on racially restrictive covenants were not going to come from the U.S. Constitution, even though the NAACP never gave up on the argument—and despite repeated rebuffs, continued to pound it all the way to *Shelley.*

There was another seeming fine point in *Corrigan* that went largely unnoticed at the time and later, but that might have made a substantial difference to the legal career of racial covenants. *Corrigan* distinguished racial zoning from private owners' racially restrictive "contracts," but a closer analysis might have gone on to distinguish those so-called contracts from the property restrictions contained in real estate covenants that ran with the land. What was the difference? The difference was that unlike ordinary contracts, which bind only those who make the contract, real estate covenants purport to bind not just the creators but also *future* owners of the covenanted properties. It would have been as if current owners A and B had agreed about what later owner C's obligations would be to later owner D. As a matter of fact, in the *Corrigan* case itself, both the plaintiff and the defendant were parties to the original covenant—they were like A and B, and the description of their relationship as contractual was accurate. Perhaps they did have obligations to each other as a matter of ordinary contract. But a rather different issue might have been presented if the parties to the case were C and D, later owners sometime in the future.

In the 1920s, this distinction between contract and property would not have struck many observers as a constitutional issue—although as we shall see, that view began to change by the 1940s as the use of racial covenants burgeoned. But even in the earlier era, or perhaps especially in that more formalistic time, property law itself might have made more of the distinction between contract and property. This was because the inherited property doctrines of the era proclaimed favoritism to the free use of property, and more specifically because the courts had only recently softened toward any residential restrictions at all that ran to later purchasers—that is to say, treating the restrictions as attached to the property rather than simply acting as personal contracts between the original parties.[14]

Some early twentieth-century real estate developers—or at least their lawyers—appeared to be concerned about potentially unfavorable legal treatment of racial covenants; as we shall see in the next chapter, the developers shaped many of their residential real estate deals to escape from negative precedents and judicial skepticism. The developers' precautions, however, largely sought to allay concerns about traditional property law, not constitutional law. From the 1920s until the quite unprecedented decision in *Shelley* in the late 1940s, it seemed that the U.S. Constitution would have no role in policing covenants as a legal route to white residents' collective "ownership" of their neighborhoods.

PROPERTY LAW AND RESTRAINTS ON ALIENATION

From the perspective of property law in the early twentieth century, the most important issue about racially restrictive covenants was a rather general one: that they might constitute unreasonable and thus illegal restraints on alienation. Alienability is the ability to buy and sell property. Since almost any regulation or private obligation can have some impact on how easily one can sell one's property, the legal concern about restraints on alienation is rather open-ended, somewhat akin to the notoriously vague contours of nuisance law, which bans uses of one's property that "unreasonably" damage one's neighbors.

For all the vagueness of the idea of restraints on alienation, however, free alienability has been a matter of concern in American law for a long time. For example, most states long ago outlawed the kind of property ownership known as the "entailed fee," a property that can be handed down only to the direct lineal heirs of a particular owner, and that cannot be sold to or acquired by persons outside the line of familial inheritance. In this move, the United States diverged from English common law. Jane Austen's novels are replete with these entailments in early nineteenth-century England; but across the Atlantic, courts and legislatures proclaimed that such entailed fees were an aristocratic holdover, and as such they were incompatible with the free alienability of property enjoyed in the (lowercase *r*) republican United States.[15]

Lawyers have often analogized property rights to a "bundle of sticks" in which each right—the right to acquire, the right to exclude others, the right to use, and so forth—is a separate stick. Alienability—that is, the right simply to sell freely to any willing buyer—has widely been thought to be one of the sticks in the property bundle. From that perspective, restrictions on alienation could seem logically incompatible with property itself, or as nineteenth-century lawyers would put it, "repugnant to the estate."[16] This would of course be a quite formalistic view, but legal thought at the turn of the nineteenth to the twentieth century *was* quite formalistic, and hence the argument may have seemed persuasive to some.

Moreover, racial restrictions in particular might have seemed especially suspect. The race of a buyer is a matter far removed from the *uses* the buyer might make of the property. Durable use restrictions might seem quite reasonable, as for example permitting residential uses but not businesses or manufacturing plants in a neighborhood. Courts had upheld such use limits against charges of restraints on alienation for decades, particularly after an 1879 decision of the U.S. Supreme Court, *Cowell v. Colorado Springs Co.*, upholding a lot restriction that prohibited liquor sales. The opinion mentioned favorably prohibitions on factories, slaughterhouses, and other uses that might disturb the "health and comfort of whole neighborhoods" in urban areas. Preventive land use restraints of this sort could stave off the later nuisance suits that might otherwise occupy the time of the residential property owners and, of course, the courts themselves. In passing, *Cowell* described as unobjectionable a prohibition on sales to "particular persons," but all the case's examples concerned noxious uses. A constraint preventing whole classes of persons from buying land, as opposed to restrictions on the uses they might make of it, would send up warning flags for traditional property lawyers.[17]

Modern lawyers like to think of themselves as more practical about law's functions and less attached to the formal categories of earlier legal thought. But even from a more pragmatic perspective, racially restrictive covenants give pause, even putting to one side the questions of racial equity that are so vastly more salient in today's moral universe. As a practical matter, any constraint that reduces the set of potential bidders for a particular property is a matter of some significance. In a smaller bidding pool, one bidder is less likely to have to compete with another, and thus with a smaller pool, competitive bidding is more likely to stop at lower levels. Thus, all other things being equal, the smaller the class of people who will bid for an owner's property, the lower the property's likely value on resale. Restraining *who* can buy necessarily affects the size of the bidding pool—and it affects it for the worse.

Modern scholars of law and economics might suggest that this issue really should be left up to the buying and selling parties, since they ought to take into account the prospect of a lower resale value when they make the original contract. On that view, any risk of a lower resale value would be internalized by the same parties who originate the restraints on alienation. If they know what they want, and if they are willing to pay the price of a lower resale value for their property, why not let them? By the same token, when future purchasers buy, they should take into account any preexisting restraints, and they will pay less for a house whose retail value will predictably be lower because of the smaller number of persons who can bid for it. Hence future purchasers too will be unhurt be the constraints, since they will pay less in the first place—or so the argument goes.

There are several scholarly responses to this "cost internalization" argument, however, and we shall see more of them later. One response might be mentioned here because it is salient to earlier courts' attitudes. That is the point that housing resale constraints may have social impacts that are not necessarily internalized by the initial contracting parties. Take, for example, the issue of home improvements. An owner may have purchased a home quite cheaply, knowing that because of various restrictions, it may be difficult to find someone else who wants it as a home later. In that case, the owner will have fewer incentives to make home improvements or even to maintain the property, by comparison with simply letting it deteriorate as a wasting asset. But neglecting the house can have deleterious effects not only on the owner's property, for which the owner pays the price, but also on the wider neighborhood—for which owner pays practically nothing.

Indeed, as we shall see shortly, it is entirely plausible that by the 1930s and 1940s, restrictive covenants were contributing to an underinvestment problem, especially in urban neighborhoods where home occupancy was shifting from white to minority. Under those circumstances, white owners sometimes found themselves prevented by covenants from renting or selling to the only persons—minority members—who would realistically bid on their properties. Those owners' inability to rent or sell must have dampened their willingness to keep up the properties. Why bother to fix those back stairs or the broken basement window, if the only people who might be interested in the property are not entitled to buy or rent? Even more important, deterioration of a few properties can set off a cascade of deterioration in a larger neighborhood, as decline in one house makes the neighboring property less appealing. Thus when owners who agreed to covenants found that they could not rent or sell, and when those same owners neglected their unsalable or unrentable properties, others were affected too, including adjacent neighborhoods where the homeowners never did sign covenants.

These kinds of consequences of racially restrictive covenants suggest one reason why the courts have frowned on all kinds of restraints on alienation, not just racial ones. The racial deed restrictions are now particularly objectionable, but they suggest a more general pattern in which a genuine social impact can follow when owners cannot freely rent or sell their properties. The impact of an alienability restraint is not necessarily internalized by those who agree to it initially, but in part may be foisted on the surrounding neighborhood.

Now, to be sure, these kinds of problems can be more than offset if the restraints themselves are valuable to a substantial class of bidders. For example, restraints to prevent noise or commercial uses might be valuable in a residential neighborhood, and they might make the properties *more* saleable as residences. Thus noise restraints do shut out a class of purchasers—those whose uses necessarily create noise or congestion—but they will attract a substantial class of purchasers who are seeking peace and quiet and who will pay more to get it. These offsetting value creations can justify what would otherwise seem to be damaging restraints; they make restraints on alienation "reasonable," in the perennial language of Anglo-American courts.

But one should notice that what creates the offsetting value is the balance of one land *use* against another land *use*. Constraints on *who* can buy a landed property, as opposed to what uses the purchaser can engage in, seem peculiarly troublesome, as they did even to early twentieth-century lawyers. The person of the owner is irrelevant to the uses that he or she might make of the property. A constraint on *who* can buy or rent only reduces the pool of potential bidders for the property, without creating any ostensible counterbalancing enlargement of value. The only value of such personal racial constraints must be to satisfy the racist preferences of the other purchasers, either directly ("I don't want to live near minorities") or indirectly ("I'll bet that when it comes time to sell this place, the potential buyers will not want to live near minorities").

Could such restrictions seem reasonable to the courts? Would what has been called a "taste for discrimination" justify them?[18] As racially restrictive covenants started to be litigated in American cities in the late 1910s and early 1920s, the courts in different jurisdictions came to different conclusions on the restraint-on-alienation question. Some, notably the Louisiana and Missouri Supreme Courts, allowed Caucasian-only racial covenants, on the grounds that these restraints on alienation were only partial and that they left a large enough pool of potential buyers even after the exclusion of those who were not considered Caucasian. The implicit message was that any drop in value from disallowing one set of bidders would be offset by another set of bidders' greater eagerness to buy, presumably because the latter group would happily give up some of their powers of alienation, in exchange for the advantage of living in a neighborhood where all the residents had to exclude everyone of a different race.[19]

Other jurisdictions, however, notably California and Michigan, took the position that once any set of bidders was excluded, it would be impossible to draw a line of reasonableness. That is to say, there would be no way to figure out whether the group of remaining bidders would be numerous enough and eager enough or not.[20] As one California court colorfully speculated, restrictions like those under consideration, which excluded ownership by those of African, Chinese, or Japanese descent, might go on to exclude "any but albinos from the heart of Africa, or blond Eskimos"[21]—that is, they would constrict the bidding pool to a very small number. For this set of courts, restrictive covenants might constrain noisy or unpleasant land uses, but they could not bar ownership to any racial group.

Having made these bracing pronouncements, however, the high courts in both these more abstemious states backed away and rescued racial restrictions by means of a different formalism. They held that restraints on "use" or "occupancy"—as opposed to sales and ownership—were not restraints on alienation after all.[22] This was not a new distinction; nineteenth-century courts had treated limits on sale or ownership as issues of alienability but had permitted *use* restrictions as not affecting alienability in the strict sense. Even so, the precedents were not so clear: as in the U.S. Supreme Court's *Cowell* case, use limits in the earlier cases had excluded such things as taverns and manufacturing plants, and had not shut the door on whole classes of persons based on their personal characteristics. Nevertheless, with these or similar formal distinctions to support them, many racially restrictive covenants, including those much later at issue in *Shelley* and the companion case of *McGhee v. Sipes*, were drafted to constrain use and occupancy by disfavored races, in addition to or instead of ownership.

As a practical matter, the decisions about racial restrictions meant that in the more fastidious jurisdictions, no one could enforce covenants that would prevent minority members from purchasing property, but covenants could still prevent minorities from using or occupying the property they purchased. The ownership/use distinction thus led to the odd conclusion that African Americans and other racial minority members might own residential property subject to racially restrictive covenants, even though they could not live there themselves. Indeed, this is exactly what happened in a Los Angeles case in the later 1920s, when two African American women bought a house that was restricted to the use of those of the Caucasian race. The court ruled that a racial restriction on *use* could not be deployed to prevent the two from *owning* the restricted property. Even though they could not live in the house, they presumably could rent it to some white occupant who met the covenant's Caucasian-race qualification. But as one legal writer tartly commented in a 1934 law review, "probably very few Negroes invest in property which can be used only by white people."[23]

To the modern ear, and indeed to some ears at the time, all this sounds like ludicrous hairsplitting, particularly in the case of residential real estate. While occasional purchasers might buy houses as investment properties, most people buy houses in order to live in them, not to rent them out. In the 1919 California Supreme Court case that upheld racial restrictions on minority use (but not sale), a dissenting judge thought the court should construe the restriction to permit owners to occupy their houses, even if they were non-Caucasians, although he would have permitted provisions against rentals to non-owner minority tenants. His reasoning was rather technical, but he may have had in mind something like the many public policies that actively support owner occupancy of residences for the sake of the security, pride, and encouragement to invest that homeownership is thought to promote.[24]

The formalistic ownership/use distinction in the racial context only arose in states that already were concerned about the effects of racial restrictions on alienability. The distinction evidently had little purpose other than to dodge the usual legal bias in favor of free alienability, authorizing developers and neighborhoods to perpetuate legal residential segregation even where there were substantial doubts about racial restrictions as a matter of property law. In effect, the distinction nominally upheld the free sale of individual property while implicitly permitting white owners to exercise a group property right—exclusive white residency in the neighborhood as a whole.

But as is often the case with formalities, one formality led to another. Perhaps no byway in the saga of racially restrictive covenants is more peculiar or more revealing than the way in which alienability considerations—including the use/ownership distinction—played out in the area of corporate law, which the next section will explore.

THE STRANGE CASE OF CORPORATIONS AND COVENANTS

Corporate owners were involved in two substantial restrictive covenant cases that roughly bracketed the era of legally enforceable racial covenants in the United States. One was a case from Richmond, Virginia, in 1908; the other a case from Columbus, Ohio, in 1943. Both raised a strange question: how would racially restrictive covenants apply when the buyer was a corporation?

First, a word about corporations. American courts, at least since the famous *Trustees of Dartmouth v. Woodward* (1819), have regarded the corporation as a "person," albeit an "artificial person" that through law is "endowed with certain powers and franchises . . . subsisting in the corporation itself, as distinctly as if it were a real personage."[25] By contrast to a partnership, the corporation is thus expressly created by law, rather than through the association or conduct of its members. But this "as if" corporate person has some differences from natural persons. Lay people often describe corporations as engaging in cognition and other mental acts, but they do not describe them as participating in physical activities or having any physical presence. In a similar fashion, judges have attributed complex and even absurd mental states to corporations, but until very recently they have been reluctant to attribute physical presence or other physical characteristics to corporations.[26] Interestingly enough, it is the more modern effort to rectify economic disparities, and specifically to encourage minorities to engage in business activity, that has opened the door to "racing" corporations.

But no such modern motives disturbed the thinking of traditional corporate law in Virginia in the early 1900s. In fact, in that era, what might have led to the racializing of corporate law was precisely the opposite idea—that of keeping minorities in their place, a place distinctly separate from white citizens. Virginia was among the most emphatic proponents of the Jim Crow legislation that swept the South in the later part of the nineteenth century, and Richmond's social practices at the time suggest the depth of the state's segregationist impulses. They had reached the point that black and white children kept to opposite sides of the street when walking to school, while black and white prostitutes kept to separate streets altogether. Prisons, schools, and other public institutions all enforced segregation, and, if anything, social activities were even more sharply policed by both laws and informal norms. Interracial fishing, dancing, and boxing, as well as pool halls, race tracks, theaters, parks, beaches, circuses, and other "tented events" were all subject to formal and informal regulation.[27]

In this meticulously separationist environment, Virginia's courts had to decide whether an amusement park corporation, owned entirely by black persons, was subject to a deed restriction that barred ownership of the property by any person of "African descent." The amusement park in question was situated on part of a faltering residential development, which originally had been destined for ownership by white homeowners. As matters stagnated in the original development plan, the developers became increasingly open to the idea of selling off some portions to one Joseph Johnson, a man who had been born in slavery. More specifically, the sale would be to Johnson's corporation, the People's Pleasure Park Company, for purposes of creating a black-only amusement park on the land. But a white couple, Dick and Frances Rohleder, had previously bought some lots in the development, and they now objected—as did the husband's brother Joe, indeed rather more strenuously. None wanted anything to do with a neighboring amusement park for African Americans, or with the patrons who would crowd the nearby streetcar line. To be sure, the Rohleders must have had mixed motives, particularly the husband's brother Joe, since he himself operated another nearby park with amusement facilities and residential rentals for black persons, as well as running a local outdoor eatery that catered to a mixed clientele. Joe Rohleder in particular got into some heated fracases with the new management of the black amusement park, and he was one of the organizers of a county "improvement association" that was formed in response to the sale.[28]

In their lawsuit, the Rohleders claimed to have been deceived, and they attempted to oust the new amusement park owners on the basis of the development's original covenants that barred title to any African American. The trial court held that the Rohleders deserved compensation because they had indeed been misled, but the judge refused to quash the sale of the park, taking a position that courts in some other states were to echo later about residential covenants: the racially restrictive covenant was invalid as an unreasonable restraint on alienation. On appeal, however, the Virginia Supreme Court sidelined this ground and instead decided the case on the basis of the corporation's identity. That identity had no race, since a corporation was an "artificial person," and hence the amusement park had not been sold to a prohibited "colored person" or "person . . . of African descent." In effect, the court took the position that a corporation by its very nature could not have a race.[29]

This decision certainly followed the standard thinking about corporations in the day, but it is still more than slightly odd, given not only the virulent climate of segregation in Virginia politics in the early 1900s, but also the Virginia courts' nimbleness in upholding racial distinctions in an array of other areas. Some contemporary commentators thought the case unduly formalistic. And no wonder; in other legal contexts, southern courts at the time managed to abstract race onto persons and things with great facility, countenancing separate white and African American schools, churches, prisons, restrooms, drinking fountains, and even courtroom Bibles. Moreover, if the People's Park business had been a partnership or some other unincorporated business venture, it could have been more easily designated as African American, through the natural persons of the venturers. What was so different about corporations?[30]

The first difference rests squarely on property. Corporations then and now have generally not been viewed as associations of co-venturers (as partnerships are).[31] The corporate form splits ownership from control, so that shareholders are not understood to be in association in a common enterprise, but simply investors, each with a property claim to the corporation's equity. But property claims make corporate ownership special, or at least they did in the early twentieth century. As we noted in regard to the 1917 *Buchanan* case overturning racial zoning, this was an era in which property and contract were treated as the most fundamental of civil rights—*civil* rights because they were distinguished from the political and social claims that were then not thought to be automatic attributes of citizenship, and *fundamental* rights because their exercise might permit individuals to prosper and ultimately to stake a claim in those other political and social arenas as well.

Indeed, in principle, the Virginia Supreme Court's refusal to racialize corporate ownership was a variant on the trial court's rejection of the covenants themselves as a restraint on alienation. Racializing corporate shares would have prevented the free purchase and sale of those corporate shares. But the Virginia high court took a narrower approach, effectively saving for another day the general legality of racial covenants, even as it exempted corporations as race-less.

There were good reasons, though, why Virginia's high court was so cautious about "racing" corporations. One of the most important advantages of the corporate form is that it can draw together a variety of investors who need not know one another personally. If the corporation were to have a race, based on the race of all or some proportion of the investors, each investor would have to keep constant watch on purchases and sales by other investors, a monumental task that would defeat the whole idea of widespread and anonymous ownership. One might also expect fraud, subterfuge, and collusion as well, since persons of the "wrong" race might purchase or sell shares in order to take advantage of corporate racial advantages or avoid comparable disadvantages. And then there are the creditors—the banks and other lenders who extend loans to the corporation. If, say, a corporation deemed to be African American had special advantages or disabilities because of its race, a lender too would presumably only extend credit with those disabilities and advantages in mind, and it too would have to monitor shareholder purchases and sales in order to keep tabs on its own risk portfolio. The necessary monitoring and verification for the "right" race could cause huge administrative costs, raising the cost of credit to corporations and greatly diminishing the advantage of the corporate form. In all these respects, corporate ownership intensifies the concerns of property ownership more generally. As we shall see in the next chapter, for all kinds of property, legal relationships have to be kept relatively simple, or property ownership can bog down in complications that undermine the advantages of property itself.

One point to note: the modern "racing" of corporations has to face many of these same complications, as seen in our more recent efforts to extend business opportunities to minority- and women-owned firms, or to address concerns that these firms might face discrimination against them. To be sure, there are strong arguments that the principles of equal opportunity may make the effort worth the costs of administration. The historical contrast is thus all the more interesting. Even in the heyday of Jim Crow, and even in a state so thoroughly committed to segregation as Virginia was at that time, the courts did not think the principles of racial segregation made it worth the costs of assigning race to corporations.[32]

Undoubtedly this unusual hesitance was due in part to the respect for property rights. During that era, respect for property could outweigh segregationist motives, as it did in the *Buchanan* case's invalidation of racial zoning, and as it also did in the rejection of race as a nuisance category in all courts, northern and southern. But there was another factor at stake too, a factor that dogged racial restrictions throughout the era of legal segregation. In addition to considerations of property—both its principles and its practicalities—courts had problems with categorizing race itself, and those problems could have been spotlighted if corporations were to be assigned a race.

The corporation cases thus revealed the awful truth behind the law of segregation: no one knew exactly how to identify race. Southern courts followed the laws of their states, and they did find ways to distinguish the races in all kinds of situations. But the distinctions were fragile indeed, and the courts did not always have an easy time making them. Virginia courts in particular had struggled since colonial days with the problem of identifying and categorizing race. They and other courts often relied on anatomical or physiological patterns like skin color, hair texture, and nose and head shape, but these courts did not allow themselves to be ensnared by biology. Race was never determined solely by scientific verification or clinical examination. Instead, it was identified by common knowledge, performance, and social cues. Indeed, throughout the post-Reconstruction South, judicially identified race was well understood to be something of a fiction—as well it might be, given the widespread patterns of interracial sexual relationships throughout the slavery and post-slavery era.[33]

At the turn of the century, the newly sharpened implementation of legally imposed segregation—in parks, schools, employment, transportation, and so on—always threatened to reveal the socially constructed character of race itself, and the members of the *Rohleder* court must have had some inkling of this. What could have raised this issue more pointedly than the race of a corporation, an entity that was not a physical person at all? Should corporate race be based on the self-identification of the shareholders? This would be highly threatening if segregation legislation were to have any bite at all, since it would suggest that people could choose their own race. Should it be the shareholders' physical characteristics or general reputations? All the shareholders, or just some percentage? On the one hand, a requirement of racial purity for the total shareholding group could have brought on a litigation nightmare and a business disaster for supposedly white corporations as well as African American ones. But on the other hand, a percentage rule could destabilize the enforcement of racial definitions on all the other fronts, from schools to water fountains to train compartments. Imagine the analogies that could be drawn about the percentages of African Americans that would be allowable for a water fountain to remain white. The emergent Jim Crow regime was predicated on race as something observable and immutable, but any method for defining corporate racial identity defied any such immutabilities. Better to leave the issue alone, then, and leave corporations "unraced."

The nagging question in *Rohleder,* however was this: if corporations had no race, what would become of racially restrictive covenants? Could they not be completely or at least substantially evaded if minority purchasers simply adopted a corporate form, as seems to have been the case for Joseph Johnson's People's Pleasure Park? By the 1920s, a commentator in the *Yale Law Journal* expressed doubts about whether other states would follow the *Rohleder* decision. A "more sensible" solution, the author said, would be to follow a precedent from California, namely that the state's laws against alien land ownership could not be evaded by the corporate form. The author did not consider whether race might not be more difficult to prove than citizenship.[34]

Interestingly enough, the evasion issue arose in South Africa in a 1920 case, *Dadoo v. Krugersdorp Municipal Council*. The South African court took the same view of corporations that the Virginia court had taken in *Rohderer*, no doubt for some of the same reasons. But the race-free character of corporations meant that minorities might evade South Africa's housing segregation laws simply by incorporation. Indeed, the case had arisen precisely because Dadoo, a merchant of Indian origin, wanted to operate a grocery store and residence in an area in which Asians could not own property.[35]

The South African court noted the opportunities for evading the apartheid statute but further observed that the issue would be mooted in future by some 1919 amendments to that statute. Evidently anticipating the problem of corporate end runs, the legislature decided that landownership restrictions henceforth would apply to corporations in which members of a prohibited race held a controlling interest—too late to block Mr. Dadoo, whose corporation had purchased before the legislative change, but decisive from 1919 on. Legislation of this sort was a step toward solving the evasion problem, but it must have brought on all the definitional and monitoring problems that race-defined corporations entail.[36]

As was observed in a handful of law review commentaries over the next decades—generally but not entirely disapprovingly—American restrictive covenants were also vulnerable to the evasions inherent in the nonracialized corporate form.[37] But a second corporate law case, decided several decades after *Rohderer* and *Dadoo*, illustrated the way that American courts dealt with this kind of evasion. Instead of giving corporations a race, as in South Africa, American courts deployed a formalism that we have already seen in connection with restraints on alienation: they drew a distinction between restrictions on *ownership* and restrictions on *use or occupancy*.

Perkins v. Trustees of Monroe Avenue Church of Christ was a case that came out of Columbus, Ohio, in the mid-1940s, shortly before the

U.S. Supreme Court ended legally enforceable racially restrictive covenants in the United States. But at the time, no one knew that the end of racial covenants was near, and, in any event, the first step in the *Perkins* story had occurred much earlier, all the way back in 1926. At that time, a set of Columbus neighbors had agreed that their lots should not be "leased, rented, sold or conveyed to any person or persons of any race other than Caucasian, nor shall any such [persons] be permitted to occupy the same . . . except as a servant."[38] Almost a generation later, in June 1945, one of the covenanted lots was conveyed to the Monroe Avenue Church of Christ, which was incorporated in Ohio. The church had a racially mixed congregation, and it planned to use the residential lot as a parsonage for its "partially Negro" pastor, the Reverend Lloyd Dickerson. Some neighbors sued to enjoin the whole transaction—the sale to the church as well as the occupancy of Reverend Dickerson.[39]

The neighbors won on both grounds in the trial court, but on appeal, the Ohio appellate court flatly rejected any injunction against the sale to the church. Why? The answer should be familiar: it was because the church was a corporation, and as the court of appeals put it (prominently citing *Rohleder*), "[i]t ought to be clear that a corporation as a legal entity can have no racial identity."[40]

Nevertheless, the appellate court affirmed the trial court's decision with respect to Dickerson's residence, for another familiar reason: the reverend could not live on the church's property, because the relevant restrictive covenant also restrained not just sale to a minority person but also *use and occupancy,* and Dickerson, the would-be occupant, was a real person rather than a disembodied corporation. To the argument that such a covenant was contrary to public policy, the appeals court commented that while "vociferous minorities of our citizens, instigated by politicians, not statesmen, clamor for judicial denial of private rights under the guise of public welfare," this court was having none of it.[41]

There is slightly more to the story, however. On appeal in the Ohio Supreme Court, Dickerson's lawyers made a very clever argument: even if he was not Caucasian, he nevertheless was a servant of the church, and thus he should be able to reside on the property under the covenant's exemption for servants (a common exemption in racial covenants). The state supreme court apparently took a dim view of this stratagem. It dismissed the appeal *per curiam,* evidently taking the position that a corporate "servant" was not the same as a domestic servant, the latter being the obvious subject of the exemption.[42]

The very next year, in 1948, *Shelley v. Kraemer* came down from the U.S. Supreme Court, and following that decision, the Ohio Supreme Court's decision was itself reversed in favor of the church.[43] All the same, it is worth noting the ways in which the courts manipulated doctrine in these cases: they were formalistic with respect to the distinction between ownership and use, but they were practical and realistic with respect to the meaning of "servant."

By mixing and matching interpretive strategies in this way, the courts managed to uphold the use of covenants to effect residential segregation. This is not to put particular blame on Ohio's courts; they were not really different from other American courts in upholding racially restrictive covenants against common law objections. But what is noticeable is the set of contortions that courts and lawyers had to undertake in order to avoid the very old-fashioned legal concerns that racial covenants raised—concerns that had a real basis in the American approach to the meaning and function of property.

Some of the same traditional concerns were reflected in other common law property doctrines that we will review in the next chapter—but unlike the big constitutional complaints and the big objections to restraints on alienation, the courts largely ignored these other doctrines altogether, no doubt because they seemed to be narrowly technical pettifoggery, at a time when courts were generally growing more relaxed about all kinds of private land restrictions. When viewed through their underlying principles, however, these unspoken doctrinal objections could have provided considerable ammunition to shoot down covenants as legal supports for neighborhood social norms of segregation. Although not much heard from, these ghosts came back occasionally to haunt racially restrictive covenants. With a modicum of imagination and a few more hints from the lawyers, courts might well have used them to rule against racial restrictions, simply on grounds of formal property law.

Pushing Down the Ghosts

Covenant Development and Unseen Legal Influences

4

In the forty-plus years before *Shelley v. Kraemer* disrupted the legal enforceability of racially restrictive covenants, litigation in the courts suggested that these instruments would go largely unpoliced either by constitutional law, property law, or the law of corporations. As we saw in the last chapter, by 1926 it appeared that the U.S. Constitution would have nothing to say about them. Somewhat more restrictively, some states' property law doctrines of restraints on alienation did limit racial covenants insofar as they applied to residential sales. But when the courts approved covenants against use and occupancy, in effect they reinstated covenant constraints on most residential sales. After all, who would buy a house that he or she could not occupy? As to corporate law, the courts followed the conventional doctrine and agreed that corporations had no race—but the occupants of corporations' property did, and those occupants were subject to use-and-occupancy racial restrictions.

These major litigated matters did not tell the whole story of the legal policing of covenants, however. Property law in particular contained still other constraining technical doctrines, and while these other doctrines barely made any overt appearance in any litigation about racial covenants, they did inform judicial interpretations of the broader-brushed citations to restraints on alienation. As a practical matter, the shades of more technical doctrines also influenced the structure of many of the early racial restrictions, and, as we shall see in later chapters, they continued to haunt residential real estate transactions for decades to come.

Like the doctrine of restraints on alienation, all these property law ghosts had important normative ideas behind them. However loosely interpreted, the doctrine against restraints on alienation stood for the principle that anyone should be able to buy, use, and sell property freely unless there were good reasons for exceptions. The property law ghosts stood for related but somewhat more precise principles. One was that living persons, rather than the dead, should control property, so that any exceptions to free alienability should not last forever. Another was that anyone affected by limitations on property should have ample notice of them. Still another was that any long-term limitations on property usage should have continuing value, primarily measured by the participants, but to some degree by outsiders' interests as well.

For several decades, proponents of racial restrictions managed to dodge the highly technical property rules that embodied these principles, and this chapter outlines how they did so. But these dodges clearly had some costs for the developers and homeowners who used them. Besides that, the larger property norms lurked in the background all along. Even though NAACP-affiliated lawyers concentrated on constitutional issues from the 1920s onward, they did not entirely neglect the property law arguments, and they especially found some use for property technicalities at the margins. This chapter explores some of the deeper intuitions that they might have found behind what seemed to be merely technical issues of property law. It does so by tracking the way that racially restrictive covenants evolved for a few decades, and by showing the influence that the ghost doctrines had on that evolution.

HOW LONG COULD THEY LAST? THE ISSUE OF TIME LIMITS ON RACIAL COVENANTS

Chronologically, one of the first property law obstacles facing developers who wanted to use restrictive covenants—racial or otherwise—was the issue of duration. Those who buy into a "nice" urban neighborhood want it to stay nice for a long time, both for their own use and to maintain resale value. This wish may take the form of long-term restrictions that permit only single-family uses—for example, in order to prevent gas stations or convenience stores from sprouting up all over; or it may take the form of similarly long-term limits on setbacks or heights in order to protect homes against overbuilt lots or tall buildings that block sunlight and air.

Turn-of-the-century developers were especially anxious to control buyers who might deviate from the developers' subdivision plans. This was because at that time, developers only set out the streets, lots, and landscaping, leaving it to the buyers to arrange for building their own homes. Given that mode of subdivision, developers did not want to see some early buyer make inappropriate building decisions that would undermine later lot sales. Moreover, home buyers themselves were aware that other buyers might pose threats in early twentieth-century urban areas, especially given the arrival of automobiles and elevator-assisted skyscrapers, among other things. In the new well-to-do suburban developments, many residential purchasers wanted to keep gas stations, cheap construction, and tall buildings at bay, for a long time. Insofar as homeowners thought that racial restrictions were a part of "niceness"—and many apparently did—they thought that racial restrictions should last a long time too. Since buyers thought that all these long-term restrictions added value, it was profitable for developers to give them what they wanted.[1]

But long duration was not treated lightly by common law property doctrines. One hoary but important legal doctrine potentially blocked the new, long-term neighborhood restrictions: the Rule Against Perpetuities (RAP). This venerable property doctrine aims to prevent any given landowner from extending his or her control over property too far into the future. Roughly speaking, the traditional RAP usually permits the owner to control land for about two or at most three generations beyond his or her ownership, but not further. It bears mention that the RAP is still one of the most dreaded formalities in all of property law, because it entails very close attention to the passage of generations; indeed, a mistake about the RAP was the central plot device in *Body Heat,* the celebrated 1981 *film noir.*[2]

In spite of its convoluted practical applications, however, the normative considerations behind the RAP are not so complex. Basically, the rule recognizes that while land and property can last a long time, times change and people change too. And this means that new generations are likely to have new views about the most desirable uses of land. The RAP gives those new generations their day, restraining the "dead hand" of the past. More subtly, the RAP protects against external third-party effects in much the same way as the doctrines of restraints on alienability discussed in the last chapter.

With the RAP as with alienability doctrines, the modern perspective of law and economics might suggest that concerns about the dead hand are overblown: on this view, when current owners impose long-term restrictions on a property, they will take into account the gains and losses that might occur to future buyers, since future buyers will pay more (or less) depending on the restrictions. But quite aside from the commonsense understanding that no owner is so prescient as to anticipate uses of the property long into the future, the RAP takes a second cut at the same concerns about external effects that drive the alienability doctrines. Over the long run, restraints on property A may affect its maintenance and character, with spillover effects on neighboring property B. Moreover, if long-term restraints on land are allowed to accrete without limit, inquiry costs for future purchasers of *all* landed property purchasers will be raised. Instead of questioning the reasonableness of particular restraints, as with the alienability doctrines, the RAP simply shuts them off after a maximum of a few generations.[3]

But all these normative considerations created potential problems for homeowners and developers who wanted the neighborhood to stay the same indefinitely. There are many exceptions and detours around the RAP in modern property law, and it is now generally thought that deed restrictions and covenants are not strictly subject to it, though courts may cite RAP policies against unusually long-lasting restrictions.[4] Those policies implicitly inform the concern for duration—albeit a more flexible one—in the doctrines limiting restraints on alienation, discussed in Chapter 3. The exact reach of the old-fashioned RAP was not so clear at the beginning of the twentieth century, however, when widespread uses of residential real estate covenants were only in their infancy. The RAP thus loomed as a threat to the new and relatively large-scale subdivisions, potentially crippling the long-term covenants whose whole purpose was to guarantee neighborhood character out into the future.

Developers could avoid the RAP in two clear ways, and at the turn of the century they did both. The first way was to limit the duration of restrictions. Because of certain technicalities within the RAP itself, a limit of twenty or twenty-one years was bound to be safe. One sees these relatively short time limits on some of the early racial covenants. But a time period of twenty or twenty-one years is not very protective for some aspects of neighborhood continuity—for example, restraints that keep houses from becoming commercial buildings—and covenants that vanished so quickly might make the neighborhood plan seem unstable to potential buyers. In fact, a 1928 survey of early subdivision restrictions showed that early development restrictions of all kinds were extending beyond the safe twenty- or twenty-one-year period, clustering around a length of about thirty-three years.[5]

How, then, did developers extend the time? Some used a second loophole that enabled them to avoid the RAP, though the method was awkward. This second loophole entailed adjusting the strict legal form of the covenant. With a straightforward covenant structure, the developer himself could enforce the covenants as long as he still owned part of the property; but as the developer sold lots, each buyer acquired enforcement rights, so that once all the lots were sold, the entire power to enforce the developer's covenants would rest with the homeowners themselves. Unfortunately, this pattern ran particular risks from the RAP, since the wishes of the original owner (the developer) effectively controlled the property long after he had relinquished his ownership interests—shades of the dead hand of the past, in which a past owner might continue to rule over current owners. But with a rather more old-fashioned legal arrangement, a developer could structure the sale to each homeowner in a different way, one in which the developer retained a certain kind of residual ownership interest.

The way to do this was to structure each purchase as a kind of conditional estate. With a conditional form, a violation of one of the covenants would cause the property to revert back to the original seller—that is, to the developer himself. The RAP did not cover this kind of arrangement, in which the developer (or development corporation) still held a possible reversionary interest and counted as a potential residual owner.[6]

One can observe this cautious reversionary structure in a number of cases involving the early racially restrictive covenants, including some of the important early state cases that upheld racial restrictions. The remedy for violation of the covenants was that the property would return to the hands of the developer—a remedy quite unlike that with which many modern homeowners are more familiar, namely a legal action by the other property owners themselves to fine or enjoin the rule breaker.[7]

The later evolution of modern remedies suggests what was wrong with the conditional or reversionary structure: the conditional estate may have provided an enforcement mechanism that evaded the RAP, but it was exceedingly clumsy. Let us suppose that a current owner parked her car in the street, in violation of the subdivision rules. A forfeiture of the entire property back to the developer would be a sledgehammer remedy for such a minor lapse. Yet failure to enforce even minor infractions might mean that the covenants would gradually erode altogether, at the cost of undermining all or part of the community plan.

There was a second problem with the reversionary structure too: when a development firm structured an urban or suburban community's management in this way, the firm had to keep up some involvement with the place, long after the initial construction and marketing was complete, and long after the developer may have wanted to move on to other projects. A third and related problem, of course, was that this remedy fell to the developer to enforce, even though the homeowners themselves had the greater interest once all the properties had been sold.

The conditional-estate structure was thus out of step with the growing specialization in American real estate development, where developers did the initial platting, layout, and legal-covenant structure, and left ongoing governance issues to purchasers and subsequent owners.[8] As we shall see in Chapter 8, the conditional-estate structure also caused trouble for more modern forms of real estate finance, because lenders could see a potential sledgehammer remedy—a reverter interest still in the hands of the seller—as too great a risk for their mortgage security interests.

As time went on, and as courts became more accustomed to private land use controls of all kinds—including racial restrictions—the risk from the RAP diminished substantially, and its concerns faded into the more general caution about restraints on alienation. The straightforward covenant form came to be more prevalent. Developers of new subdivisions sold out entirely, leaving the homeowners themselves to take over covenant enforcement through homeowners associations that could use more nuanced remedies like injunctions and fines for infractions, instead of the draconian forfeiture of whole properties. The homeowners, after all, were the ones who really cared about infractions, and fines or injunctions allowed them to enforce the rules with sanctions more closely tailored to the problems.

But given the ghost of RAP considerations, it took some time before anyone could be certain that this more convenient structure would work. Back in 1919, the California Supreme Court had upheld racial occupancy restrictions in the *Los Angeles Investment* case referenced in Chapter 3, but the restrictions in that case were structured as a part of a conditional estate with a reverter clause; and the court strongly hinted that it might not look so favorably on the pure covenant form.[9] After all, the pure covenant form passed forward all rights and obligations and enforcement power to later owners. However practical that arrangement might be, from the RAP perspective, the question was whether a developer's plan could continue to rule later owners when the developer himself was no longer on the scene. The California court never talked explicitly about the RAP, but it took until 1928 before that court clearly accepted the pure covenant form for racial restrictions, whereby the homeowners themselves acquired the right to enforce covenants against one another directly—as opposed to relying on a remedy that involved forfeiture to an intermediary development firm that had retained a residual ownership interest.[10]

In the end, the Rule Against Perpetuities gradually lost its scare power as a common law constraint on restrictive covenants. Even in the earlier part of the twentieth century, private land use restrictions of all kinds were becoming more important to real estate development practices. The courts were evidently willing to relax rules, like the RAP, that would have severely undercut their use. As unattractive as racial restrictions now seem in retrospect, for developers and courts at the time, they were just one of a number of subjects in the emergent use of private land use controls. Racial covenants appeared to piggyback on the early twentieth-century courts' willingness to accommodate new land use control practices more generally.[11]

As a practical matter, RAP considerations did have some effect, however, just because of the earlier methods that developers and homeowners had used to evade the RAP or RAP-like considerations in the doctrines about restraints on alienation. A number of early racial covenants had avoided the RAP by setting time limits of twenty or twenty-one years. This meant that many of these covenants looked as if they were about to expire in the 1930s and 1940s, and by that time the real estate industry had become thoroughly invested in promoting racial covenants. Renewing the covenants conjured up a different ghost, however. Covenant renewal would take place among neighbors who were already homeowners—no sales of property were involved. But another older property doctrine made it difficult to get any covenants started outside the context of a property sale. As with the RAP, almost no cases explicitly talked about this second ghost, but in the actual structuring of racial covenants one can see that it too was something of a scare factor.

HOW DO YOU KNOW ABOUT YOUR OBLIGATIONS, AND TO WHOM ARE YOU OBLIGED? THE PROBLEM OF LATER-INSTITUTED RACIAL RESTRICTIONS

A critical feature of any kind of covenant running with the land is that it is not simply a contract. A covenant that runs with the land binds later owners of a property, even though they are not the people who negotiated and agreed upon the restriction in the first place. Because of this characteristic, covenants raise a number of questions that are out of the ordinary in simple contract law. One of the most serious is this: what should happen to the covenants if a new purchaser buys the property without knowing about them? Unlike an ordinary contract, the buyer was not a party to the original bargain. Should the buyer be bound anyway? And if so, to whom? Suppose there are a hundred people who claim that, through the covenants, they have some rights over what the new owner does with the property? Does the owner have to placate all of them? How does the owner know whether they really do have claims against his or her property?

All running covenants raise issues like these, issues relating to notice to subsequent purchasers—notice both of their obligations and the scope of those obligations. Because covenants that run with the land might well be unknown to later buyers, and because multiple persons could claim to be beneficiaries, these covenants are especially sensitive to issues of notice and scope. For those reasons, among others, the older common law had some limitations that were specific to covenants. One doctrinal limit that dealt especially with notice acquired the exceedingly odd name of "horizontal privity," but it had a very practical purpose: it would not permit covenants to run to later purchasers unless the covenants themselves appeared in major documents of transfer.

Horizontal privity was scarcely ever alluded to in any major litigation, but the doctrine was a genuine if unspoken threat to a type of racial covenant that became especially widespread after 1920. Those were the covenants that were not created by developers at the beginning of a new subdivision, but rather began as agreements among neighbors, long after the first purchases of the properties had occurred. These after-the-fact covenants trailed the developer-orchestrated covenants by several years, but they were especially important in older urban areas that were fully built before racial restrictions became standard practice in new developments. We shall see much more about these covenants in subsequent chapters; this is not only because they were so important in older cities like Chicago, Detroit, and St. Louis, but for other reasons as well, notably because they had a number of practical and legal vulnerabilities.

The ghost doctrine of horizontal privity was one of those vulnerabilities. Even though few jurists talked about it explicitly, this oddly named doctrine had an impact on the ways that racial restrictions were written, and even more on the ways that they were enforced.[12] Despite the rather forbidding nickname, horizontal privity was really about a simple matter of fairness: making sure that future purchasers realize that they may be bound by a covenant that runs with the property they buy. To effect this end, horizontal privity required, to put it briefly, that the original parties to a covenant had to have one of a specific set of relationships to the property in question. Generally speaking, no promises or covenants could run with the land and bind future possessors unless the covenants were created in conjunction with a *lease* or *sale* of the property. The underlying reason appears to have been notice: sales and leases would normally be accompanied with noticeable documentation. Subsequent purchasers would be likely to look into these documents or find them in the chain of title, and thus they would find out about the duties created by their predecessors in title.[13]

In new subdivisions, developer-initiated covenants easily met the horizontal privity requirement; if a developer inserted a "Caucasians only" clause in every deed before selling any of the properties, every potential buyer (or her attorney) was sure to find a reference to the restrictions in the deed or in a document search of past deeds. On the other hand, neighbor-initiated covenants did not come along until later in the life of the neighborhood, outside the context of any property transfers, and thus these neighbor petitions were more problematic from the perspective of notice to later purchasers. They could be recorded, but they were not part of major transfer documents like sales or long-term leases.

There were some instances of this type of racial covenant in the early 1900s—that is to say, the after-the-fact neighborhood racial covenant, where a group of homeowners agreed among themselves not to sell or rent to nonwhites, and further agreed to pass on these obligations to later purchasers. Indeed, the covenant in *Shelley v. Kraemer* itself was based on a neighbor agreement that dated back to 1911. But covenants in the form of neighbor agreements faced an uncertain fate in the first years of the century. In that respect, the experience of one very important location—Harlem, New York—was instructive.

In the early 1900s, New York's expanding black population started to move from downtown and midtown locations up into Harlem, then an affluent suburban area within the city, albeit one with a certain softness in the real estate market at the time. In response to this emerging influx, some local property owners tried to round up their neighbors to get them to promise that none would sell or rent to nonwhites. Some even tried to keep down the numbers of persons who might have been exempted as servants—the maids and janitors and other service personnel.[14]

But the New York courts gave the old owners no help in enforcing these agreements. Even more important, according to Gilbert Osofsky, a leading historian of Harlem in this era, the owners themselves could never keep up a unanimous front. Covenants were neither a sufficient signal to assure the white owners among themselves, nor a sufficient warning to stave off the new entrants. Black real estate dealers disregarded warnings to stay away from "covenant blocks"—no Hawk/Dove game here—and antiblack neighborhood agreements quickly unraveled, as white owners sold or rented to the newcomers and Harlem turned into a vibrant black mecca.[15]

By the 1920s, however, and in different locations, neighbor agreements became much more prevalent and much more acceptable in the courts. The NAACP and other civil rights proponents argued that white neighbors started to deploy restrictive covenants as a substitute for the racial zoning that the *Buchanan* case outlawed in 1917. Indeed, in the 1930s, a remarkable opinion by the Maryland Supreme Court strongly supported that narrative, though the case was unimpressed with potential constitutional implications. In 1938, *Meade v. Dennistone* upheld neighbor agreements in Maryland; with a barbed comment about the inexplicable character of the Supreme Court's *Buchanan* decision against racial zoning, the Maryland high court observed that "all agree that something ought to be done," and it was only to be expected that Baltimore's white neighborhoods would take their own legal precautions against the African American influx.[16]

Aside from neighbor covenants as a response to the *Buchanan* case, an alternative or perhaps additional explanation for their rapid spread may have derived from the race riots of the late 1910s, especially those in Chicago in 1919. These serious disturbances may have softened any skepticism the courts had held toward racial covenants. In addition, the courts may have tolerated this type of covenant simply because by the 1920s, the courts were more willing to countenance private land use controls of all kinds, ignoring any ways in which racial restrictions might be more problematic than others. Whatever the reasons, from the 1920s onward, a number of cases upheld these after-the-fact neighborhood agreements against would-be sellers or renters to minority members, as well as against the minority persons themselves.

But the cases also suggest another feature of these irregular kinds of covenants: that these neighbor agreements often emerged in areas that were older and less modish than those with developer-originated covenants. Some of these neighborhoods were established working-class or ethnic neighborhoods; but since those were as likely to turn to threats or violence as to covenants, they were not the majority. Instead, neighbor-covenanting areas were more likely to be the somewhat embattled middle-class neighborhoods that seemed to lie in the direct path of minority expansion, like Harlem in earlier years or Chicago's Hyde Park later, or like some of the buffer areas of St. Louis that formed a "ring of steel" around minority areas.[17] In addition, whereas the developer-originated deed restrictions in the 1920s included race merely as one element in a larger plan for an "exclusive" and "high class" private community, the neighbor-driven restrictive covenants had no other elements at all. Their creators fixed all hope for gentility on promises of racial exclusion.

Those who pushed for neighborhood covenants were at least dimly aware of the horizontal privity problem—that these covenants, even if recorded, were not part of a major title transfer—and they tried to get around it in various ways. One way was a proliferation of what might be called bells and whistles. The Harlem property owners early in the century paid one another one dollar at the time they agreed to the covenants, obviously in an effort to make the proceedings seem more formal. By the 1920s, for the white neighbors in an area near Washington's Dupont Circle, the price had gone up to five dollars. Later on, some neighborhood covenants required the signatories to include the covenant in the next deed of sale, thus getting the restriction into a major document of transfer at some future time. Many of the other neighbor covenants were almost ludicrously formalistic, loaded with "whereas" clauses and "the said parties" and "consideration of the premises" and the like, often following model covenants created by real estate professionals.[18]

In spite of these simulacra of formality, the neighbor covenants in fact tended to be considerably sloppier than the developer restrictions. Developers could draw up a set of covenants and place a reference to them in every deed in the new subdivision, before any lot was sold. By contrast, to get neighbor covenants under way later, individual persons with a particular interest collected signatures door to door, and in the process they were apt to create numerous irregularities and ambiguities. Sometimes they failed to get necessary signatures from spouses; sometimes the signatures lacked the necessary formalities; sometimes the documents themselves failed to say anything about proportions of signatories in a neighborhood that would be required it order to make the agreements valid for those who had signed. These and other technical problems were useful later to local civil rights lawyers, who learned to exploit them in fighting off covenant enforcement.[19]

While the neighbor covenants were always vulnerable to irregularities of this sort, they did find a path around the general problem of horizontal privity. Their path, ironically enough, was to call on the courts' jurisdiction in "equity." When the spokesmen for neighborhood covenants went to court to enforce these racial restrictions, they sued to *enjoin* sales or occupancy rather than to collect damages (the normal remedy in civil suits)—that is, they sued for a type of remedy that is only available when damages are inadequate. This procedural move put the case in the court's "equity jurisdiction" rather than its normal jurisdiction "at law." In the latter, cases at law, decisions may be made by a jury of lay persons, and to guide their actions, the courts generally are supposed to act in a relatively rule-bound manner. By contrast, cases in equity traditionally give all authority to the supposedly learned judge, who attempts to do justice with a somewhat more relaxed view about the legal rules—including privity rules for covenants. This is because equity jurisprudence comes into play only where strict adherence to the legal rules might lead to unfair results or insufficient remedies.

Here again it matters that these covenant cases were about property. Unlike most civil legal issues, real property issues generally call on the courts' equity jurisprudence. Every piece of real estate is considered to be unique, and equity deals especially with unique cases where the remedy at law—money damages—is thought to be inadequate for the injury. In earlier years, when none of the subdivision covenants enjoyed an entirely certain legal status, developers and those who bought homes from them also called on the courts' equity jurisprudence to enforce the original covenants. Thus by the 1920s, when the neighbor-driven covenants became more prevalent, courts had become accustomed to enforcing covenants through equitable remedies like injunctions. But equity jurisprudence was particularly important for the neighborhood agreements, because they (and not the developer covenants) had to avoid the ghost of horizontal privity.[20]

All the same, the neighbors ran some risks in requesting the courts to exercise their powers in equity. After all, the overriding consideration in equity jurisprudence is fairness. By the 1940s, some judges were beginning to observe that it was not exactly fair to keep minorities bottled up in urban ghettos, particularly through the neighbor-driven covenants that were not confined to specific developments, but that might instead expand indefinitely through signature collection.[21]

But as we shall see, those objections were to come later. In the 1920s, the principal fairness concern in covenant cases was simply notice to a buyer that the property was restricted by a covenant. All that was required to enforce a covenant at equity was that the purchaser *knew* of the earlier obligation when he or she bought—after all, that was the point of the old legal horizontal privity rule in the first place. Technical horizontal privity, itself a kind of assurance that later occupants could find out about the restrictions by looking at major documents, was not necessary if the occupant actually knew about the restriction, or if the occupant had notice from the official records office, even though the documents on file were not major ones like deeds.[22]

This of course raises an important question: *did* subsequent minority buyers or occupants know about the neighborhood agreements that purported to keep out nonwhite residents? In some cases they clearly did, as in Harlem at the beginning of the century. In that time and place, enterprising black real estate brokers and purchasers knew perfectly well about the old-time white residents' frantic efforts to keep them out, and they prided themselves on breaking the neighborhood agreements wide open. That could be just a case of New York cheekiness, but it was helped along by the New York courts' skepticism about such agreements at that early stage in the history of racial covenants.[23]

Those who later wanted racially restrictive neighborhood agreements to act as legal instruments made sure to record them, so that later purchasers would be on notice. Recording is not a complete answer to the notice issue, however. Some documents can appear in the records but have no legal effect. For example, in an old-fashioned recording system, information is gleaned by tracking successive conveyances of real estate interests, and if there is a break in the chain of conveyances, another conveyance outside the chain need not be attended; such an unmoored document is rather picturesquely called a "wild deed," and it may have no effect.[24] Similarly, in order for a document to give record notice and count as part of the chain of title, one has to believe that it is a valid instrument in the first place; but until the state courts began to enforce these neighborhood covenants in equity in the 1920s and later, there was a certain circularity to the assertion that they really did give notice of any legal obligations.

Even when their judicial acceptability became clearer, a recorded neighborhood agreement might give only limited information about the covenants to a potential buyer. Depending on how the instrument was drafted, and how carefully signatures were collected, the potential buyer might find the record of the neighborhood racial restriction that ran with the property but might not learn how many other lot owners could enforce the covenant, or which owners they were without searching some other set of nearby properties as well. Moreover, since many of these neighborhood agreements only took force upon the signature of a given percentage of the residences on a block or set of blocks, a potential buyer might receive ambiguous or mistaken information from a search of the neighbors' titles, who might or might not hold title from a previous owner who had actually signed the agreement. This is not a mere technicality, because a purchaser would very much want to know who (if anyone) could enforce a covenant. Among other things, if there were only a few "beneficiaries," a potential purchaser might be able to pay or otherwise negotiate her way out of a covenant.

Still, on the issue of actual knowledge of the racially restrictive neighborhood agreements, it bears recalling that the entire history of legally enforceable racially restrictive covenants was relatively short, and highly contentious too. Given that none of the neighbor-driven racial restrictions had been in place for more than a few decades at most, one might surmise that many of the white sellers were the very people who had signed the covenants in the first place, and one might suppose too that their minority purchasers also actually knew about and willfully violated neighborhood covenants aimed at keeping them out, even if many were more diffident than their insouciant Harlem compatriots had been in the early 1900s. In Washington, D.C., for example, in the middle-class neighborhood whose racial covenants were upheld in the Supreme Court's *Corrigan* case, segregation quickly eroded as African American buyers used straw purchasers, or passed for white, or simply bought when white owners abandoned the covenants.[25]

This is not to say, however, that minority purchasers or renters always did know that their acts were breaking some earlier agreement. As we shall see in the *Shelley* case itself, the buyers did not appear to know about the neighborhood agreement that purported to forbid their entry, and it appeared that they would not have tried to make the purchase if they had known that they were not wanted. For them, the old neighborhood agreement would have had its assigned function of signaling and intimidation.

Moreover, the litigated cases are generally not a good sample on this issue of information. These cases undoubtedly selected for instances in which everyone did know of the restrictions, because some white actors or a noisy "neighborhood improvement association"—egged on by local real estate councils—cared enough to try to enforce them, while other white and black actors wanted to break them. As one prominent NAACP lawyer observed at a 1945 conference, racially restrictive covenants were usually only enforced if some self-selected agitators were especially active in stirring the pot.[26]

But another lawyer at the same conference noted that it was expensive to litigate these cases, a fact that dampened the neighboring homeowners' enthusiasm for doing so.[27] The more the white owners' enthusiasm was dampened, of course, the less likely it was that a minority family's entry would arouse militant opposition, at least in areas where the white neighbors were reluctant to resort to threats and violence. Given the patterns of neighborhood change in many major cities, there were doubtless many racially restrictive covenants that buyers and sellers forgot about or did not know about, or that simply fell apart for lack of enforcement. If racially restrictive covenants had remained legally enforceable for a longer period, the questions of notice and knowledge at the heart of horizontal privity might well have come to the fore more sharply.[28]

Obviously, the issue of notice or knowledge was not the only equitable consideration at stake in the enforcement of racially restrictive covenants, and certainly not the most important one, given the difficulties that minority members had in finding housing. But notice or knowledge was at least *one* issue in basic fairness. Neighborhood agreements in particular raised the problem that racial covenants, unfair in themselves, might be doubly unfairly enforced against minority families who did not even know about them. It was only this secondary or derivative unfairness—having the rug pulled out—that horizontal privity addressed. But had the courts paid closer attention to it, they might have ruled against many of the racial covenants that most sharply limited minority housing opportunities as a practical matter: the neighborhood agreements that spread across older urban neighborhoods from the 1920s onward.

Perhaps the most important contribution of the ghost doctrine of horizontal privity in the history of racial covenants was this: it forced a substantial class of racial covenants, the neighborhood agreements, into the equity jurisprudence of the courts, because the courts could only enforce such irregular covenants as a matter of what they called equity. For racial covenants, equity jurisprudence at first asked only the narrow question of notice to purchasers, a pattern that did nothing to help the minority members who refused to take the dove role when they defied covenants that they knew about. But as time went on, as we shall see in Chapter 6, at least some judges started to think that equity should have a broader meaning. Some used equity doctrines to invalidate covenants that seemed antiquated, and a few began to question the equity of the whole pattern in which white neighborhood residents could use the law to intimidate minority residents. Indeed, one might well think that the most important equity consideration with respect to racial covenants was not whether those affected knew about them; it was rather whether such covenants should exist at all. The next of the ghost doctrines might have addressed that kind of issue.

WAS IT WORTH IT? THE PROBLEM OF VALUE IN RACIAL COVENANTS

If we needed more, perhaps one tip-off that courts prior to the twentieth century were suspicious of all running covenants was their creation of a kind of catch-all limitation that was specific to these instruments. This was the requirement that before a covenant could run to a subsequent owner, it had to "touch and concern land." What did this mean? The answers could be either very rigid or very vague. One notorious example of rigidity was the question of whether promises to pay money could run with the land. Early judicial decisions on covenants took the position that promises to pay money had no necessary connection with land, and hence they were simply contracts between the promising parties and would not run to later owners of the properties. Unfortunately, this line of reasoning would have doomed modern planned communities, with their dues and common funds for maintenance and repairs.

As planned communities became more prevalent, New York's highest state court met the challenge in a very important case, *Neponsit Property Owners' Association v. Emigrant Industrial Savings Bank* (1938). Here the court very sensibly decided that a beach community's covenants requiring money dues would run with the land to subsequent purchasers, at least where the unpaid dues were collected through a lien against the property, itself an equitable remedy. But *Neponsit*'s explanation of the new dispensation was singularly unhelpful: a promise touched and concerned land when it "affect[ed] the legal relations" of the parties, and otherwise not. But whether such a promise affected legal relations was of course the whole point at issue.[29]

In some measure, the amorphous touch-and-concern requirement seemed to be akin to horizontal privity, in that it was aimed at providing notice to purchasers. A subsequent purchaser of a restricted property is more likely to be aware of an obligation if the obligation has something to do with land—a promise to maintain a sidewalk, for example. But the touch-and-concern requirement goes beyond that simple guideline and speaks to other objects at the heart of property law as well. The requirement helps to assure that real property does not become too loaded down with idiosyncratic restrictions. In this sense, the touch-and-concern doctrine overlaps with the judicial distrust of restraints on alienation, and like other technical covenant requirements that became more or less absorbed into doctrines about restraints on alienation, touch-and-concern issues were seldom mentioned specifically in the cases about racial covenants.

We glanced on the simplifying aspect of property law in connection with the RAP, but it is central as well in doctrines of touch and concern and restraints on alienation. Simplification has caught the attention of several modern property scholars. Their work builds on a characteristic of property law—and a difference from contract law—that we have emphasized in connection with covenants: property relations are durable, affecting not only people who might originally want a set of arrangements, but successive owners as well, who are increasingly remote from firsthand knowledge of the earlier transactions. Hence it is important that any obligations attached to landed property take relatively simple and standardized "off the rack" forms, like driveway easements or mineral rights, so that successive owners do not have to worry that they might be walking into some odd or idiosyncratic arrangement that they were not expecting. By contrast, an ordinary contract can set out innumerable complicated obligations, because the parties negotiate for themselves, and presumably they know all the intricate details of their bargains. Besides that, contractual obligations normally will not outlast the original parties to the deal, so that ignorant successors in interest are not often in the picture.[30]

As with the more general doctrines about restraints on alienation, a major function of touch and concern was to keep covenants relatively simple, and within the bounds of purchasers' expectations. Taken together, these simplifying doctrines traditionally carried a cost: they meant that covenant arrangements were rather coarse grained by comparison to contract. The gain of simplicity, though, is that a large real estate market can function smoothly, accommodating persons who are strangers to an area and who do not know the intimate details of prior owners' wishes. Thus what have often seemed to be the excessive formalisms of property law are, paradoxically, a part of the law's drive to keep property categories relatively straightforward, so that property may be more easily bought and sold.

A related point about touch and concern again links this covenant doctrine to the more general legal disfavor toward restraints on alienation: the doctrine attempted to protect arrangements whose benefits outweighed their costs, while peeling off the rest as temporary caprice. Generally speaking, touch-and-concern doctrines have cabined real estate covenants to those promises that most people would understand as enhancing the net value of all the properties in question, taken in their entirety. For example, a front lot owner might find it annoying to have to follow a prior owner's promise to trim the trees. But the front owner's annoyance should be more than offset by the back owner's greater gain from maintaining a view. A deal that enhances net value is the kind of thing that neighboring owners might be expected to negotiate, that they would want to pass on to subsequent owners without having to renegotiate, and that subsequent owners themselves would notice. Precisely because such arrangements are value enhancing, they are not likely to catch a subsequent purchaser by surprise.

Now, let us return to racial covenants specifically. How do racial covenants fit this general requirement that covenants touch and concern land by enhancing values? This was a question that was only obliquely raised in covenant litigation, but the ghost nevertheless haunted the subject. In an early state supreme court case on racial covenants, the Louisiana high court observed in 1915 that these conditions on land ownership would be invalid if they were "founded on no substantial principle but merely in caprice"; and a little over a decade later, a study of covenants in planned communities mentioned that covenants of all kinds could only run to subsequent owners if they were value enhancing.[31]

In the era when racially restrictive covenants were emerging, many people in fact did think that these restrictions enhanced collective land values, including middle- and lower-middle-income people who rejected other kinds of controls on their property.[32] But the big question for racially restrictive covenants was this: in what way does it touch and concern land that an owner is African American or Chinese or "Mongolian"? What do those personal characteristics (supposing that they can be defined—not always an easy matter) have to do with the usual promises about hedge trimming, building design, and lawn ornamentation? The race of a purchaser or occupant seems particularly implausible as an issue that touches and concerns land, since a person's race bears no obvious connection with the land *uses* normally associated with the touch-and-concern doctrine. Instead, as the African American defendant asserted in Michigan's first major case on racially restrictive covenants, the restriction treated him as if his very person constituted some kind of nuisance—that is, someone whose mere presence damaged the neighboring property. He was right, and, as we have seen, nuisance law would not countenance treating someone's person as a nuisance. His *actions* could be a nuisance, but not his person.[33]

But in the context of covenant law in the 1920s and later, it seemed entirely obvious that his race by itself was indeed relevant to property values. Why? Simply because white owners thought so. As we shall see, their view was supported by a steadily increasing drumbeat from surrounding institutions. Real estate professionals' appraisal manuals reported that property values dropped for white people if African Americans or other nonwhite persons moved into a neighborhood. Real estate boards, no doubt many sincerely believing that they were serving their customers, stated that it was unethical to introduce racial elements that would be "detrimental" to property values in a neighborhood. Perhaps most influential of all was the Federal Housing Administration, newly created in the early New Deal to insure residential loans. The FHA specifically encouraged racially restrictive covenants in its underwriting manual, the document that acted as a guide to selecting the mortgages that could receive FHA insurance, on the ground that "inharmonious" racial groups diminished housing value.[34]

With all these respectable institutions asserting that racial mixing would cause property values to drop, and acting on that asserted belief, it should not be surprising to find that property values *would* in fact drop when neighborhoods were integrated. Institutional support for racial restrictions was a case of what we will shortly take up in the next chapter as an example of "norm entrepreneurship," helping to create or reinforce norms of exclusion in early- to mid-twentieth-century urban areas.

For their part, the courts seemed to take it for granted that higher resale values lent legal support for racially restrictive covenants, and they appeared to assume that as a matter of course, white purchasers would naturally want the same racial restrictions that earlier owners had had—even if their own later sales would be limited to white purchasers. Thus Michigan's highest court ruled in 1927 that covenants that barred "persons . . . injurious to the locality" included African Americans, at least with evidence that they had been so intended, as well as evidence that the presence of this racial group would diminish property values. Thus too, California's highest court in the mid-1940s noted matter-of-factly that the influx of African Americans had caused a drop in property values.[35]

Once the courts made the assumption that subsequent white purchasers would see the value of an earlier racial restriction, and that they would not be surprised by the restriction and instead would wish for the entire neighborhood to be bound by it, then courts were effectively ruling that racial covenants touched and concerned land. But in making this seemingly easy assumption about white owners' views of minority neighbors, the courts effectively implicated themselves in racial covenants, putting an imprimatur on a whole set of social preferences and bolstering the social norms that enforced them. As we shall see, this is a point that could have been given much greater significance in the demise of judicially enforceable racial covenants in *Shelley v. Kraemer*, where the acts of judges were counted as an important element of state action in enforcing covenants.

In the meantime, however, the courts basically ignored the ghost doctrine of touch and concern along with those other ghosts, the Rule Against Perpetuities and horizontal privity. These doctrines stood for important property law principles that reined in any private efforts to cabin the free flow of property—principles favoring finite duration of any constraints, along with notice, simplicity, and general value enhancement. But the doctrines had funny names, names that made them sound like throwbacks to a more formalistic legal era. Perhaps their funny names were their undoing.

If one can put racial restrictions to one side, the growing judicial leniency toward land use covenants was not particularly objectionable. Indeed that more liberal posture made possible a number of important innovations in American real estate. Most of the other covenants were innocuous reassurances about common homeowner preferences, dealing with such matters as setbacks, residential usage, and homeowner association membership. Some judicial decisions of this era, like New York's *Neponsit* case discussed earlier, effectively made newer forms of real estate development possible by a permissive reading of the common law rules. With a careful parsing of the rules and a close examination of the legal infrastructure that would be necessary for private planned communities, courts began to permit matters that might not have been allowed under earlier covenant law—matters like money dues and the role of homeowners' associations as enforcers of community rules. Without those changes in the legal regime, today's condominium developments and other planned communities would have been well-nigh impossible.[36]

Thus it may be that racially restrictive covenants were simply swept along with the tide of the courts' more relaxed attitude about real estate covenants of all kinds. On the other hand, it may also be the other way around: perhaps judicial sympathy with racial restrictions helped to create the more general relaxation. Perhaps both are true. But one thing is important to bear in mind: the early twentieth century's most significant real estate covenant cases do not suggest that racial restrictions played a leading role in inducing the courts to accept new legal forms for residential communities. Chronologically, racial restrictions came later than other kinds of residential restrictions, suggesting that all the leading players hesitated at least somewhat to exclude whole classes of citizens from the emergent patterns of property ownership. At least some of their hesitation was undoubtedly due to concerns about whether these kinds of restrictions would be valid.

In any event, as we shall see in Chapter 6, the ghosts came back to haunt racial restrictions. It will be recalled that even though it was seldom named, the unspoken doctrine of horizontal privity forced many covenants, particularly the neighborhood covenants, into the courts' equitable jurisdiction. Meanwhile, the equally unnamed doctrine of touch and concern required that covenants have some recognizable continuing value. These two ghosts united to spook racial covenants in the later 1930s and 1940s, as courts applied another equitable doctrine—that of "changed circumstances"—to nullify some racial covenants because they no longer had value to the immediate parties. Some isolated opinions began to go even further, demanding that racial covenants pass the test of value for the entire community, not just for the white neighborhoods.

The ghosts were not so dead after all.

The Calculus of Covenants

5

In this chapter we will pause to calculate, in at least a rough way, the ways that a white homeowner or prospective homeowner in the first few decades of the twentieth century might have assessed the various options if she wished to live in a segregated residential community. As we shall see in this comparison, there were reasons for favoring racially restrictive covenants as the method. But as we shall also see, the covenant option was sufficiently onerous for individuals that they needed the help of "norm entrepreneurs"—a second topic that we will take up in this chapter. We will conclude with a few words about their opposite numbers, the "norm busters," but the latter will appear in greater numbers in the following chapter, on the emerging challenges to racial covenants as the twentieth century turned twenty, then thirty, then forty.

RESIDENTIAL SEGREGATION: COMPARING THE METHODS

Let us consider the position of an urban white person who lived sometime in the first few decades of the twentieth century, and who wanted assurance that she would live in a segregated neighborhood. It would probably be a mistake to assume that the many white people who shared this preference viewed themselves as doing something terribly wrong. Such a person might rather have borne no particular ill will toward

African Americans or any other racial or immigrant group. Unlike the southern landowners who hoped to capture the labor of African Americans on the cheap in the Reconstruction era, this person may have had no desire whatever to exploit such groups and may have even had some regret when she concluded that these groups were likely to bring danger and disorder to a neighborhood—a conclusion that she might have reached, ironically enough, from reading the alarming reports of socially conscious journalists, settlement house workers, and others who attempted to call attention to the plight of the many new minority arrivals who were pouring into early twentieth-century American cities.[1]

Alternatively, she might have concluded that simply because many others held this opinion, the presence of these groups would destabilize the value of her property. Moreover, she may have noticed that other white residents were starting to figure out ways to ensure that their own neighborhoods would remain segregated, and she might have worried about being left behind in an area with what was to her an uncomfortably high proportion of minority members as well as falling property values.[2]

How, then, would she keep these groups at arms length from her residence? What were the options to consider, and how might she have weighed the costs against one another?

Harassment. One option was what we have euphemistically called informal means: threats, intimidation, and harassment escalating to violence. These methods had some advantages: not only were they often effective in fending off specific would-be minority entrants, but they also sent a frightening message to any other unwanted minorities who might have been thinking of moving in. Then too, the short-term cost was usually low for the individual white homeowner. The relevant measures were cheap—rudeness or insults on the street, defacing the garage, throwing eggs, tomatoes, or rocks at the house—and they could be done alone or with a few friends, without the need to coordinate with others. But the effectiveness of these acts depended on a longer-term "investment" in neighborhood cohesion. In many neighborhoods, not all the neighbors would necessarily approve, no matter how much they disliked neighborhood integration. Harassment would likely be ineffective without the approbation or at least acquiescence of other neighbors; the perpetrator or perpetrators would have to rely on the others not to undermine their acts by defending the newcomers or by calling the police. Particularly as these acts escalated into violence, they would carry risks for the perpetrators and their allies.

Then too, there is simply the matter of illegality. Illegal intimidation and violence can carry a particularly strong signaling function. These measures tell the outsiders that they are in danger, while telling the insiders that their neighbors are holding the line, and telling all parties that the perpetrators themselves will take risks in their determination to keep the neighborhood as it is. But this kind of signal, in contrast to legal methods, suggests that the neighborhood norm enforcers have no particular support in the larger community—quite the contrary. That is another reason why self-help enforcement of group claims is more likely to occur in close-knit, tightly bound communities than in more dispersed ones—and even there, self-help is often surreptitious.[3]

From a short-term individual perspective, then, informal self-help exclusion methods might have been relatively cheap and easily organized. But these extralegal measures actually relied on a longer-term, intangible "social capital," a kind of neighborhood solidarity that could take considerable time to develop, and that might have to be strong enough to defy the disapproval of the larger community. Those kinds of neighborhood bonds certainly could not yet have been in place in the new "additions" or subdivisions that were springing up in and around growing cities at the turn of the twentieth century. It is thus not surprising that, as we have seen, these new subdivisions turned to other means to ensure segregation, particularly racial covenants. This is not to say that violence and covenants never overlapped; they definitely did, particularly in the older neighborhoods where racial covenants were not part of an original subdivision plan but were rather introduced later through door-to-door neighborhood drives. Even in the older neighborhoods in which covenants came to coincide with illegal intimidation, the turn to covenants appeared to be more likely in less tightly knit areas, where the neighbors were uncertain about one another's plans and motives when faced with possible minority entry.[4]

Covenants, of course, were a legal method, but as we saw in Chapter 2, they were not the only legal option in the early twentieth century.

Legal segregation methods introduced formal institutions to help enforce neighborhood segregation, but they had other kinds of costs. Once a white homeowner in a more loose-knit or new community had rejected informal or illegal methods, how might he or she have evaluated the various legal options?

Nuisance law. Nuisance law at one time must have seemed to be an available route to segregation, even though, as we saw in Chapter 2, fairly early in the twentieth century the courts and commentators settled the point that no neighbor could be designated a legal nuisance simply because of his or her race. On the other hand, there continued to be indirect ways in which the courts might countenance something like racial nuisance claims. These might include suits against activities or venues associated with minority groups—certain churches or bars or laundries or other business establishments. Even those indirect versions of racial nuisance law had drawbacks, however. The largest of these was the multiperson Prisoner's Dilemma or collective action issue: the purported nuisance was likely to be felt across a number of different homeowners, and this meant that anyone bringing a nuisance suit had the additional burden either of organizing the neighbors or of bearing all the litigation costs alone. Either option would be a time-consuming and potentially expensive matter. It would be tempting to hang back to see if someone else would undertake the task—which could mean that nothing would happen. Another drawback was that nuisance claims are decided on a notoriously case-by-case basis, and hence even if the white homeowner won a case here or there, that case would not necessarily send a more general signal, particularly if she were suing indirectly, for such matters as purported noise or congestion. She might win Case Number 1, but in Case Number 2, new questions would arise: What kind of noise? How much congestion? Nuisance, then, was probably never much of a live option for the white homeowner; it was too expensive, too uncertain, and presented too many collective action issues.

Zoning. Racial zoning had been another option for neighborhood segregation before it was ruled unconstitutional in *Buchanan v. Warley* in 1917. As we also saw in Chapter 2, a number of municipalities attempted to do an end run around *Buchanan* after the case was decided, and this pattern suggests that zoning continued to have some definite attractions as a method for segregating neighborhoods.

David Bernstein, in his commentary on the *Buchanan* case, argues that no matter how bad racial covenants may have become in later decades, public zoning legislation by race would have been considerably more pernicious. The logic is simple self-interest: zoning enlists third parties—in this case the municipal authorities—to enforce social norms of segregation legally; thus zoning would have enabled white residents to externalize the cost of enforcement onto the taxpaying public at large, including the minority citizens most disadvantaged by these schemes. On the other hand, without zoning, the owners had to do the enforcing themselves. With either nuisance or covenants, the white homeowners had to take norm violators to court, with all the aggravation and expense that this entailed. Once the white residents themselves had to bear the cost of neighborhood segregation, Bernstein argues, they undoubtedly did some damage, but not so much as if they had been able to call on the public authorities.[5]

Bernstein certainly has a point, and zoning may well have been a preferred route to neighborhood segregation had *Buchanan* and the follow-up cases not ruled it out. In fact, there were some other advantages to zoning as well, advantages that did not go unnoticed by residential developers by the 1920s. Zoning could apply to older urban neighborhoods, where it was too late for developers to institute racial covenants into deeds *ex ante*. In addition, zoning potentially could overlay great swaths of territory, because it did not need to apply simply within the confines of an individual subdivision. As a public measure rather than a private property control, zoning had no issues with the Rule Against Perpetuities, and in theory it could last indefinitely. Zoning was also more flexible than covenants; if zoning restrictions did not work out, they could be changed through the political process, rather than requiring the consent of all or some supermajority of the original covenantees. Finally—a point that was to become more obvious in later decades—zoning could affect racial geography through income-related restrictions, especially large-lot requirements and others that ultimately came to be known as "exclusionary zoning."[6]

But with all those reasons in zoning's favor, zoning and especially explicitly racial zoning was not necessarily the perfect tool for neighborhood segregation. First, although zoning would permit the neighbors to foist the cost of establishing and enforcing segregation onto the public, the public authorities rather than the developers and white residents would ultimately control the decisions. Public processes can be slow and fraught with difficulties, requiring quite disparate interests to agree on a strategy. Zoning limitations based on race might or might not have been adopted in the first instance in any given city, particularly in cities like Chicago, where African Americans were beginning to have some political influence even in the early twentieth century. Baltimore is an interesting case in point. Although Baltimore's racial zoning ordinance became the model for others, the city of Baltimore itself had a great deal of trouble finding an ordinance that would work for it, legally and politically.[7]

Moreover, public officials might not have enforced any given zoning ordinance in the way that the neighbors wanted, particularly in settled urban areas. The subsequent history of zoning for other purposes is instructive for what could have happened to racial zoning. Municipal zoning is rife with small-scale changes, with "spot" rezonings of uses and buildings, variances, special exceptions, so-called preexisting nonconforming uses, and the like.[8] A second issue about zoning, then, is that its flexibility could have backfired for the white neighbors, destabilizing the racial uniformity of their neighborhoods.

Still a third issue was the technical structure of explicit racial zoning. The Baltimore/Louisville ordinance contemplated only two racial types, white and African American, but many cities had other minorities, including various groups from Latin America, southern and eastern Europe, and Asia, including the rather oddly designated "Mongolians" of some covenants.[9] Finding a metric for their separation could have been tricky, while redefining them as all white or all black could have undermined racial categorization more generally, as in the "racing" of corporations discussed in Chapter 3.

Racial covenants. Explicit racial zoning, of course, was off the table after the 1917 *Buchanan* case, just as explicit racial nuisance was off the table even earlier. While real estate and banking professionals could do much to foster residential segregation by their steering and lending practices, after racial zoning fell away, restrictive covenants were the only method left for explicit, legal enforcement of segregation throughout neighborhoods. But it is not entirely clear that our white homeowner would have preferred zoning to covenants even if *Buchanan* had upheld racial zoning. Obviously, from the perspective of white homeowners, racially restrictive covenants did have the major disadvantage that Bernstein pinpointed: the developers and then the neighbors themselves had to pay the costs of creating and enforcing these covenants.

But covenants had some countervailing advantages. One was duration. By the later 1920s, the Rule Against Perpetuities was a diminishing threat to covenant continuation, as courts appeared to accept covenants without concern about a long duration. If anything, durability issues worked in favor of covenants, because of the flexibility issue mentioned above: zoning can change as can any ordinary legislation, through a majority vote of a governing body, whereas in the absence of some agreement to the contrary, covenants generally cannot change without the consent of all the beneficiaries. Even where consent requirements are relaxed by agreement to something like a supermajority, the requirements for alteration almost always make covenants much more tenacious than the politically malleable zoning mechanisms. In addition, covenants can last indefinitely in the official records, sending out a signal of neighborhood preferences even when no individual homeowner would be willing to spend the time and money to defend them in court.[10]

Most important, developers and neighbors could take charge of the covenants' content without the impediment of political compromise. Developers in particular could orchestrate whole packages of restrictions, including race along with many other features—like architectural features, building restrictions, landscaping requirements, and homeowner association dues—that were basically beyond the authority of politicians to impose on homeowners, particularly in an era in which aesthetic regulation was legally unacceptable. Racial covenants that were set up after the fact in older developments, through neighbor-generated petitions, did not include any features except race; but like zoning (and unlike subdivision covenants), they had no predetermined boundaries, and potentially they could expand without limit, so long as someone could collect the necessary signatures from the neighbors.[11]

With all their advantages, however, the use of racial covenants did present some problems, some rather reminiscent of the problems associated with racial nuisance cases. As with nuisance, these covenant issues too can be lumped under the rubric of collective action—the multiperson Prisoner's Dilemma. The post hoc racial restrictions in already-settled older neighborhoods had the most trouble, right from the outset: there was no developer to orchestrate matters in advance, and someone with an interest in the neighborhood had to take the initiative to collect the necessary signatures for a common front against minority encroachment. To get that project underway, as we will see in the next section, the neighbors often needed the help of a neighborhood improvement association or some outside institution.

On the other hand, developer-created racial covenants in new subdivisions had an easier time at the outset, since developers could insert all the restrictions they wanted into deeds prior to sales. But for developer-created covenants as well as neighbor-created ones, enforcement was still a collective-action Achilles' heel. Who would undertake the legal procedures necessary to stop some minority person from coming into the neighborhood? Individual white residents might feel special incentives to do so, especially if the unwelcome newcomer moved in directly next door, but insofar as the first entrant acted as an entering wedge for other minority members who would follow, the white resident who went to court in effect shouldered a burden for the rest of the white neighbors. Not surprisingly, many white homeowners preferred simply to move away, leaving the neighbors to cope—or not cope—with the problem as best they could.

Developers were well aware of the collective action issue and the ensuing enforcement problem, not only for racial covenants but for the other land use restrictions that they instituted in what they called their "high class" suburbs. These developers regularly discussed enforcement methods in their trade journals and at meetings and conferences. As discussed in Chapter 3, a developer could structure his subdivision ownership arrangements as a set of conditional estates or "defeasible fees," retaining the right himself to enforce against homeowner infractions. But as also discussed in Chapter 4, this enforcement method had several problems. For one thing, the usual remedy—reversion to the developer—was far too heavy-handed for minor violations, although a racial violation probably would not have been considered minor. But in addition, there was an incentive problem: a developer's interest in enforcement was likely to diminish after he finished a project. Even though developers, especially high-end developers like Kansas City's J. C. Nichols, often had an interest in maintaining a reputation for durable quality in their past projects, an offsetting factor was that many wanted to get on to some other planned community, and not to be bothered with the thankless task of monitoring resident behavior in already-completed developments.[12]

Following the early lead of Nichols's upper-class planned communities in Kansas City, the developers found their ultimate solution to the collective action problem in a device that is still with us today (though of course not for racial covenants): the homeowners' association, a built-in governance structure through which the developer could hand over enforcement powers to an interested but organized group—that is, the owners themselves. Even today, of course, covenanted communities still have issues over enforcement of various restrictions, with some residents finding the homeowners' associations too slack and others seeing them as too picky and intrusive.[13]

Of all the options for legal residential segregation in the early twentieth century, then, covenants had some major assets. But their greatest obstacle was that in the more or less loose-knit urban communities—the newer developments in town or in the suburbs, the urban areas with more turnover and fewer crosscutting ties—residents and neighbors were not really capable of overcoming collective action problems on their own, either for the creation of covenants or for their enforcement. Something had to set these racial covenants in motion, and something had to impel the neighbors to keep them going. The next section takes up the norm entrepreneurs who undertook those functions. The main categories were developers, real estate brokers, and the officials of a financial institution much influenced by both: the Federal Housing Administration.

THE NORM ENTREPRENEURS

Toward the end of the nineteenth century, it was no mystery that many white urban residents preferred not to share their neighborhoods with African American and other generally less affluent minority groups.

Back in those years, occasional small-scale covenants and local ordinances popped up with the plain or thinly veiled intent to keep out black persons, Asians, or other minority groups. These measures may have flamed out in the courts, but they revealed the preferences of white residents to stick with their own kind.[14]

White attitudes appear to have hardened even more at the turn of the century, as urbanization picked up. Indeed, the arrival of rural southern black people in larger cities alarmed even the more settled African Americans in those locations. Long-settled urban minority communities had worked out their own versions of a modus vivendi with the surrounding white neighborhoods, but a burst of uneducated and unsophisticated rural in-migrants made some African Americans fear a kind of guilt by association.[15]

They were right. As more African Americans arrived in cities, white residents appeared to grow more nervous about having *any* African American neighbors. Those whites with money could do something about it, thanks to the work of new kinds of subdivision development.

Developers. During the early decades of the twentieth century, developers started to turn into "community builders," inventing larger-scale plats complete with scenic landscaping and building restrictions to guarantee neighborhood stability. Until the 1930s and 1940s, these developers did not normally build houses, but they rather left it to lot owners to manage construction of their own residences. But in order to maintain some overall control over the physical structures—especially during the development stage, when the sale of lots was still incomplete—developers relied on elaborate sets of deed restrictions to channel the ways that lot owners might construct their homes. The developers seemed only to be meeting their well-to-do purchasers' tastes when they promised racial exclusion along with minimum lot sizes, park spaces, amenities, and pricey and harmonious homebuilding.

Not all the new, high-end community builders of the early twentieth century did include racial restrictions in their subdivisions, particularly those founded at the beginning of the era. The developers of Baltimore's Roland Park in the 1890s soft-pedaled restrictions generally, but they particularly avoided racial restrictions on the advice of their lawyers that such restrictions might not be legal—a fairly common view until the early 1910s, when Roland Park itself adopted racial restrictions.

Similarly, the Van Sweringen Company's luxurious Shaker Heights development outside Cleveland, initiated in 1913, included no overt racial restrictions in its covenants. But the Van Sweringens included covenant restrictions that required the developers' or the neighbors' consent to any sales within the subdivision—restrictions that in fact excluded both racial and religious minorities. Many developers undoubtedly thought that no African Americans could assemble the funds to move into the luxury homes created by these early planned subdivisions. Jews were a greater concern, though a matter of some disagreement. J. C. Nichols, the developer of Kansas City's opulent Country Club District, included antiblack restrictions in his projects as early as 1908, but wavered on the question of Jewish entry.[16]

Given the increasing comfort levels of the courts that we saw in Chapters 3 and 4, high-end developers soon lost most concerns about the legality of racial covenants. By the early 1920s, racial covenants had become sufficiently common that the developers of Los Angeles's Palos Verdes Estates would refer to them as "the usual restrictions." In 1928, the Institute for Research in Land Economics and Public Utilities in Chicago published Helen Monchow's extensive study of the role of all kinds of covenants in subdivisions. Along with material on building restrictions, homeowners' fee charges and so on, Monchow tallied up racial restrictions. Of the eighty-four subdivisions that she studied—most of them at the higher end—she noted that forty had racial restrictions on ownership or occupancy, and that most of these were in the more recent subdivisions.[17]

As time went on, even higher-end developers began to organize somewhat more modest subdivisions, with covenants (including racial covenants) and homeowners' associations. As developments reached toward families further down the income scale, the general set of restrictions was likely to be more limited. In one subdivision in Albuquerque, for example, deed restrictions placed a racial clause alongside a stricture against placing any buildings (including barns and garages) closer than one foot from the property line, suggesting that the subdivider was probably not aiming too high. Another deed (though this may have been a division of a single large lot) had a racial restriction together with a prohibition on outdoor privies (but not outhouses). But high class or low, racial covenants were much in demand. New working-class subdivisions sometimes did not want even the elementary restrictions against commercial and manufacturing uses, since those uses constituted their workplaces. Nevertheless, buyers into those subdivisions did demand racial covenants. Racial covenants were clearly popular across class lines in white communities.[18]

Not all working-class or middle-class neighborhoods could rely on developers for racial covenants, however. Those that were built very early in the century were more likely to lack racial covenants. If the white neighbors in these older urban areas wanted to have such covenants, they would have to take measures after the fact to get them. Here is where another class of norm entrepreneurs could help: the real estate brokers.

Brokers. Real estate brokers emerged as a professional group at about the same time that developers began to concentrate on larger-scale projects, and indeed these brokers were for a time very closely allied with the high-end developers of the early twentieth century. One of the important moves toward broker professionalization was the founding in 1908 of the National Association of Real Estate Exchanges, soon to be known as the National Association of Real Estate Boards, or NAREB.[19] Members of NAREB and its state and local affiliates took the name "realtor," and they were generally among the more well-to-do brokers. They were particularly concerned about sharp or shoddy sales practices, through which competitors would steal away their deals or damage the reputation of the entire trade. To curtail less fastidious types and perhaps to tighten up entry into the business by the much-denigrated "curbsiders"—operators who plied their trades on the spot, with no real office locations—NAREB and its affiliates wrote up rules of good practice; and to bolster these rules, the groups also worked to establish state licensing requirements. The first NAREB Realtors' Code of Ethics was adopted in 1913, and by the end of the decade, the realtors' associations had enjoyed some success in getting state legislatures to adopt licensing requirements.[20]

These brokers' professional groups took the position that segregation enhanced real estate values, at least for their white clients, and their stance was reflected in NAREB's Realtors' Code of Ethics. From 1924 to 1950, Article 34 of Part III of the code ("Relations to Customers and the Public") included the followings statement: "A Realtor should never be instrumental in introducing into a neighborhood a character of property or occupancy, members of any race or nationality, or any individuals whose presence will clearly be detrimental to property values in that neighborhood."[21]

Even before the adoption of this plank, professional real estate brokers had considered African American entry to white neighborhoods as highly detrimental. Rose Helper, in her blistering 1969 report on racial practices and views among brokers, documented the actions of their professional organizations in urban areas all over the country. In 1924, according to Helper, the New York Realtors Association inquired of the Birmingham Real Estate Board how people in the South managed to "'prevent negro encroachment on white residential territory," only to be informed that such events did not occur in Birmingham, and that if any of the local real estate professionals were to sell a lot to a black person in a white neighborhood, he would "'meet . . . with serious embarrassment of one sort or another.'"[22]

Aside from New York, Helper cited Chicago, St. Louis, Detroit, Salt Lake City, Milwaukee, and various California cities (including Berkeley), among others, as locations where real estate brokers' groups took some steps to curtail African American and Asian entry into white neighborhoods in the early 1920s. Some of the practices she described have now come to be known as redlining and steering. In 1923, for example, the St. Louis Real Estate Exchange adopted by referendum a plan by which all the members would sell or rent to African Americans only in certain specified districts. Apparently other local boards passed similar measures. Some boards, like those of New Orleans and several California cities, expressed some concern about black and other minority needs for housing, but they too hoped to fill those needs by designating or creating separate districts for minority groups.[23]

Around the same time, professional real estate boards became key players in organizing "property owners' associations" and "neighborhood improvement associations" to try to stave off what they considered to be African American invasions into existing white neighborhoods. Indeed, local members of the brokers' organizations often maintained what contemporary commentators Herman Long and Charles Johnson called a "strategic relationship" with these associations. Detroit historian Thomas Sugrue describes the property owners' and neighborhood improvement associations as originating with real estate developers for the purpose of enforcing racial covenants. He asserts that by the 1940s, in spite of some other activities, their "*raison d'être*" was to resist minority neighborhood entry.[24]

Through their connections to neighborhood associations, local real estate boards in the 1920s and later became strongly engaged with the new kinds of racially restrictive covenants, those instituted *ex post* in older areas through neighborhood drives. Chicago was a city with many such older neighborhoods, and the Chicago Real Estate Board became a leader in orchestrating neighborhood covenant drives. Following the Chicago board's lead, real estate organizations elsewhere too began to promote model standard-form agreements through which neighborhood associations could collect signatures for these post hoc restrictive covenants.[25]

Helper described the racial steering provision of the Realtors' Code of Ethics as reflecting a widespread viewpoint in the 1920s, and indeed an emergent norm among realtors all over the country. As racial steering indeed became the norm among real estate brokers, it should come as no surprise that, according to a poll of California real estate boards in 1927, these boards regarded racial covenants as critical vehicles for controlling the "color question." If they could get covenants in place, the boards, presumably acting in what they regarded as their customers' best interest, could invoke legal norms to solidify the results of their own racial steering.[26]

Aside from promoting racial covenants through their organizing activities, the real estate brokers, together with the new developers, were soon to find a powerful new vehicle to turn racial residential restrictions into standard practice. This vehicle was a creation of New Deal legislation: the Federal Housing Administration.

The Federal Housing Administration. Marc Weiss, in his study of the "community builders" of the first half of the twentieth century, emphasized the degree to which the land use and property concepts first created by private developers and real estate entrepreneurs influenced public agencies at all levels. This was not by accident. The various segments of the real estate professions, led by NAREB, lobbied hard for measures that followed their own ideas of appropriate practices—state licensing requirements to discourage the "curbsider" brokers; local planning and zoning regulations that followed at least the basics of high-end developers' concepts of quality residential development; and, finally, at the federal level, financial arrangements that would pump new life into subdivision development of the type favored by the community builders.[27]

The Depression created a crisis in home foreclosures, and overcoming this crisis was high on the New Deal agenda. The Federal Housing Administration (FHA) was created in 1934, and it became the flagship of the New Deal's housing finance agencies. But from the outset, NAREB members staffed the new FHA, and these private professionals' policy choices were soon embedded in FHA lending practices.[28] Among those policies was a general approval of residential segregation, along with a particular solicitude for white neighborhoods.

Even before the FHA emerged as the centerpiece of New Deal housing finance efforts, federal efforts to counter the Depression-era lending crisis were already taking race into account. In 1933, the Home Owners Loan Corporation (HOLC) was created to refinance the many defaulting home mortgages, and it quickly moved to map out urban areas by risk factors. Such factors as the age and condition of housing stock entered into the risk map—but so did the race of the residents, with minority or mixed-race areas being considered higher risk. But whereas HOLC itself made loans even in areas deemed risky, the new FHA would use the HOLC maps effectively to redline by race.[29]

The FHA followed the HOLC with a new home loan guarantee program that was to revolutionize housing finance. Prior to the 1930s, most home loans required down payments of one-third, and they had relatively short durations, typically five to seven years, which might (or might not) be extended or renewed at the end of the loan period. FHA loans changed all that. They did so by insuring home loans of a type that the HOLC had initiated and that, over time, would became standard: the loan with a 20 percent down payment (or less), and a thirty-year fixed and self-amortizing mortgage.[30]

Lower down payments and extended repayment periods brought home mortgages within reach for a vastly larger group of potential purchasers, and indeed, over time, these mortgage patterns turned homes into the primary capital asset for most Americans. Easier mortgage terms normally would have put lenders at greater risk. But because FHA loan guarantees shifted much of this risk to the federal government, banks could participate without jeopardizing their own safely—or at least, this was the case after the FHA convinced state and federal banking regulators to exempt FHA-insured loans from the previous loan-to-value requirements. But those exemptions were not available to other mortgages at the time, with the result that the homeowners who were eligible for FHA loans enjoyed much more favorable terms than their conventional loan counterparts. FHA loans soon came to dominate residential lending, particularly in suburbs. By 1938, FHA-insured loans accounted for a third of all new U.S. housing loans.[31]

In order to cycle as much lending as possible through the system, while also protecting the federal fisc, the FHA itself had to attend to the security of its loans. To that end, the agency created an underwriting manual—a kind of checklist of the characteristics that a residence should have in order to qualify for FHA insurance.[32]

Not surprisingly, given the prevalence of former private real estate professionals staffing the new FHA, the *Underwriting Manual* reflected private developers' and brokers' views of the kinds of features that made housing values stable and secure. Those features clearly included racial segregation. In a section on "Protection from Adverse Influences," the *Manual* stated bluntly that "[a] change in social or racial occupancy generally leads to instability and a reduction in values" (par. 233). Thus property evaluators were to investigate the surrounding areas for the presence of "incompatible racial and social groups" and to assess whether the location might be "invaded" (par. 233) or suffer "infiltration" by "inharmonious racial groups" (par. 229). The *Manual* specifically noted that deed restrictions on "racial occupancy" could create a "favorable condition" (par. 228). In the section on subdivisions that were still in the development stage, the *Manual* recommended deed restrictions that included, among other matters, ". . . (g) Prohibition of the occupancy of properties except by the race for which they are intended" (par. 284(3)).[33]

The FHA was by no means the only institution that brought about urban segregation; patterns of ghettoization were already well established in American cities by the 1930s.[34] Nor was the *Underwriting Manual* concerned exclusively with race. But the *Manual* had a profound effect on the proliferation of racially restrictive covenants, as it did on a more general standardization of real estate development. With its approbation of racial covenants, the *Manual* added another layer of legal normative force to what historian Thomas Sugrue described as white homeowners' sense of entitlement: that they had a right to live in segregated neighborhoods, and that government would protect them in that right.[35]

As housing finance eased through FHA loan guarantees, more developers in the 1930s began to build actual houses on their subdivisions, rather than doing the platting, infrastructure, and landscaping and then letting the purchasers do their own building. These larger-scale projects moved down the income scale, well into the range of middle- and lower-middle-class buyers, and they gave larger and larger classes of people an interest in housing values.[36] Whether or not developers believed in segregation, they wanted to sell these new houses, and that meant that they wanted their housing stock to qualify the purchasers for FHA loan guarantees. This in turn gave them a powerful motivation to satisfy the *Underwriting Manual*'s directives, among other things for racial restrictions in new housing. A deed restriction in a Milwaukee suburban development in 1940 illustrated the FHA's influence: in limiting occupancy to "person[s] of the white race," the subdivision documents prominently stated that this provision was "according to FHA property standards." A 1947 study of the previous decade's racial covenants found many such explicit references to FHA standards in the subdivisions that included race restrictions, particularly the larger subdivisions.[37]

But whereas in earlier decades, high-end developers had included racial covenants to ensure that only the "right kinds of persons" could buy lots and build in expensive new suburbs, now developers included racial covenants in middle-tier projects in order to allow their buyers to qualify for FHA-insured mortgages. Minority borrowers did not normally qualify to buy in the new developments and suburbs. Their very persons would undermine the covenants that supposedly made these mortgages safe for publicly backed mortgage insurance. And generally speaking, they did not qualify for FHA loans in existing urban neighborhoods either, because their presence supposedly rendered those neighborhoods "transitional," or otherwise insecure. Without FHA financing, mixed neighborhoods fell behind in funds available for refurbishment as well as new construction, contributing to the relative physical decline in these areas.[38]

Large-scale, prebuilt housing developments were still in their early stages in the 1930s and early 1940s, and the Second World War temporarily slowed these developments.[39] But even as the war approached, the elements for a new spatial pattern of segregation were already in place. As we shall see, that pattern only became fully visible after the war's end, when the veterans came home and demanded housing, and when developers met their demands with mass housing projects that would meet the FHA standards—including racially restrictive covenants. By that time, it seemed, something that local governments had been forbidden to do through regulation—racial zoning—was about to be effected for the new suburbs by the federal government, more or less inadvertently, through the back door of "voluntary" and "private" assistance—loan programs for housing that effectively mandated racially restrictive covenants.

A reprise and a preview: norm entrepreneurs and norm busters. Between the 1920s and the early 1940s, the norm entrepreneurs for racial restrictions seemed to have made up much of the ground that was lost in *Buchanan v. Warley,* the 1917 case that overturned racial zoning. They made up this ground with the support of other legal instruments and legal norms. Covenants, themselves a legal instrument, were becoming standard practice, especially in new suburban developments. Covenants had also spread—although with more muted success—in older urban neighborhoods as well. New federal home-lending practices gave another very powerful legal support to the racial restrictions that would limit suburban homes to "Caucasian only."

Most of these norm entrepreneurs were or had been business people, and they undoubtedly thought of their own actions as protecting the interests of their largely white buying clientele—in particular, protecting their customers' property values from declining. As for the FHA, even aside from the influence of private real estate professionals, government officials thought it was their duty to the taxpaying public to protect loan guarantees as much as possible, particularly as their loan guarantees extended ownership to people previously unable to buy. That meant favoring the neighborhood stability that they thought racial covenants would bring, while excluding the neighborhoods whose "inharmonious elements" might cause instability, property value decline, and a consequent hitch in mortgage repayment.[40]

But it is hard to think that the success of the norm entrepreneurs did not also contribute to the general white attitude that housing values would crash and burn if minority members were to enter a white community. In a development that must have been particularly disappointing to the NAACP, mainstream lawyers would soon ratify this attitude under the auspices of the American Law Institute, an organization composed of eminent judges, attorneys, and legal scholars. In 1944 the Institute issued a revised *Restatement of Property,* a kind of compendium of the best current legal practices in to the field. Civil rights proponents may have hoped that this new *Restatement* would give heed to some faint new legal misgivings about racially restrictive covenants, but no such thing happened. Instead, in the section on restraints on alienation, the authors concluded that these restrictions were acceptable as a matter of state law policy, for the familiar reasons: supposedly they were reasonable restraints on alienation because they maintained property values and alleviated social tensions.[41]

The ALI's point about social tensions was especially significant, because it suggests in a very muted way that in the absence of formalized legal restrictions, a threat of violence was tacitly understood to be the informal enforcement mechanism for norms of exclusion. Perceived property values and violence went together. Thanks to new federal loan policies, white persons who would have been renters in an earlier era now could become owners, with a greater financial stake in their residences. These owners' fear of losing their housing investments fueled the threat of violence, and a lengthy urban history of racial confrontations made that threat credible. Legal racial covenants, on the other hand, could give a clear and apparently socially acceptable signal to minority outsiders that they were not welcome in a white neighborhood, while reassuring white insiders that their own and their neighbors' property values would remain intact, without the need to resort to force or to rely on those who would. And even to white neighbors to whom racial covenants seemed unattractive, covenants must have seemed preferable to the alternative: a perpetual open war along the frontiers between white and minority neighborhoods.

To return, then, to our white homeowner at the beginning of this chapter: whatever the truth of the matter, how could she fail to believe that racial exclusion was important for her property values, when so many respectable institutional players told her so? How indeed, when the voices ranged from the "best" developers, to the "reputable" real estate agents, to the federal government itself, along with the most distinguished members of the legal community? In turn, how could these views fail to turn into a self-fulfilling prophecy—that is, race *did* affect property values, because so many people thought that it did? And finally, how could she fail to take an interest in the legal norms that would protect her property values peacefully—property values that were now of compelling interest to many more people, thanks to the extension of homeownership through easier lending? Indeed, federal policies seemed to assure such a person that not only was she entitled to own a home, but she was also entitled to have that home in an all-white neighborhood.[42] Her attitudes reflected a situation in which social norms reinforced legal norms, and vice versa—and in which norm entrepreneurs had played a major role.

Interestingly enough, the very success of the norm entrepreneurs created its own backlash and encouraged norm *breakers* who came from two very different directions. First were the civil rights oriented organizations and the minority press. Over the decades, NAACP members and their allies grew increasingly vocal in their criticism of legal supports for segregation, including racially restrictive covenants. Second, and very different, were the less-than-respectable brokers. Growing white fears of minority entry, taken together with increasingly serious limitations on minority access both to housing and to housing finance, created arbitrage opportunities for what came to be called "blockbusting" brokers. In a pattern that went back at least to the entry of African American residents into Harlem in the early years of the century, these brokers could frighten the white neighbors with rumors of minority entry, then buy cheaply on their own account, and then sell or rent on expensive terms to growing urban populations of African Americans and other minority purchasers, who had few other opportunities.

In the next chapter we shall see how all these trends and all these characters came together, beginning with the experience of a particular city: Chicago.

6 The Emergence of the Norm Breakers

In the last chapter we considered the calculations of a white person trying to decide among various means to keep her neighborhood segregated, and we considered why she might choose racially restrictive covenants. Those covenants gave internal signals of assurance to her white neighbors that they were all committed to "saving the neighborhood." In this chapter we shall consider the outsiders who were also supposed to receive the signals, particularly the African Americans from whom the white neighborhood was to be "saved." Of special interest will be the gradual shift through which some of these outsiders stopped paying attention to the signals that would exclude them, and instead began to challenge them.

Covenants had costs to the insiders, as we noted in the last chapter. But they had even clearer costs to the outsiders. The most obvious cost was that racial covenants limited housing opportunities for the excluded "non-Caucasians," a cost that became steeper with growing minority urbanization, and acute in some cities during the Second World War.[1] A more subtle but very real cost was dignitary: covenants were a formal statement that white people regarded African Americans as undesirable neighbors per se, no matter what their personal characteristics or achievements. In this dignitary sense, it could not have been a trivial matter that racial covenants were also legal instruments. As a matter of public record, covenants announced a formal legal norm reinforcing social norms of racial exclusion.

However, breaking racial covenants also had costs for outsiders. First, breaking racial covenants meant moving into a neighborhood in which one had received a very clear signal that one was not wanted—a signal that seemed to be backed by the courts of the larger community. Second, the norm breaker would be exposed to threats from several directions. As one Chicagoan ruefully remarked, "anything you do makes you a lawbreaker," facing all the aggravation and expense that might follow in a white-dominated legal system. But even more probable than a lawsuit would be insults and slights, and possibly also more overt harassment and even violence. Those who led the way, the "pioneers" who were the first covenant breakers in a neighborhood, were likely to be most at risk of bearing all these costs. Indeed, norm breaking posed collective action problems that in some ways mirrored the collective action problems of those who tried to create and enforce racial covenants. On both sides, it would be easier to let someone else make the first move.[2]

Norm breaking, then, called for norm-breaking entrepreneurs and allies, just as covenants themselves required norm entrepreneurs and allies. Who might these norm-breaking entrepreneurs be? One type of norm buster would be an individual—preferably an idealistic, stubborn person who had some financial assets. We shall see this person in the black real estate dealer Carl Hansberry, though there were certainly others as well. Another might be a business that backed someone like Hansberry, and here we shall see the Supreme Liberty Life Insurance company as well as the *Chicago Defender* newspaper. Still another might be an organization whose mission it was to break norms of segregation, and here of course we will see the NAACP, with its local and national groups and its increasingly professional national legal team.[3] A quite different kind of norm-busting entrepreneur would be an individual businessperson who saw potential for financial gain in breaking segregation norms; here we will see the renegade real estate dealers, later to be called "blockbusters" and "panic peddlers." And finally, we shall see alliances for norm-breaking entrepreneurship coming from an entirely different direction: the national government, increasingly embarrassed in its foreign policy by the persistence of legal segregation.

In this chapter we will also take note of the targets that the norm-busting entrepreneurs chose. Although civil rights lawyers made large constitutional arguments all along, much norm breaking about racial covenants started small, and it started at the weakest links among these covenants: the older urban neighborhoods with the most vulnerable kinds of restrictions, those created by neighborhood drives. In spite of the great weight of social practice and legal authority that gathered behind racially restrictive covenants of all kinds from the 1920s through the 1940s, the neighbor-driven covenants in particular had an assortment of small weaknesses that lawyers could exploit.

Much of the best-known law on racially restrictive covenants came from just a few jurisdictions, indeed just a few cities: Los Angeles in California, St. Louis and Kansas City in Missouri, Detroit and Pontiac in Michigan, and Washington, D.C. Although Chicago was not on the list for reasons that we will explore shortly, most of the others, like Chicago, were among the urban areas mostly densely packed with racial covenants.[4] In these cities local NAACP-affiliated lawyers persistently challenged racial covenants over the course of the organization's long and ever-more-organized assault. Their legal efforts seemed only marginally effective until the major victory in *Shelley v. Kraemer* in 1948, but they still managed to chip away, adding to the uneasiness about covenants in some of the pre-*Shelley* era's major legal decisions about these instruments, and adding to a shift in more general consciousness about the injustice of these devices. One major place where this chipping-away process gathered force was Chicago, even though in the end, the city and its state left only oblique marks on the legal history of racial covenants.

NORM BREAKING EMERGES: THE CHICAGO EXAMPLE

From outward appearances, Chicago and the Illinois courts seemed puzzlingly quiet in the emerging legal challenges to racial covenants—puzzling because Chicago was a big, sophisticated city, with a large and growing African American population throughout much of the era in which racial covenants were legal and enforceable. Moreover, unlike the even larger New York, this city came to be shot through with racially restrictive covenants, aimed especially at keeping African Americans out of white neighborhoods. Coinciding with the expansion of covenants were a variety of factors that one might expect to result in major litigation: black Chicagoans made major gains in politics; from 1905 on, they had an outspoken newspaper voice in the *Chicago Defender*; and they had a talented NAACP chapter that increasingly focused on the eradication of racially restrictive covenants.

With all these elements in place for combat, why then was Chicago (and Illinois) so little represented in the record of major legal assaults on these restrictions? An important answer is simply that appearances are deceiving. In fact, Chicago's civil rights lawyers continually fought racially restrictive covenants with practical, technical, and theoretical arguments. The energetic and resourceful University of Chicago Law School graduate Earl Dickerson was a prominent member of the NAACP from the 1920s onward, and he spearheaded drives to get Chicago's bar and political organizations to reject racial covenants.[5]

Under Dickerson's leadership, the Chicago civil rights lawyers successfully argued *Hansberry v. Lee,* a covenant case that reached first the Illinois Supreme Court in 1939 and then the U.S. Supreme Court in 1940. *Hansberry* provided one of the few major pieces of legal good news prior to *Shelley* in the NAACP's long campaign against covenants. But as luck would have it, the issues in the case veered off into procedural territory, leaving the underlying validity of the racial controls untouched.[6]

And so it was for the remainder of Chicago's contribution to the legal history of racially restrictive covenants. Chicagoans' widespread use of racial covenants—and other Chicagoans' very vocal opposition to those covenants—would become widely known and influence national attitudes. But in the end, through a mixture of chance and strategy, the city's battles would produce no major case law on the validity of racial covenants.

At the same time, however, Chicago presented a kind of capsule version of other cities' experiences with covenants. In examining that capsule version, we will get a Chicago-style overview—that is to say, a big and boisterous one—of the tactics that proponents used to promote racial restrictions, and the countervailing tactics that minority lawyers would develop to combat those restrictions.

The backdrop to covenants. Even in the early years of the twentieth century, Chicago had a substantial African American population, attracting a number of migrants from bordering states. During those days, while black Chicagoans clustered in several distinct parts of the city, there were many areas that had *some* African American residents, and none that had *only* African Americans. In the years leading up to and during the First World War, however, the city attracted greatly increasing numbers of migrants from the rural South. They were pushed by ferocious racism and agricultural failures in the South and pulled by the hope of greater personal liberty and economic opportunity in Chicago, a city that had rightly or wrongly become a beacon for those qualities.[7]

The needs of war production, along with the blandishments of the *Chicago Defender*—carried south by Illinois Central Railroad conductors and widely read among southern blacks—opened the door to vast numbers of southern migrants, many of them uneducated and unaccustomed to city ways. Between 1910 and 1920, Chicago's black population grew from just over 44,000 to just under 110,000.[8] As more migrants arrived, majority prejudice became ever more marked. So did the squeeze of housing opportunities into just a few localities, primarily a narrow "Black Belt" running south from downtown and some blocks west of Lake Michigan. Allan Spear, a leading historian of the twentieth-century ghettoization of Chicago's South Side, argues that even prior to the First World War, the swelling black population, the increasing ambition among the city's African Americans, and the growing racial hostility in the city, all pushed Chicago's black leadership to turn increasingly to a strategy of self-sufficiency rather than to larger plans for integration.[9]

The newcomers obviously put an enormous strain on Chicago's existing African American institutions. But they also brought some opportunities. In particular, their sheer numbers made Chicago's politicians pay attention. African Americans began to make inroads into the city's electoral machinery early in the century, building their own ward organization and electing their first black alderman by 1915, and not long afterwards putting black politicians in the state legislature and in Congress.[10]

In turn, these political successes were noted elsewhere, thanks to the wide national circulation of the *Defender*, and they made Chicago seem an even more attractive destination for southern black migrants. Unfortunately, those same migrants generally were not sophisticated voters, and their votes often went to the most corrupt elements of the city's political machine—people who may not have been well-equipped or well-disposed to address the migrants' genuine problems.[11]

Among the most serious of those genuine problems was housing. As new migrants crammed into existing African American areas, whites moved out and the borders of the Black Belt expanded—moving toward the south and west. None of this made for good race relations. Indeed, according to historian Spear, housing was the most bitterly contested of all the issues separating the races in the city.[12]

Chicago neighborhoods had a long history of neighborhood organizations that worked to provide a variety of local services and amenities, but even in the early 1900s, some of these neighborhood improvement and property owners' associations began to contest black expansion. Their efforts were perhaps best documented on the South Side between Lake Michigan and Cottage Grove Avenue, a hotly contested area that includes Hyde Park and the University of Chicago, along with Woodlawn, the area just south of the university.[13]

In early 1917, the Chicago Real Estate Board floated the idea of racial zoning. But prospects for racial zoning dimmed considerably that year, when the Supreme Court's *Buchanan* decision overturned Louisville's racial zoning ordinance. Thus in Chicago as in other cities, restrictive covenants were soon to emerge as the only remaining legal means to enforce racial residential segregation. With the active encouragement of the real estate board, the property owners' associations increasingly turned to racial covenants to preserve their neighborhoods, instead of looking to broader-based initiatives toward the same ends. Racially restrictive covenants came to be widely deployed in Chicago from the 1920s onward, taking off in the late 1920s, declining during the Depression years when the real estate market was soft, but making a comeback as housing demand tightened significantly during the Second World War.[14]

The terrible Chicago race riots of 1919 undoubtedly played a role in the accelerated pace of racial covenants beginning in the 1920s. The riots began on July 27, 1919, when some young black men encroached on what the white locals thought was "their" area at a lakeshore beach. In the ensuing melee, a young black man in the water was stoned and drowned, while a nearby police officer refused to arrest a man who seemed to be a ringleader. More fights soon erupted at the beach, and thereafter violence and arson spread through the city, ebbing and flowing over the next week. By the end, some thirty-eight persons had been killed, and massive amounts of property had been destroyed.[15]

Those dreadful days prompted the appointment of a commission that produced a remarkable study of race relations in the city. The 1922 report, entitled *The Negro in Chicago,* documented not only the riots but also the background difficulties that black Chicagoans faced. While the commission's report rejected segregation as the answer to Chicago's race problems, there were many others who viewed the riots as decisive proof that the races could not mix. One Chicago alderman renewed the call for racial zoning after the riots, perhaps thinking, like the politicians in other cities noted in Chapter 2, that a different type of racial zoning could evade *Buchanan*'s negative decision on zoning two years earlier.[16]

No such formal rezoning occurred, though various groups of prominent Chicagoans—including members of the Riot Commission—discussed an informal route to segregation, whereby Black Belt housing would be improved and expanded in the hope that African American residents would stay put. But nothing came of such plans, and black Chicagoans still remained effectively pinned down in overcrowded and rundown black areas of the city.[17]

The *Chicago Defender* complained regularly about ghettoization over the ensuing years, but Chicago's African American leadership did not mount any immediate major attack on racial covenants. Why were these covenants not challenged more aggressively in the earlier period? If historian Spear's thesis is correct, by the time that racially restrictive covenants began to place white neighborhoods legally off limits to African Americans, Chicago's black leaders were already well accustomed to treating problems on a self-help basis, rather than demanding integration. Moreover, over time, the very success of the city's African American politicians meant that they became deeply imbued in the political machine's go-along-to-get-along ethos. Some black politicians themselves had ambivalent views about racial covenants. They hated the disrespect that covenants symbolized, and they wanted more space for the black community to expand, but as one was to observe somewhat later, "I don't want Negroes moving all over town. . . . I'd never get re-elected if Negroes were all scattered about."[18]

Norm entrepreneurship in Chicago's racial covenants. Meanwhile, racially restrictive covenants flourished in the city. The riots of 1919 had convinced many of Chicago's most respectable elements that only residential separation could preserve peace (and property values), and that only racially restrictive covenants were a foolproof method for this end—at least within the law. Real estate brokers and banks could help, of course. Even at a time when most of Chicago's African American vote still went to Republicans, as the party of Lincoln, the prominent liberal Republican Chicagoan Nathan MacChesney wrote the 1924 NAREB section of the Realtors' Code of Ethics discussed in Chapter 5—the section that warned brokers away from activities that might lead to racial mixing. MacChesney, who at the time was general counsel to NAREB, went on to draft an additional model real estate licensing act, which would have enabled a state to remove the license of any real estate broker who engaged in "misrepresentation" or other "unbecoming conduct"—strictures that could be interpreted to bar brokers whose deals violated racial covenants. Illinois was one of thirty-two states that eventually adopted this model licensing act. This was an important point for Chicago; most white brokers were not members of the elite Chicago Real Estate Board, and they might not otherwise have followed the board's Code of Ethics on matters of racial steering.[19]

Finally, in 1927, while MacChesney was still general counsel to NAREB, he drafted a standard form of a restrictive covenant. He was apparently emboldened by *Corrigan v. Buckley*, the previous year's Supreme Court ruling that racial covenants presented no constitutional issues. His model borrowed from the *Corrigan* covenant, although as it ran on to several pages in length, it loaded on considerably more bells and whistles to the simple thirteen-line agreement in *Corrigan*. But with minor modifications, this covenant could be used not only in Chicago but in other cities as well. Its adherents trumpeted it as "constitution-proof," and it was especially useful for bringing covenants to already-existing neighborhoods as a peaceable and legal method to secure segregation. Members of the Chicago Real Estate Board trotted it out for meetings of property owners, churches, and civic groups all over town to promote neighborhood covenant drives, adding a how-to pamphlet that was euphemistically entitled "Choose Your Neighbors."[20]

Even with a canned model and a book of instructions, however, it was not a simple matter to get these covenants up and running. For one thing, precisely because African Americans had already made a mark in Chicago politics, proponents of residential segregation needed to choose their language carefully. When the Chicago Real Estate Board campaigned to get neighborhood organizations to adopt racial covenants, it took account of the touchiness of race questions, describing its efforts only as designed "to protect and stabilize property values in residential districts in certain sections of Chicago." Similarly, property owners' and neighborhood improvement associations in the South Shore and Pullman neighborhoods asserted that their covenant drives aimed only to limit the entry of "undesirables."[21]

Chicago in the 1920s did see a number of new residential developments, particularly in the more outlying city areas and the suburbs; there, racial restrictions covered entire new subdivisions as part of the development plats. Since much of Chicago had been built out earlier, however, the bulk of the 1920s covenant campaigns concentrated on only one kind of arrangement—that is, the post hoc neighborhood agreement represented by MacChesney's model, rather than the *ex ante*, developer-created covenant structure. But after-the-fact covenants faced several problems. First was the difficulty of recruiting the neighbors themselves. Someone had to do the work of going door to door to collect signatures—not an easy chore, especially since neighborhoods tended to get involved in covenant campaigns only when minority group members were on the verge of moving in, by which time some owners no longer wished to be bound by covenants. One Chicago Real Estate Board official later recalled that in neighborhood covenant drives, the covenant forms were usually written so that they would go into effect with the signatures of only 75 or 80 percent of the properties. "We never got 100 per cent in every block," he explained.[22]

His statement revealed not only the difficulties of garnering unanimity, but also, with his reference to "we," the central role that real estate professionals played in these covenant drives in older neighborhoods. The experience of the north side Uptown area in 1928 gave an example of the obstacles, as well as the institutional interventions. In the wake of increasing racial diversification in homes and businesses, some alarmed residents started a covenant campaign there, but volunteers soon lost their enthusiasm. The campaign only picked up when the neighborhood organization—spurred on by the Chicago Real Estate Board—hired a paid employee for the job.[23]

To overcome a typical collective action problem—who would be the "first mover"?—the covenant promoters attempted to recruit major institutions and prominent citizens as early signatories in the process of "breaking in a book." At the end, when some owners still held back, a neighborhood association might try to embarrass the free riders by publishing the laggards' names. But the costs of all these efforts added up. One association's campaign in the 1920s cost between $25 and $100 per property owner, a considerable sum in that era. And once finished, neighborhood associations faced the prospect of starting all over again in a few years. This was because, unlike covenants in some other locales, the Chicago covenants generally were drawn up to last for about twenty years—perhaps reflecting a concession to wary owners, but possibly also reflecting lingering concerns about the dreaded Rule Against Perpetuities, discussed in Chapter 3. On the ground, what this meant was that a whole new wave of covenant campaigns would have to be cranked up in the 1940s, as the earlier agreements approached their expiration. But by that time, racial covenants were starting to attract more visible hostile firepower.[24]

Second to what might be dubbed these upstream issues of recruitment were the downstream issues of enforcement. Neighborhood agreements were notable for their failures to meet formal requirements—a spouse's signature missing here, a typing mistake there, an improper notarization on the next page. As we shall see later in this chapter, civil rights lawyers all over the country learned to exploit these technical defects in defending their clients from eviction from covenanted properties. Moreover, because the neighborhood agreements never could jump through all the hoops required for covenants to run at law—the old-fashioned horizontal privity requirements in particular—they were particularly dependent on the courts' special equitable jurisdiction for enforcement. As we shall see, this too gave lawyers an opportunity to undermine covenants piecemeal, through arguments deriving from equitable precedents.

Meanwhile, minority Chicagoans sometimes simply ignored the covenants, moving into neighborhoods whether or not they were restricted. Landlords filled vacant apartments with nonwhite tenants, covenants or no. During the Depression years of the 1930s, when white buyers were harder to find, some white sellers were more than willing to go along with a sale to a minority purchaser. Even an occasional individual lender might break ranks with general mortgage practice, championing the right of a landlord or seller to deal with whomever they chose in spite of covenants—no doubt a better option than foreclosure for both the owner and the lender.[25]

Against this array of resistant forces, nothing would make covenants start—and last—unless the norm entrepreneurs intervened. That might mean an initiative by a few particularly enterprising neighbors or an active neighborhood improvement association, often led by a real estate board member, or it might mean that some more powerful entity got involved. On the city's South Side, the University of Chicago was a particularly important institutional supporter of racial covenants, at least for a time; but throughout the city, many banks, churches, and large and small businesses also lent legitimacy to covenant drives. Some parts of the city lacked such imposing institutional norm entrepreneurs or supporters, however—as in what was then the somewhat decaying Oakland neighborhood north of Hyde Park, where both Asian and African American residents entered the covenanted neighborhood in the 1930s and 1940s without significant incident. By 1947, the year before the Supreme Court's decision in *Shelley v. Kraemer*, one study estimated that more than three thousand black families were living in Chicago properties that had covenants against their presence.[26]

THE NORM BREAKERS EMERGE

Even when white neighbors were willing to take on the legal expenses entailed in expelling an "undesirable" neighbor, they faced an increasingly savvy set of technical defenses thrown up by the lawyers for African American clients. Significantly, they also faced an increasingly uncertain audience before the Chicago judiciary, a group of elected officeholders who were always influenced to some degree by the city's ever-bubbling politics. At least one municipal judge declared that racial covenants were unconstitutional. This was an opinion that had zero precedential value, but it still served as a straw in the wind about the changing politics of race. Indeed, those changing politics may have discouraged white owners and neighborhood associations from lawsuits, and may have kept them from appealing when judicial decisions went against them—all of which made it less likely that Chicago and Illinois would produce major precedents on racially restrictive covenants.[27]

Because of the difficulties and costs of creating racially restrictive covenants in the first instance, and then making them stick in a neighborhood later, working-class neighborhoods like the Back of the Yards did not bother with them. Tight-knit neighborhoods like these had other ways to keep out unwanted minorities, notably intimidation. Chicago's racial covenants, like racial covenants elsewhere, gravitated toward middle-class neighborhoods, where the residents could afford the expense of covenant drives, and where the white residents undoubtedly preferred the legal system to brute force.[28]

By the same token, at least some minority buyers who defied covenants may have also gravitated toward the middle class—that is, they were people who could afford to get a mortgage and buy a home, even without much help from FHA policies, and who were willing to take the risk and pay the price to get their chance at the American Dream. In Chicago, this meant that a middle-class area like Hyde Park and its surroundings would become what commentators St. Clair Drake and Horace Cayton called "contested areas."[29]

Thus it may not be accidental that the one major Chicago covenant case—the one that made its way to the history books and the law school casebooks—was instigated in an area adjacent to Hyde Park, by the well-to-do real estate dealer Carl Hansberry, together with Harry Pace, then the president of the Supreme Liberty Life Insurance Company. The Supreme Liberty Life Insurance Company was a Chicago institution much involved in African American real estate mortgages. It was especially important in the 1930s and later, given African Americans' difficulties in securing FHA loan qualification; its longstanding general counsel was NAACP lawyer Earl Dickerson.

After taking advice from Dickerson, Hansberry joined Pace to buy properties and break the covenants of the Washington Park neighborhood.[30] Washington Park at that time was a largely white area just south and west of Hyde Park, the neighborhood where the University of Chicago was located. Although the matter was somewhat ambiguous, university officials first supported racial covenants in that neighborhood, but somewhat later they appeared to soften their position, hoping to turn Washington Park into a kind of middle class black buffer area that would relieve the pressure on Hyde Park itself. The neighborhood association's lawsuit against Hansberry and his co-defendants ultimately failed—and with it, the particular set of covenants that governed Washington Park—but procedural questions would deflect the case away from the civil rights lawyers' big target, the legality of racial covenants altogether.[31]

In addition to his real estate activities, Hansberry was an active member of Chicago's NAACP. Many years later, his daughter said that he had been a man who was convinced that the "American Way" was the appropriate vehicle by which to combat racism. While he tried to prove his point with his legal attack on racial covenants, as she recalled with some bitterness, his family suffered months of taunts, blows, and threats.[32]

To challenge the racial restriction on his house, Hansberry used a method that had become increasingly prevalent: a cooperating white straw purchaser would buy and then resell a covenanted property to a minority purchaser. He had tried this method a short time earlier with a rental unit, when a cooperating white woman sublet a covenanted apartment to him and his family, claiming that they were cousins. When she was successfully sued by the neighbors, however, the Hansberrys left the apartment.[33]

But in May 1937, armed with a mortgage from the ubiquitous Supreme Liberty Life Insurance Company, Hansberry and his wife, Minnie, purchased a covenanted building through another white intermediary, this time a real estate speculator (another type of norm breaker that we shall see again). The night that the family moved in, they were greeted with two bricks through the front door. Within two weeks, as Dickerson had warned, a neighbor sued under the auspices of the Woodlawn Property Owners Association, which included the Washington Park subdivision. Meanwhile, Harry Pace, a man whose career had migrated from music entrepreneur to insurance executive at Supreme Liberty Life, had moved into another covenanted property in the same neighborhood. Although Pace was of sufficiently mixed origin that some said he later passed for white, he too became a defendant in the lawsuit, along with several white—or perhaps one should say whiter—

participants, all of whom were accused of conspiracy to violate the restrictions. The *Hansberry* case immediately attracted the attention of the *Chicago Defender* newspaper, which among other things sharply criticized the otherwise progressive University of Chicago for its role in trying to keep the neighborhood white. Marches, protests, and debates followed, some led by the university's own Negro Student Club.[34]

As it turned out, Hansberry's broadside attack on racially restrictive covenants foundered on the white "co-conspirators." One of them, James Burke, had helped to orchestrate the straw sales to Pace and Hansberry. Burke earlier had been an active member of the Woodlawn Property Owners' Association, but at the time of Hansberry's lawsuit he had had a falling out with the organization. This may well have been at least in part because, like many homeowners in the Washington Park neighborhood, he now thought it hopeless to find white purchasers for homes there.[35]

The problem for Burke was that several years earlier, his wife had been the plaintiff in a lawsuit that upheld the very covenants that Hansberry and Pace now defied—along with Burke himself as an arranger. The Woodlawn Property Owners' attorneys convinced the trial judge that Burke himself, as a co-signer of the covenants, was a member of a class of people represented in the earlier suit, and that as such he was now barred from denying the covenants' validity. He was now challenging the covenants on the ground that too few owners had signed on—a typical flaw for neighbor-driven covenants—but the property owners' association argued that this issue had been resolved in the earlier case, and that as a member of the class that had successfully defended the covenants in that suit, he could not now gainsay the earlier finding.[36]

When the *Hansberry* case came to trial, it was this procedural issue that swayed the judge, who obviously saw in it a key to what he thought was Burke's two-faced activity. On appeal, the Illinois Supreme Court affirmed the lower court's ruling against the defendant covenant breakers, focusing on the same procedural issue, and deciding that the ruling in the earlier case was now binding on the current defendants. That procedural issue deflected a straightforward decision on the issue most central to the *Hansberry* covenant breakers, however: their charge that the covenants were invalid either as a property matter or a constitutional one.[37]

Nevertheless, the case galvanized the Chicago civil rights bar, whose confident and capable young African American lawyers argued all the way to the U.S. Supreme Court. There they finally won a victory—but of course not on the issue of the general validity of racial covenants. Instead, the case turned on the question whether Burke's peripheral involvement in the earlier suit barred him and his fellow defendants from challenging the covenants' validity in this later case. When the Supreme Court reversed the Illinois court and decided that the defendants could litigate the substantive issues after all, the Woodlawn Property Owners' Association effectively gave up the case—although it did not give up the more general effort to create and enforce racial covenants.[38]

Modern civil procedure casebooks and legal texts continue to reference the Supreme Court's decision in *Hansberry v. Lee*. It was an important case in determining the legal effect of a class action lawsuit, even though it sidestepped the validity (or invalidity) of racially restrictive covenants. And in fact, something came out of the case that was even more dramatic—very literally—than a Supreme Court opinion about racially restrictive covenants might have been. In 1959, *A Raisin in the Sun* opened on Broadway, a play that was destined for enormous success. It had been written by Lorraine Hansberry, Carl Hansberry's daughter, about a family living in Chicago's Washington Park area sometime in the late 1940s or 1950s. The play demonstrated the great symbolic significance of owning a home for working-class African Americans at the time—as well as the racial obstacles that stood in their way. Although the Hansberrys themselves had been well-to-do, unlike the family depicted in *Raisin*, and although the time of the play was at least a decade later than Lorraine Hansberry's experiences, the characters' sentiments surely were informed by her childhood memories of her family's harrowing travails during the lawsuit.

Lorraine Hansberry's play did not overtly focus on racial covenants—the white antagonist in the play instead wanted to buy the family out of its dream home—but well before that literary work appeared, her father's lawyers had fixed their sights on covenants. Indeed, over the early 1940s, some advocates thought that their sights were too firmly fixed, fearing that the covenant issues were draining attention and resources away from the more pressing issues of better housing for minorities, without respect to covenants. Nevertheless, Chicago became the opening venue for a series of national NAACP conferences beginning in 1945, convened with the chief purpose of organizing a major assault on racial covenants. The only question was how and where. To some degree by accident, and to some degree by plan, the answer to the "where" question would be St. Louis, Detroit, and Washington, D.C.[39]

Chicago NAACP lawyers developed a case of their own to carry the torch, but some in the national NAACP were wary—including Thurgood Marshall, who had by this time established a leadership role in the national organization. The Chicago case, *Tovey v. Levy*, was not far along in April 1947, when St. Louis lawyer George Vaughn forced the issue by petitioning the U.S. Supreme Court to hear a case of his own. NAACP attorneys in several other cities scrambled to add petitions from other racial covenant cases, including a Detroit case and two cases from Washington, D.C., which the Court ultimately did agree to hear. And so in the end, not Chicago but those other cities would become ground zero for the final legal challenges to racially restrictive covenants.[40]

All the same, it was big, brawling Chicago that set the stage for the legal norm breakers. The city had certainly had its norm entrepreneurs for promoting racially restrictive covenants, including leaders in the real estate business. But norm breaking needed entrepreneurs too, and while Chicago lagged at the outset, it went on to produce some good ones, at a time when it mattered. Through the *Defender*'s publicity, through the local civil rights lawyers' capable strategies, through the support of homegrown financial institutions like Supreme Liberty Life Insurance, and through the personal toughness of a man like Carl Hansberry, Chicago's negative experiences with racially restrictive covenants came before the eyes of the nation and stayed there. Chicagoans on both sides illuminated the tactics, the moves and countermoves, that other American cities would experience in the gradually emerging challenges to racially restrictive covenants.

MOVING TOWARD *SHELLEY*

Lawyers associated with the Chicago NAACP brought home a victory in *Hansberry*, and indeed the case was an important marker for African American civil rights lawyers' turn toward the courts and toward direct legal challenges to segregation. But the case's procedural redirection made it a very thin gruel for opponents of racial restrictions as such.[41] Even after *Hansberry*, and up until *Shelley v. Kraemer* was decided eight years later, things went on more or less as they had in the past for civil rights lawyers in court, in Chicago as in other cities. They lost again and again on their major claims that racially restrictive covenants constituted unconstitutional state action.

Nevertheless, their challenges succeeded in keeping the injustice of racial covenants alive as a political issue. Their litigation also forced white neighborhood organizations and real estate interests to bear the expense of enforcement. Certainly those costs must have led to the abandonment of many covenant arrangements, as occurred in Chicago's Washington Park area after the *Hansberry* decision. And finally, as in *Hansberry* itself, the civil rights lawyers managed to pick away at the legal margins of racial covenants, attacking them on technical grounds such as signature problems and recording irregularities. Indeed, shortly before the *Shelley* case, there were enough of these seemingly penny-ante tactics that Scovel Richardson, an African American lawyer in St. Louis and an important covenant challenger himself, put together a small compendium for the use of other covenant opponents all over the country.[42]

Unsettling the opposition: the meaning of race. From the perspective of modern legal scholarship, a particularly intriguing technique of NAACP lawyers in the 1940s was their challenge to the very concept of race itself. This was a strategem that had its origins decades earlier—at least as early as the organization's location of an almost-white "black" man in the old case upholding railroad segregation, *Plessy v. Ferguson*. Among other arguments, Plessy himself had asserted that as an "octoroon," he was not African American, and that his relegation to a "colored" rail car damaged his interest in a good reputation.[43]

The NAACP lawyers retooled the maneuver for the racial covenant cases, but now they argued that race was not so easy to discern. Carl Hansberry's co-defendant, Harry Pace, could easily have been a case in point, since he could have and perhaps later did pass for white, but by the 1940s, the argument did not really hinge on anyone's actual color. Instead, it was a way to catch would-be covenant enforcers off guard, although at a deeper level it represented the beginnings of an overt challenge to the category of race itself. At the 1945 Chicago conference on racial covenants, the eminent civil rights lawyer Charles Hamilton Houston urged that all the NAACP lawyers try to undermine racial definitions, describing the effort as an educational technique that might shake up white covenant enforcers. By that time, he was speaking from experience, having grilled the plaintiffs about their racial perceptions in *Hurd v. Hodge,* the Washington, D.C., case that was to be decided in tandem with *Shelley.*[44]

Houston was in fact extending a technique pioneered by Detroit lawyers Willis Graves and Frances Dent, who had already made racial identity a central issue in *Sipes v. McGhee,* the Michigan case that was to become the national NAACP's companion case to *Shelley.* The McGhees were in fact quite fair-skinned, and Graves and Dent thoroughly flummoxed a white neighbor by asking how he knew that the couple moving in next door were "Negroes" (the answer: "I have seen Mr. McGhee and he appears to have colored features. They are more darker than mine . . ."). In addition, the lawyers also called as experts two members of the Wayne State University Department of Sociology and Anthropology. The professors stopped short of the modern view that race is a socially constructed category rather than a natural one, and instead they adopted the more cautious position that only experts could recognize racial differences.[45]

The Michigan Supreme Court was unimpressed with this tactic, however, curtly accepting the neighbor's identification as sufficient evidence. The state supreme court did not mention a point that had apparently swayed the circuit court below, however: the defendants themselves had self-identified as African American in some earlier legal documents. If they were expert enough to identify themselves as black, it seemed, so was their white neighbor. What also went un-noted was the point that for segregation laws, it could have been dangerous ground indeed to leave racial designations simply to self-identification—here as in the older issues that we saw in Chapter 3 about the race of corporations. But it would be left to later decades to interrogate more thoroughly the legal category of race.[46]

Changing neighborhoods, changing attitudes, "changed circumstances." In addition to the small-bore challenges to signatures and the like, one other pre-*Shelley* legal attack on racially restrictive covenants did have some moderate success: lawyers deployed a standard equitable principle in covenant law called "changed circumstances" or "changed conditions." According to this doctrine, courts of equity would not enforce covenant restrictions that had outlasted their purpose or had lost their value. We have already seen this underlying idea in property law doctrines like restraints on alienation and covenant law's more specific requirement that covenants touch and concern land. Like those doctrines, the changed circumstance doctrine relates to a land restriction's ongoing *value*. All these legal categories may seem overly technical to anyone unfamiliar with real estate law, but they represent a simple commonsense idea: covenants made at an earlier time by Owners A and B will not be enforced at a later time between Owners C and D, unless the covenants are likely to retain some reasonable value to landowners affected by them.

Interestingly enough, the equitable changed circumstance doctrine is one of a very few through which an owner can lose a property right, even a partial one, without consent or some neglect of his or her rights. There is a reason for this exception: real estate covenants of any type typically give large numbers of owners a set of mutual rights over one another's properties, as for example in subdivision restrictions on building styles. Because of the number of owners involved, those who want to renegotiate obsolete restrictions can face high transaction costs and advantage taking (or "strategic bargaining") by other individual owners; hence more than many other property interests, these covenants need some mechanism for post hoc readjustment.

The changed circumstance doctrine serves this need. Although courts have generally applied the doctrine only reluctantly, they occasionally did so in the 1940s in the case of racially restrictive covenants. When they did, they implicitly acknowledged important demographic and attitudinal changes in American cities: on the one hand, a continuing and accelerating pattern of African American urbanization, and on the other a newly emerging white suburbanization, such that even racist white owners had little to gain from enforcing racially restrictive covenants in their increasingly black neighborhoods.

During the World War II years, black urban areas expanded as more minority members moved to the edges of their ever more crowded neighborhoods—even though, by all contemporary reports, the minority regions grew nowhere nearly enough to satisfy housing needs. In a striking example, Detroit's African American prewar population of 160,000 grew by another 60,000 by 1943—and that meant 60,000 persons with very few housing options. Predictably, African Americans pushed out from existing ghettos, and in doing so they put increasing pressure on the white residents' collective control over "their" neighborhoods. And predictably too, one white response to the wave of new urban pressure was violence, that cheapest of all enforcement mechanisms for segregationist norms for close-knit urban communities. Violence broke out in Detroit in a particularly dramatic way in 1942, when a white mob—including the Ku Klux Klan—stoned and beat the African American war workers who attempted to move into the newly available Sojourner Truth housing project. As it turned out, that disturbance was only the prelude to a full-blown race riot in Detroit the following summer.[47]

White outrage was not always strong enough to generate violent norm enforcement, however. A second and newer response suggested that even white residents did not think it worth the effort to keep the neighborhood for themselves. This newer response was white flight, particularly after the war drew to a close and the suburbs started to open up. People moved to the suburbs for many reasons, but one was to escape urban neighborhood change. As described in Chapter 5, FHA mortgage insurance policies called for restrictive covenants until well after the war was over, while developers targeted their primary purchasers and kept the new middle-class developments largely white. The burgeoning suburban developments offered white urban residents a third alternative to what must have seemed to be two unattractive prospects: either staying put as minorities entered the neighborhood, or resorting to violence to stave them off. The catch with flight, however, was that every white departure made racial transition even more difficult to resist in the urban neighborhoods left behind.

Another response, of course, was to remain in the city and to fall back on existing racially restrictive covenants. When minority buyers attempted to acquire the homes vacated by departing white families, some of the neighbors, bolstered by respectable city real estate interests, treated racial covenants as their chief bulwark against change, and they did what they could to hold the line by enforcing the covenants. But there was a major problem with holding the line through covenants: covenants could deeply cleave the interests of the white homeowners. When minority members started to move into adjacent areas, the owners of restricted properties sometimes found that the pool of white bidders had effectively dried up, and any who remained were likely to make only paltry offers. Meanwhile, the owners were legally stuck: they were precluded by the racial covenants from selling their properties to the African Americans who would have bid more. Some white homeowners in these circumstances simply broke the covenants and went ahead and sold to minority purchasers. In Chicago, some white owners and real estate dealers went even further: they organized to *prevent* the enforcement of racial covenants, attributing these efforts to wealthy outside interests.[48]

When breakaway white owners like these were challenged by their neighbors or the local improvement association—or perhaps the outside real estate interests who hoped to buffer more distant white residential areas—they became defendants along with their minority renters or buyers. And it was at this point that they claimed that changed circumstances had made the racially restrictive covenants valueless. What value could there be in a white-only covenant when the neighborhood had already changed so much? As we shall see, by the mid 1940s, changed circumstance cases began to cause some judges to reassess the enforceability of racial restrictions more generally. But even before that, changed circumstances became a potential doctrinal path for knocking down restrictive covenants in the very areas where they mattered most to pent-up minority families: that is, the urban neighborhoods that were already at a border between white and minority. It was in those areas where minority members had already breached the barriers or seemed about to do so, and where others were most likely to look for housing opportunities. And it was in those labile border areas where the changed circumstance doctrine made possible a kind of wary cooperation between restricted white sellers or landlords and the minority renters or buyers who wanted to move into their forbidden properties. What the courts called changed circumstances meant that for at least a few fleeting moments, the interests of these groups were aligned—aligned against covenants.

The Blockbusters. The numerous instances of urban racial transition created other strange bedfellows as well, most notably one type of norm-breaking entrepreneur that became especially controversial. Some enterprising real estate brokers realized that there was arbitrage money to be made in racial succession. In fact, real estate brokers had noticed this for a long time, even in the days before racially restrictive covenants were widely adopted. Early in the twentieth century, both black and white speculators in Harlem observed that white people were likely to sell cheaply when black neighbors started to move in, and they took advantage of these opportunities to buy at panic prices, even when it meant breaking open ineffective neighborhood agreements not to sell to minorities. In those same early years in Chicago, Jesse Binga, an important black banker and real estate agent, honed the art of purchasing properties on the cheap in transitional areas, a practice that may have been a factor in the bombing of his house and office seven times in a single year (1919–1920).[49]

Two or three decades later, the demographic changes of the 1940s created many more arbitrage opportunities, and speculative practices settled into a widely decried pattern. By encouraging minority entrance into white neighborhoods, or by simply spreading rumors of such moves, the real estate dealers who would come to be known as blockbusters could fan the flames of racial fears and then pounce on the bargains, ultimately reselling the properties to willing minority buyers.[50]

These practices seemed highly unsavory, and the brokers who engaged in them were widely denounced for fomenting trouble for the sake of cashing in. But on closer examination, the ethics of blockbusting appear in a much more ambiguous light. In its own way, blockbusting was a kind of norm entrepreneurship—or more accurately, an entrepreneurship in norm busting, breaking down white neighbors' resistance to minority entrance.

It was undoubtedly true that in taking advantage of white fears, blockbusting brokers had much to gain by inflaming those fears even more. But there is another side to the story. In the later 1940s, the name of one of these norm-busting brokers, Raphael Urciolo, floated through the controversies over racial covenants in Washington, D.C. Urciolo's blockbusting tactics turned him into a defendant in *Hurd v. Hodge*, the Washington case that paralleled *Shelley*. At the trial, Urciolo claimed to be interested only in making as much money as possible. But he also stated flatly, "I don't believe in covenants at all," and he observed that if he were given a choice between selling to a "colored" or foreign purchaser, as opposed to a white purchaser, he would always sell to the minority or foreign person, because that buyer had so much more difficulty in finding a house.[51]

Needless to say, Urciolo was in bad odor with the Washington Real Estate Board, whose code of ethics reflected the usual bar on sales practices leading to racial mixing; in fact, the board had already expelled him by the time that *Hurd* was litigated. But it is hard to see such a figure simply as the enemy of racial justice—especially when some who fought hardest for racial justice saw him as a friend. The question of cooperating with blockbusting brokers came up at the NAACP's 1945 Chicago conference on restrictive covenants. Some of those present wanted to keep a distance from these very controversial middlemen. But Charles Houston, who would soon argue the *Hurd* case, was probably thinking of Urciolo when he asserted that the brokers performed a useful service in the long campaign against racially restrictive covenants. Chicago lawyer Loring Moore agreed with Houston: the organization's challenges to covenants, he said, depended on these brokers who would act as "law breakers."[52]

War, Cold War, and expanding horizons. The Second World War and its conclusion created a critical juncture for racially restrictive covenants. Many African American and other minority soldiers had served their country's cause in the war effort, and some had died for it. Because the war itself entailed a struggle against fascist and Nazi enemies, it raised profound questions about racism at home. When fighting such enemies, how were Americans to explain or rationalize our own discrimination against our own fellow citizens? During the war, the NAACP and sympathetic commentators—notably the Swedish economist Gunnar Myrdal in his influential 1944 book, *An American Dilemma*—hammered ever more insistently on the deleterious effects that segregation and discrimination had had on African Americans and their life chances.[53]

By the end of the war, these considerations were starting to rumble faintly in the courts, and perhaps it was to be expected that the first noticeable tremors came via the equitable changed circumstance cases that had already begun to rattle racial restrictions. In two important courts, the California Supreme Court, and the federal District of Columbia Circuit Court of Appeals, two minority opinions by highly respected judges suggested that judicial support for racial restrictions was beginning to crack. In a 1944 case from Los Angeles, *Fairchild v. Raines,* the majority decided that the trial court should consider whether minority influx in the vicinity of a covenanted area was a sufficient change in circumstance to make compliance with white-only covenants unjust for the affected lot owners. But California Justice Roger Traynor's concurring opinion went further, taking a cue from the NAACP's emerging strategy of detailing the social circumstances behind individual cases. Traynor argued that the covenants' validity should be decided not simply in light of the affected property owners, but also in the light of the entire public's interest in adequate housing space for all the city's residents.[54]

A few months later, in the case *Mays v. Burgess,* which concerned a very wide stretch of neighbor covenants in Washington, D.C., a clearly troubled majority decided that neighborhood change had not undermined the covenants' enforceability for the affected properties. But Judge Henry Edgerton's dissent, rather like California Justice Traynor's opinion in *Fairchild,* argued among other matters that equitable enforcement of a covenant should take into account more than simply the immediate parties and affected property owners. Equitable enforcement, Edgerton asserted, should also consider the changed public interest of the entire city, in which minority residents had come to be severely constrained by white-only covenants.[55]

Edgerton's opinion raised constitutional issues along with the property law questions, and lower courts too were starting to raise broad questions of fundamental rights, if anything even more vehemently. Late in 1945, the well-known black actresses Louise Beavers, Ethel Waters, and Academy Award winner Hattie McDaniel took part in a real-life drama when they were sued for breaking racial covenants on their residences in Los Angeles's Sugar Hill neighborhood. NAACP lawyer Loren Miller, fresh from his changed circumstance arguments in the *Fairchild* case, represented the actresses, and very successfully as it turned out. Municipal Judge Thurmond Clark threw the case out after a visit to the neighborhood, declaring that it was time that African

Americans enjoyed their full rights under the Fourteenth Amendment of the U.S. Constitution. "Judges have been avoiding the real issue too long," he said. A little over a year later, a county judge in New York's Queens county upheld a racial covenant on the basis of overwhelming precedent, but not before he delivered a pointed quotation from an earlier Supreme Court opinion, to the effect that racial distinctions were contrary to American principles and to the purposes for which the war was fought. Meanwhile, in May, 1945, the High Court of Ontario declared a covenant restriction against "Jews or persons of objectionable nationality" to be void as against "public policy," prominently citing the new United Nations Charter. Civil rights lawyers were soon to cite the case and the charter in their arguments against restrictive covenants.[56]

With the war's end and the newly unfolding Cold War, a new kind of public policy concern about racial restrictions was indeed emerging. Patterns of continuing segregation caused serious embarrassment to the United States, over against a Soviet rival that consistently pointed to racism and inequality as inherent defects of America's political and economic structure. President Truman appointed a new Committee on Civil Rights, and in its 1947 report, *To Secure These Rights,* the committee commented on the foreign policy consequences of segregation at home. Housing discrimination did not go unnoticed in this report; among other matters, the authors singled out racially restrictive covenants as a problem and called upon the Justice Department to intervene in challenges to their validity.[57] The Justice Department—joined by an impressive array of civil rights, labor, and religious organizations—did just that the next year when the *Shelley* case came before the U.S. Supreme Court. Among other things, the Justice Department's amicus brief cited a letter from the State Department, detailing the embarrassment that segregation caused for American diplomacy.[58]

But another less-discussed factor may also have played a role in spotlighting racially restrictive covenants: the mad rush to suburbanization at the conclusion of the war. It was clear that unless something happened to halt them, racial covenants were going to be an even larger part of the nation's new suburban demographics. In late 1947 and early 1948, the first several thousand homes went on sale in the huge and quintessentially middle-class new Levittown development on Long

Island. The deeds to these modest new homes included racial restrictions. Under pressure from the NAACP, the FHA had recently dropped its explicit preference for racial covenants in the 1947 *Underwriters' Manual,* but it still accepted those covenants, and the *Manual* continued to advise mortgage investigators that neighborhoods with "user groups" who were "congenial" were more likely to be stable and attractive. After years of racial covenants, lenders undoubtedly understood what these euphemisms meant. If racial restrictions mattered to lenders, they would matter just as much to the mass housing developers of the postwar era, because without the possibility of a standard long-term FHA-insured mortgage, many of the developers' targeted customers would not be able to buy a house at all.[59]

Levittown's first sales thus forecast a future in which legal residential segregation would expand exponentially. In this future, it seemed, racially restrictive covenants would be the rule not just for some relatively small "high class" communities, as in the developer restrictions in the early part of the century, and also not just for the highly motivated or panicky white urban dwellers, as in many of the older urban areas covered by neighbor-driven restrictions since the 1920s. Instead, racially restrictive covenants seemed poised to reach out into a whole new geography of a suburbanizing, white middle-class America.

It was at this juncture that the Supreme Court decided to take the case of *Shelley v. Kraemer* from St. Louis, the companion case *McGhee v. Sipes* from Detroit, and the closely related *Hurd v. Hodge* from Washington, D.C.

The Great Dilemma for Legal Norms

Shelley and State Action

7

In the middle of August 1945, an African American couple, J. D. Shelley and his wife, Ethel, bought a house on Labadie Avenue in St. Louis. Their white neighbors Louis and Fern Kraemer were not pleased. Neither was the local improvement association, nor the St. Louis Real Estate Exchange, a citywide brokers' organization that was particularly active in promulgating and enforcing racial covenants. With the association's and the Exchange's very active support, the Kraemers filed suit to prevent the Shelleys from taking possession of what they had thought would be their new home. The Kraemers' claim was based on a racially restrictive covenant that the neighbors—including the seller's predecessors—had imposed on themselves in 1911, with the standard prohibition: the house was not to be used or occupied by "any person not of the Caucasian race." Meanwhile a group of black real estate brokers saw the case as a potential vehicle for opening up more of the city for their own clientele, and they came to the defense of the Shelleys.[1]

Some months earlier, in November 1944, a similar story had played out in a neighborhood in Detroit. Orsel and Minnie McGhee, another African American couple, purchased a house and got somewhat further than the Shelleys—they actually moved in. But their white neighbors, Benjamin and Anna Sipes, were just as displeased as the Kraemers would be a few months later. The Sipes sued the McGhees to remove them from possession, basing their claim on a neighborhood restrictive covenant very similar to that on the Shelleys' property: it also prohibited the use or occupancy of the house by any person except those of the Caucasian race. The McGhees then turned to the local NAACP for their legal defense, and their lawyers were soon to be joined by the national NAACP legal staff.[2]

Together, these two local disputes were to become the basis for one of the best-known constitutional law decisions of the twentieth century.

DECISION AND DOUBTS

By the time these two local lawsuits surfaced, as we saw in last chapter, the NAACP had committed itself to combating racially restrictive covenants. But on the other side, local and national real estate organizations were highly interested in defending covenants. The two sides threw their legal staffs behind their respective claims as the *Shelley* and *Sipes* lawsuits wound their way through the judicial systems of Missouri and Michigan. Eventually both states' highest courts upheld the covenants, relying on existing state and federal precedent.[3]

The U.S. Supreme Court, after receiving mountains of briefs from a remarkable range of organizations, reversed both state supreme court decisions in the highly publicized 1948 case *Shelley v. Kraemer.* In a major departure from what most people thought was the clear legal precedent, Chief Justice Vinson wrote for the Court that no state courts could enforce these racially restrictive covenants. They could not do so, the Supreme Court announced, because judicial enforcement of racially restrictive covenants would be an exercise of state action, denying equal treatment of the law in violation of the Fourteenth Amendment to the U.S. Constitution.[4] Having disposed of the Michigan and Missouri decisions with this very controversial interpretation of state action, the Court turned its attention to a pair of cases that had originated in Washington, D.C. The city of Washington is a federal enclave, and not a state, and hence the Fourteenth Amendment's prohibition on discriminatory state actions does not apply in Washington, at least not directly. Nevertheless, Vinson's second opinion for the Court held that it would violate public policy to permit federal courts to enforce racial covenants in Washington when the same devices were not judicially enforceable in the states.[5]

Shelley was a bombshell in several ways—or so it seemed. It had important implications for the NAACP's litigation strategy, particularly in vindicating the use of social science literature to bolster civil rights claims. Proponents of racial covenants had long cited their formal equality—that is, both blacks and whites supposedly could avail themselves of these covenants—but the use of social science data cut hard against the notion that equal protection could be served by this kind of formalism, without accounting for the ways that legal devices played out in the real world. *Shelley* gave strong support to this approach, and the NAACP would use social science materials extensively—although sometimes controversially—in the major school desegregation and other antidiscrimination cases in the coming years, deploying social science findings to attack the formalistic versions of equality inherited from *Plessy v. Ferguson*'s separate but equal doctrine.[6]

As a practical matter too, *Shelley* had important consequences, simply by summarily denying legal enforcement to all racially restrictive covenants. As we saw in Chapter 3, these kinds of covenants had been uniformly upheld for decades in state and federal courts, and even in the Supreme Court's own 1926 decision in *Corrigan v. Buckley*, albeit on formal jurisdictional grounds.[7] Meanwhile, as we have also seen, despite deepening criticism of racial covenants and their weakening hold in the cities, these restrictions were still widespread in urban and especially suburban areas throughout the United States. They had enjoyed the support of local neighborhood organizations and real estate brokers, the national real estate industry, the elite members of the bar, and even the Federal Housing Administration, on the ground that they reduced racial conflict and stabilized housing values. But with *Shelley*, it seemed, all this would change. Racially restrictive covenants were the last legal means for enforcing housing segregation against willing buyers and sellers, and once those means fell, so it seemed, segregation would have to loosen—not only in housing but on all the other fronts supported by residential segregation.[8]

As is now well-known, this was not to be: the case opened up previously forbidden housing to minorities, but did little to end segregation as a practical matter. In fact, as we shall see in the next chapter, the case did not even dispose of racial covenants; these continued to be inserted in deeds, often taking their enforcement from social norms rather than legal ones.

But this chapter takes up a different issue, that of the construction of legal norms. Changes in *social* norms almost certainly had an important impact on the Court's change of heart in *Shelley*, but legal norms have their own internal imperatives. One of those is that any major legal change be justifiable within some legal framework. In certain important ways, the *Shelley* decision failed that test. While its very expansive reading of state action seemed at the time to be an important victory for civil rights advocates, subsequent history was to show that the case was juridically isolated—a kind of dead end.

Here a brief review can help to sort out the constitutional issues at stake in *Shelley*, all originating in the Reconstruction amendments from the years immediately following the Civil War. As we saw in Chapter 2, the Thirteenth Amendment was the first of these Reconstruction amendments; it bans slavery, and its provisions apply to all actors, public or private. As we also saw in Chapter 2, it was this amendment that undercut the most egregious of the later nineteenth-century southern landowners' efforts to impose a new version of servitude on the ex-slaves, under the guise of labor and debt contracts. The NAACP legal team in *Shelley*, however, rested their case's civil rights arguments not on the Thirteenth Amendment but rather on the next Reconstruction Amendment, the Fourteenth, which among other things requires the states to provide all persons within their jurisdictions the equal protection of the law.[9]

As we saw in Chapter 2, the Fourteenth Amendment had been the basis for the NAACP's victory over racial zoning in the *Buchanan v. Warley* case in 1917. The Fourteenth Amendment, however, is directed not at individuals but at *states*, and until the *Shelley* case, the courts had normally understood state action to mean legislation or some other measure initiated by public actors. It was for this reason that so many courts had rejected civil rights lawyers' charges against covenants: racial covenants, the thinking went, originated in private actions, and the mere act of going to court did not make them subject to the Fourteenth Amendment's limitations on state action. After all, lots of people go to court for private matters—say, to sue for an automobile accident or enforce a sale contract—and their acts scarcely seem official when they do so. As was also noted in Chapter 3, courts clearly are public bodies, and in that sense it is obvious that judicial enforcement entails the power of the state. But insofar as there is anything at all that is considered private law, arranged between private actors with no official capacity, then those actors of necessity must be able to resort to the courts to vindicate their private rights. Racially restrictive deals may have looked mean-spirited and not civic-minded, but they also still looked private, initiated and enforced by private parties rather than public officials, even when private parties used the courts.

But *Shelley* seemed to brush aside the cautious distinctions between state action and private action. It did not matter that no public legislature had adopted a neighborhood's racially restrictive covenants, or that no one in an official capacity took part in their creation or enforcement. It did not matter that the only thing that appeared to have happened was that at some point private developers had reached deals with home purchasers to exclude certain races, or homeowners had agreed with other homeowners to do the same, and that they or the persons who had bought their houses had used the courts to vindicate these ostensibly private arrangements.

According to *Shelley*, judicial enforcement was the element that turned these arrangements into state action. But that assertion raised a serious problem: so sweepingly formulated, *Shelley* seemed to leave little room for any private legal rights at all. After this case, the touchstone for state action apparently would be nothing more than resort to the courts. With that, it seemed, every private claim, at least when vindicated in court, could be labeled state action, subject to the same constraints that apply to official actors and policies. Such a view would have enormously expanded the scope of federal authority over discrimination, bringing federal antidiscrimination law right down to individual actions—a refusal to rent a single room in one's home, for example, or refusal to offer membership in a club.

But this too was not to be. The "judicial action equals state action" formula would have simply pulverized any distinction between private and public legal actions. The courts of the United States soon proved themselves unwilling to take that radical a step. Later decisions by the Supreme Court backtracked from *Shelley*'s broad formulation and suggested that the bare potential for judicial enforcement, taken alone, would *not* transform what are considered private arrangements or preferences into state action, even when those private relationships entailed something as distasteful as racial discrimination.[10]

The Court's retreat seemed to mean that *Shelley* itself would have no further application, precisely because it had made such an all-encompassing pronouncement—that judicial enforcement of covenants was state action. As we shall see in the next chapter, the real estate industry met the case with such skepticism that those professionals carried on business as usual with racial covenants, on the assumption that the case would be overturned or at least corralled.

It bears mention that *Shelley*'s wider ineffectiveness extended to the legislatures as well. In the 1960s, at the urging first of President John F. Kennedy and then of Lyndon Johnson, Congress wrestled with its first serious efforts to pass a broad swath of federal antidiscrimination legislation, ultimately covering the areas of employment, housing, and "public accommodations," such as restaurants or hotels. But the *Shelley* case gave no substantial jurisprudential support to these legislative efforts. While the wide range of new congressional legislation probably made the state action question less salient over the long run, the new laws still made a nod to the distinction of state action versus private action, steering clear of simple one-on-one instances of personal prejudice, such as a racial preference in renting one apartment in a residence. Congress could have done the same if *Shelley* never been decided.[11]

Thus *Shelley*'s very breadth was its jurisprudential undoing, undermining the traction that it might have had as a more focused legal weapon against discrimination. This point raises another question: was there some other way the case might have addressed the state action issue, in such a way as to make the case more helpful to legal norm setting in later civil rights areas? When we turn to the theories that were available to NAACP lawyers in 1947 and 1948, we will find that several other possible approaches emerged, some of them popping up and falling back in various stages of the litigation, others lying in the background all along. The following sections recount some of these possibilities and how they were (or were not) argued.[12] From the perspective of this book, the most interesting will be those theories that might link legal norms to social norms, treating racially restrictive covenants as state action precisely because their enforcement solidified a set of pervasive social norms. But there were other approaches on the table as well, beginning with a kind of end run around the state action problem.

AVOIDING THE STATE ACTION PROBLEM: DEPLOYING THE THIRTEENTH AMENDMENT

One way to deal with the state action question was to sidestep it. The lawyer for the Shelleys was George Vaughn, a member of the St. Louis NAACP, but one with his own ideas about the best way to prosecute the case. Unlike the national NAACP lawyers, Vaughn wanted to deal with his clients' problem under a statute based on the Thirteenth Amendment—the amendment banning slavery—as well as or perhaps instead of the Fourteenth. While the Fourteenth Amendment claim necessarily involved a state denial of equal protection or due process of law to its residents, the Thirteenth Amendment's prohibition on slavery applied to all actors, private as well as public. No one is supposed to enslave anyone else.[13]

An argument deriving from the Thirteenth Amendment presented difficulties of its own, of course: it required the lawyer to assimilate the client's problem to enslavement. One route to this end was to treat denial of the right to contract for property as a mark of slavery. The basis for this position was the 1866 Civil Rights Act, passed shortly after the Thirteenth Amendment; the act proclaimed that all citizens in the United States had the right, among others, to enter into contracts in the same manner "as is enjoyed by white citizens." Vaughn argued that this act rendered racial covenants void. But there was an old problem with the 1866 Civil Rights Act: from a very early date, lawyers had doubted that the Thirteenth Amendment's ban on slavery really was broad enough to support this statute. Congress soon moved to bolster the statute by passing the Fourteenth Amendment, with its guarantee of "equal protection of the laws." The Fourteenth Amendment was ratified in 1868, but unfortunately for the *Shelley* plaintiffs, this Amendment introduced the familiar state action problem: it asserted that no *state* could deny equal protection of the laws, and insofar as the 1866 Civil Rights Act now depended on the Fourteenth Amendment, the statute too was read to require state action.[14]

Despite these issues of constitutional doctrine, by the mid-1940s Vaughn's Thirteenth Amendment strategy had already acquired some precedent, at least indirectly. As legal historian Risa Goluboff has argued, at that time, certain kinds of civil rights claims were not so squarely seated on the Fourteenth Amendment's equal protection clause as they may now seem to be in retrospect. Goluboff has probed a whole series of cases beginning in 1939, cases in which the Justice Department's new Civil Rights Section contested abusive southern labor practices, especially in agricultural labor camps. In part in order to avoid the Fourteenth Amendment's state action predicate, the department's new section of civil rights lawyers rested their arguments on the Thirteenth Amendment's prohibition of slavery.[15]

As Goluboff notes, the Civil Rights Section's strategy was something of a stretch for existing law, since the employer/employee relationships at issue took the form of contracts, ostensibly voluntary ones. But as we saw in Chapter 2, the stretch did have some precedent in the labor context, where Thirteenth Amendment arguments had invalidated peonage contracts with farm workers early in the century. Extending the slavery analysis beyond labor issues to housing segregation clearly would been an even more lengthy stretch. Nevertheless, attorney Vaughn may have been on an interesting track with his argument from the Thirteenth Amendment and the civil rights statute based on that amendment. As with workers who were deceived and bilked in the migrant camps, the contractual justification for restrictive covenants in housing seemed quite inadequate when it came to home purchasers like the Shelleys, who had not even known that their house was subject to racial restrictions.

But more important, Vaughn's argument from the antislavery amendment was and continues to be a reminder that enslavement itself means more than the simple fact that one person owns another. Although attorney Vaughn may not have been aware of it, the famous seventeenth-century political philosopher John Locke had described the slave not only as one who was *owned by* another, but as one who himself could not *own* property. While Locke's position was not historically accurate, since some slaves in fact owned property and even bought their own freedom, that fact in itself suggests an important analogy between slavery and the inability to acquire property. A slave—or indeed any person—who cannot own property cannot escape her condition. She cannot buy her freedom from her owner, and indeed she cannot even buy a horse or a bicycle or a car to run away. As we saw in Chapter 2, white planters after the Civil War appeared to understand this analogy when they refused to sell property to African Americans, as part of their plan to keep their nominally free former slaves in servitude. An argument resting on the Thirteenth Amendment, then, might have served as a reminder that the ability to own and dispose of property is a powerful talisman of freedom.[16]

But in order to operate in a manner that even approached enslavement, the denial of the right to own property had to mean more than simply the inability to buy a particular house from this or that individual owner. An individual refusal to deal might be unpleasant and insulting, but it would not have disabled the Shelleys or others from owning property altogether. The problem had to be put in a larger frame: that a whole class of important properties was closed off to them. Only some larger barrier—not just a handful of individuals or even a number of neighborhoods who refused to deal—could disable their right to acquire and dispose of property, and as such function as an emblem of slavery.

Hence the analogy to slavery, using the Thirteenth Amendment argument, would have required some fleshing out, some reference to a larger pattern, rather than a simple individual refusal to deal, or even a whole neighborhood's refusal where other neighborhoods were open. In that sense, a campaign against covenants based on the Thirteenth Amendment might not have entirely escaped a problem akin to the Fourteenth Amendment's state action problem: both required some larger pattern of action, some larger social preclusion of minority members' ability to acquire and dispose of property. Here both the Thirteenth and Fourteenth Amendment arguments might have been much aided by reference to the classic property law coolness toward restraints on alienation: such restraints are considered reasonable only if they do not exclude too large a class. And as we shall see, a reference to social norms might have helped to illustrate just such a widespread exclusion—social norms reinforced by the then-legal racial covenants that spread out in a network across urban and new suburban neighborhoods.

Having said all this, the authors of this book are highly sympathetic to the kind of argument that attorney Vaughn was trying to raise. Indeed, as we shall see in a later chapter, the Thirteenth Amendment and the Civil Rights Act of 1866 reappeared in an important Supreme Court case that was decided at almost the same time that Congress deliberated the 1968 Fair Housing Act.[17]

Back in the late 1940s, however, any vindication of an argument founded on the Thirteenth Amendment might have made it easier to attack widespread discrimination by nonstate actors over the next decades. As historian Goluboff suggests with respect to the labor cases, a Thirteenth Amendment campaign might have led in different directions from the Fourteenth Amendment equal protection litigation, where the most immediate major targets turned out to be public institutions like schools and parks. Thirteenth Amendment litigation might have put economic relationships at center stage earlier in the civil rights struggle—not just labor relations, though those would have been important, but also constraints on minority contracting and property ownership.[18]

But in the *Shelley* case as with other civil rights litigation, for what undoubtedly seemed at the time to be good strategic reasons, the national NAACP effectively sidetracked Vaughn's Thirteenth Amendment foray and reshaped the *Shelley* litigation. They rested their case on the more favored Fourteenth Amendment grounds of governmental denial of equal protection—grounds that thereafter dominated civil rights litigation. And this, of course, leads back squarely to the question of state action: how could the mere judicial enforcement of ostensibly private agreements amount to state action?

STATE ACTION AS JUDICIAL OVERREACHING

One particular tactic might have solved the state action puzzle persuasively in *Shelley*, but the NAACP had good reasons to avoid it, especially after the planning and effort that it took to get racial covenants before the U.S. Supreme Court. This solution, though simple, would have undermined the case's larger impact, because it depended on the very specific facts of *Shelley* itself. The covenants on the Shelley's house were, in three words, full of holes. Their lawyer could easily have argued that any state court that enforced such a miserable set of covenants had to be bending over backwards to do so. On that account of the case, the state court was making up the law—hence in this specific instance, judicial action itself really was state action.

Here is the way the facts looked: The Shelley's bought their house at 4600 Labadie Avenue in St. Louis in 1945. The racially restrictive covenant to which it was supposedly subject was a neighborhood agreement dating back to 1911. As we have seen in earlier chapters, restrictions arising from neighbor agreements often had technical problems and gaps in coverage, and the Labadie Avenue agreement certainly fell into that category. The original agreement had been signed by only thirty owners out of thirty-nine in the designated area, covering forty-seven parcels out of fifty-seven. When the case went to trial, the trial court noticed these numbers and ruled that the covenants had never gone into effect since the owners must not have wanted to be bound unless they could achieve 100 percent unanimity among themselves.[19]

But spotty coverage was only one of the problems with the *Shelley* covenants. Back in 1911, five of the nonsigning owners were in fact African Americans, and in the intervening years African Americans had lived continually in the neighborhood. The Shelleys themselves claimed quite convincingly that they had not known of the restrictions at all. Indeed, how would they have known, unless they were actually told? The mixed character of the neighborhood gave them no notice that they should inquire about restrictions. As Mrs. Shelley said at trial, "I see other people on the street, that's why I bought it." That is to say, Mrs. Shelley was not a conscious norm breaker, or as some of her contemporaries said of those who violated racial covenants, a "law breaker." She was not looking for trouble, and she would have gone elsewhere if she had noticed the signals. But what she saw was a neighborhood that was mixed.[20]

In fact, their problematic purchase had been orchestrated by an African American minister and part-time real estate dealer, who had arranged to have the property purchased first by an intermediate straw white buyer. The minister no doubt did know about the restrictions since he made a substantial profit from the sale to the Shelleys, a fact that drew a sharp rebuke by the trial judge. But rather like the block-busting real estate lawyers who believed in doing well by doing good, he evidently pocketed the money and said nothing about the matter to the Shelleys.[21]

What was left over for notice to the buyers was the recording system. The racial agreement on the Shelley house had indeed been recorded. But because the restriction had arisen from a neighborhood agreement rather than a developer's deed restriction, it did not appear in the

Shelley's own deed—supposing that they might have looked at that—and apparently it did not appear in any other earlier major document of sale either. Readers may recall from Chapter 4 that the older common law rules of so-called horizontal privity would have disallowed it, because those rules would not enforce any purported covenants based on such post hoc neighborhood agreement. Indeed, the whole point of that older privity doctrine was to make sure that covenant obligations were located in the conventional transfer documents like deeds or long-term leases, where new buyers would be more likely to notice them.

Finally, there was another damning feature from the perspective of older doctrine: restrictions had to touch and concern land before they could be held to burden future purchasers. This touch-and-concern concept generally required that covenants carry a benefit to some identifiable land, for two reasons. First, there is no point in enforcing a land restriction that does no landowner any good. Second, a purchaser of a burdened property is more likely to notice a restriction that actually benefits some other property and is more likely to ask about obligations to those other owners. For example, the buyer who observes that all the houses in a subdivision are made of red brick might ask whether there is some neighborhood requirement to that effect. But even on the racist assumption that white owners in the Shelleys' neighborhood might benefit from racial restrictions on their neighbors' properties, it would have been quite a feat to identify the value of these particular restrictions, since African Americans had been a substantial part of the neighborhood mix all along. Indeed, the surpassing irony of the *Shelley* case was that the Shelleys pled for a lifting of covenant restrictions in a neighborhood that apparently was already integrated. If there was a so-called benefit to anyone, it would most likely have been to more distant white neighborhoods—neighborhoods that St. Louis real estate dealers typically protected by promoting a "ring of steel" of racial covenants in buffer areas around the black ghetto.[22]

The Missouri Supreme Court, however, upheld the restrictions in the face of all these frailties. As was necessary with neighborhood agreements, the case was brought under the court's jurisdiction at equity rather than at law, since none of the neighborhood agreements ever met the formal requirements for covenants to run with the land under traditional common law doctrines. When it acted under the auspices of equity jurisprudence, a court could dispense with formal common law requirements, and instead it could look only to the question whether the deal was fair and known to the parties. Specifically, for covenants running with the land, the equity question was this: did the purchasers know, or should they have known, about the covenants that would keep them out?

On that issue, the Missouri Supreme Court was satisfied. Because the restriction did appear somewhere in the land records, those records provided constructive notice to the Shelleys that they could not occupy the house, whatever the couple might or might not have known in fact. Presumably if they did not know of a recorded agreement, it was their own fault; they should have chosen a more honest agent. Their lapse, apparently, was no reason to force their unwelcome presence on the objecting white neighbors. The court was not unsympathetic to the housing difficulties that African Americans faced, but it did not think this was an issue that the courts could address, apparently not even in their equitable jurisdiction.[23]

Moreover, the court overturned the ruling below—that is, that these particular neighborhood agreements had been defective for want of 100 percent approval by all the owners of all the parcels. Nonsense, said the Missouri Supreme Court: back in 1911, the neighbors could scarcely have expected the African American owners to agree to restrictive covenants that would have prohibited their occupancy, and hence the signatories must have expected some gaps all along. As to the question of whether the covenants actually benefited anyone, the Missouri court only circumspectly hinted that holding the line against further African American encroachment was enough to give the covenants value to the white neighbors.[24]

Thus in upholding these quite questionable property restrictions, the Missouri Supreme Court rejected every objection, including a trial court finding that was arguably a mixed question of law and fact—a finding that would not normally be disturbed by an appeal court that was itself not directly in touch with the factual evidence.[25] In ruling as it did, the Missouri Supreme Court, the final arbiter of the meaning of the state's law, appeared to go out of its way to uphold covenants about race that might well not have been enforceable for other subjects—unenforceable in the conventional cases at law because of the failure of formalities, and unenforceable at equity because of the weakness of notice to the purchaser or genuine value to any enforcing party.

It is in that sense that one might have understood the U.S. Supreme Court's statement that judicial enforcement of *this* racially restrictive covenant was state action: on that reading, the Missouri state court took extraordinary steps to uphold a *racial* restriction that otherwise had scant legal support. Francis Allen, a judicial clerk for Chief Justice Vinson in 1948 and later a law professor, wrote a retrospective article on the case many years later, in 1989; there he suggested that the justices had thought that state courts might be going out of their way to enforce racial covenants, creating a kind of common law of racial covenants differing from ordinary property rules. If so, this overreaching would be judicial action of a piece with legislation—that is, official action that made something legal that otherwise would not have been. Indeed, in the 1926 case *Corrigan v. Buckley*, when the Supreme Court had found no state action for federal constitutional jurisprudence in some Washington, D.C., racial covenants, the Court had commented that a judicial decision might count as state action if it were so contrary to law as to amount to "mere spoilation." The upshot, then, would be that the Supreme Court could call the Missouri court's decision state action because the state court was stretching the law on behalf of a racial restriction—mere spoilation of conventional covenant law.[26]

One problem with this approach, however, is that it would have required the Supreme Court to delve into Missouri's law and become a kind of second guesser of the true content of each state's law—contrary to the usual view that makes each state supreme court the final arbiter of that state's law. The U.S. Supreme Court traditionally has been reluctant to engage in this kind of policing of state courts' interpretation of their own body of state law, both because of the intrusiveness of such forays and because of the potentially overwhelming burden on the Court's own caseload. But the issue does resurface from time to time; for example, in recent years, state courts' decisions about their own property law have raised the ire of some advocates, who argue that these decisions have diverged so far from prior law as to amount to "judicial takings" of property.[27]

But even supposing that the Court in 1948 had been willing to fault the Missouri court for state action through judicial overreaching, that particular spin on the case would have presented civil rights lawyers with a major practical problem. The charge of judicial overreaching would have meant that the *Shelley* decision would reach no further than the particular situation of that case—a legally weak set of covenants, taken together with a state supreme court that was altogether too eager to pump life into these legally questionable discriminatory agreements. More artfully drawn covenants might have escaped.

Would such a limited interpretation nevertheless have had an impact on covenants? The answer is probably yes. Such a decision could have taken a major bite out of racially restrictive covenants in American cities in the 1940s, especially where covenants were created by post hoc neighborhood campaigns. These neighbor agreements dominated the racial covenants of the older big cities, but as we have seen in earlier chapters, they frequently suffered from ambiguities and irregularities; the weaknesses of the *Shelley* covenants were by no means unusual or simply idiosyncratic. Even a narrow understanding of *Shelley*—effectively demanding that state courts apply the more rigorous legal standards of ordinary covenant law to racial restrictions—would have doomed quite a number of these neighborhood racial agreements, effectively de-covenanting large swaths of older urban areas.

What the narrow judicial-overreaching spin on *Shelley* would have left intact, however, was the other class of racially restrictive covenants, the developer-driven restrictions that originated with new residences, and that dotted the i's and crossed the t's of ordinary covenant law. On top of that legal fact lay another social fact: suburban tract housing was to be the future of American residential development in the postwar years. With huge, brand-new suburban communities like Levittown emerging in the postwar era, and with the Federal Housing Administration's recent history of favoring loans in racially covenanted areas, developers were highly likely to insert formally correct racial covenants into new deeds, thus exploding the racing of property into vast new areas of housing. The covenants that appeared in the first Levittown sales sent a signal that unless the courts interpreted state action more broadly, residential apartheid, however widely it spilled out of the cities and into the suburbs, could be classed as merely a private matter, untouched by the U.S. Constitution.

STATE ACTION AS PRIVATE TAKEOVER OF PUBLIC FUNCTIONS

The NAACP's national leadership clearly did not want the constitutional status of racial restrictions to be decided by a small-bore technical decision about some specific racial covenant like the one on the Shelleys' home. These leaders had not even wanted to use the *Shelley* case as the vehicle to bring covenant issues forward, perhaps at least in part because the dubious Labadie Avenue neighborhood agreement could again tempt the Supreme Court to decide simply on narrow or technical grounds, as it had in 1940 in Chicago's *Hansberry v. Lee* case—important for issues of procedure, but not for racial covenants. Who would want to see that happen again?

To get a widely sweeping decision, the perfect test-case covenants would have been a set of developer-created deed restrictions, incorporated in original deeds. Those would have met all the formal requirements for running with the land, and they would have much reduced the messy issues of notice and technical irregularity, thus bearing down squarely on the constitutionality of racial covenants as a matter of principle. But in spite of the organization's careful effort to find just the right case—as it had succeeded in doing in *Buchanan v. Warley,* the racial zoning case thirty years earlier—the NAACP's leading lawyers found that this time they could not so closely manage the litigation. George Vaughn, the Shelleys' St. Louis lawyer, was too much of a maverick. He could not be talked out of carrying his case as far as it would go in the courts, creaky and technically vulnerable covenants and all. When he petitioned the U.S. Supreme Court to reverse his loss in Missouri's supreme court, he forced the national organization's hand. To keep him from arguing the case on his own, and to lessen the chances that the Supreme Court might make a decision that turned once again to technical niceties, the Detroit NAACP petitioned for certiorari on *Sipes v. McGhee,* which was then joined with the *Shelley* case before the Court.[28]

Like the covenant on the Shelleys' house, the covenant in *Sipes* was not entirely ideal for a pure constitutional attack. It too came from a neighborhood agreement rather than a developer deed restriction, but at least *Sipes* got rid of one or two of the case-specific questions that had much affected *Shelley*'s case history. In *Sipes,* there was no question whether the covenant had ever been intended to take effect; the covenant stated on its face that it would take effect upon the signature of 80 percent of the owners within the affected area. Moreover, although as neighborhood agreements, neither covenant began as part of a real estate transfer and hence was not initially in a formal deed, the *Sipes* covenant only dated from 1935—considerably more recent than *Shelley*'s 1911 date and hence presumably fresher in memory in the mid-1940s. Putting to one side the parties' "constructive" notice through the land records, the question of *actual* notice never became an issue in the case, suggesting that the McGhees did know that the property was restricted. A few questions arose about technical problems with the signatures on the agreement, but these were decided in accordance with accepted state law precedent.

With *Sipes* as a companion case to *Shelley,* then, it was considerably harder to slip around the big issues through technical detours. Even more important, it was harder to make the case that only judicial overreaching could cause a state court to approve some legally rickety set of racial restrictions. The *Sipes* covenant, though not perfect, was still pretty much a garden variety affair. If judicial enforcement of the *Sipes* agreement were to be classed as judicial state action, some factor other than overreaching had to explain it.

But what was that factor? If judicial enforcement of these seemingly private agreements were to be classed as state action, the courts would have to face the same old problem: *any* judicial decision resolving private disputes might somehow turn into state action, subject as such to constitutional constraints. That transformation seemingly could spill over from real estate covenants to ordinary contract enforcement to trespass cases or defamation claims—or to any other ostensibly private claim. What, then, might distinguish racially restrictive covenant cases from the rest of the run-of-the-mill private civil actions that make up such a large part of most courts' normal work?

By the late 1940s, thanks in large part to the work of lawyers affiliated with the NAACP, the Supreme Court had opened up a potential route to make such a distinction. In a handful of cases in the preceding years, the Court had ruled that ostensibly private entities could be subjected to constitutional limitations if they effectively took over functions normally performed by public bodies. One such case was *Smith v. Allwright,* a case involving voting rights, or more specifically, the NAACP's challenge to Texas's "white primary." Electoral discrimination was an issue for the Fifteenth Amendment, which protects citizens' right to vote against racial discrimination, but like the Fourteenth, the Fifteenth Amendment is directed at governmental action.

State election officials had argued that the Texas Democratic Party was merely a private organization, and that as such it could control its own membership and exclude African Americans; hence there was no state action when blacks were unable to vote in the party primary. This was at a time, of course, when the Republican Party had very little presence in the southern states, and when those states' Democratic primaries effectively determined the outcome of state elections. In *Smith,* the Supreme Court had rejected the claim that the party could discriminate at will because it was merely a private entity. Instead, the Court ruled that the primary election could be attributed to the state because this group's choices were effectively a part of the state's own electoral process.[29]

In planning for *Shelley,* civil rights lawyers strategized to show something akin to a private takeover of state functions. Although the NAACP lawyers did not cite the *Smith* case in their own Supreme Court brief, other civil rights organizations did, and the NAACP lawyers' own arguments were closely related to the public-takeover position. Pursuing their new litigation strategy of invoking social science literature, they attempted to persuade the Court that racially restrictive covenants were both widespread and damaging to minorities. If racial covenants truly did control widespread housing patterns, then the NAACP had been right in the position it had taken ever since the old *Buchanan* case outlawed racial zoning: that restrictive covenants were racial zoning by another name. Their arguments suggested a pattern aligned with the public function cases; with racially restrictive covenants too, ostensibly private organizations—the neighborhood improvement associations, the real estate boards, the major developers—had effectively appropriated a governmental function and were using the courts to enforce what was in fact a form of racial zoning.[30]

Indeed, the history of public and private land use controls in the United States gave some support to the takeover argument. As we have seen, one of the first types of American zoning was racial zoning, whereas the use of covenants for segregation only became truly popular after the *Buchanan* case—suggesting that what seemed to be merely private arrangements had instead simply picked up where public zoning left off. The point was made explicit in the 1938 Maryland case, *Meade v. Dennistone,* where the state's highest court openly and quite angrily stated that racial covenants had necessarily substituted for the outlawed racial zoning. The Justice Department's long amicus brief for the United States particularly hammered on the continuity between racial zoning and racial covenants.[31]

A critical issue for the takeover argument, however, was whether racial covenants had acquired a sufficiently widespread grip as to dictate the choices of the general public. Unfortunately, it was generally not entirely clear what percentage of any city actually had racially restrictive covenants. Even in a location like Chicago, where racial covenants were certainly known and very much used in areas of racial transition, other areas managed to stay segregated without covenants.

All the same, if there had been a concerted policy to contain African American expansion, controls on areas adjacent to black neighborhoods would have been the primary strategy, particularly in older cities, where restrictions had to come through laborious post hoc neighborhood covenant drives. A number of covenant proponents did indeed behave as if they were following such a boxing-in strategy—described by the NAACP's magazine, *The Crisis,* as the "iron ring," and by St. Louis attorney Scovel Richardson as the "ring of steel." As we saw in Chapter 6, Chicago's real estate board, so instrumental in organizing neighborhood drives for racially restrictive covenants, focused on areas where the residents felt themselves immediately threatened by spillovers from nearby minority areas. The strategy was even more pronounced in St. Louis, where the *Shelley* case originated. The St. Louis Real Estate Exchange was especially active in proposing and enforcing covenants, openly coordinating the city's numerous so-called neighborhood improvement associations in order to put up an impenetrable wall of racial covenants around minority neighborhoods. Indeed, the Exchange made itself a trustee to the neighborhood racial covenants, so that the Exchange itself could enforce them. In light of this activity, George Vaughn's brief for the Shelleys in the Missouri Supreme Court argued that the Exchange was a part of a conspiracy to deprive his clients of their civil rights.[32]

The guiding intuition behind the public takeover arguments, then, was that the pervasiveness of racially restrictive covenants, or at least their strategic location, made them inescapable for racial minorities in any given jurisdiction. That inescapable character linked racial covenants to another major Fourteenth Amendment case of the era, *Marsh v. Alabama* (1946), in which the Court had held that the efforts of a company town to quell religious proselytizing constituted state action. In *Marsh,* the managers controlled every part of the town. By parallel reasoning, where covenants were in place widely, minorities could not get away from housing discrimination. Arguably, this was why private covenantors could be said to have taken over the work that zoning did, thus acting as state actors: they actually directed the public's choices.[33]

One might observe that the whole takeover argument is closely related to antitrust principles against agreements in restraint of trade. If competing businesses make too many and too tight agreements that control much of the market for some product, their acts are very likely to raise prices and limit opportunities for consumers. Even more salient in property law, the public takeover position would have acted as a kind of constitutional refutation of the American Law Institute's 1944 *Restatement of Property* and its commentary on restraints on alienation. As noted in Chapter 5, the *Restatement* had maintained that wide-reaching racial covenants were legally acceptable, but even the document's authors circumspectly acknowledged that this view was contrary to the general policies of property law—policies that both favored alienability in general and that particularly disfavored alienability constraints where they cut off large numbers of persons. Contrary to the *Restatement*'s position, the public takeover argument would have reinstated a more traditional view of restraints on alienability: any restraints that effectively disabled large classes of people from ownership could not be enforced. Although the property law arguments of the day were soon overshadowed in the constitutional blaze of *Shelley,* Dudley McGovney's influential 1945 article made roughly this attack on the *Restatement* before going on to his state action analysis, and so did the brief for the United States in the *Shelley* case itself.[34]

The public takeover position in effect attempted to reconstruct state action from the fact of pervasiveness. The idea of *state* action, however, seemed to imply something more directive than simply a widely held set of preferences. However disagreeable those preferences might have been, they could still have been a mere aggregation of a "taste for discrimination"[35] that was held by a large number of individuals. State action, on the other hand, implied that residential segregation was somehow compulsory—compulsory in a way that went beyond the individual developers who satisfied individuals' tastes for discrimination by inserting racial covenants into deeds, or groups of neighbors who decided to restrict their own freedom of sale so that they could keep their neighborhoods white.

For the public takeover argument, the question was whether the very fact of a widespread pattern sufficed for a constitutional claim of state action. Widespread dispersion alone might have been enough to trigger the traditional property law's doctrines against restraints on alienation. It might even have been enough, in an odd way, for a Thirteenth Amendment claim that covenants constituted a badge of slavery, if these covenants were so pervasive as to foreclose minority members from normal transactions with property. But could widespread dispersion of a practice, taken alone, add up to enough compulsion to count as state action?

In the public takeover argument, the element of compulsion focused on minority members, who found themselves frozen out of normal market transactions. But a different focus might have bolstered the claim of compulsory force: that is, the way that racial covenants enforced social norms, affecting not only minority members but white residents as well. The next section will take up several interlocking factors—some from the history of racial violence and some from property law—that might have looked to social norms as the compulsory factor that could turn the judicial enforcement of racial covenants into state action.

STATE ACTION AS THE ENFORCEMENT OF SOCIAL NORMS

One path through *Shelley*'s state action dilemma went largely unexplored at the time, although there were hints here and there. But it is a path that leads deep into the relationship of social norms to legal ones—

particularly as both kinds of norms play out in property relations. In brief, the path would have been this: upholding racially restrictive covenants implicated courts in enforcing social norms, or, as the contemporary legal language put it, in the enforcement of "custom"—and custom counted as a form of state action in longstanding civil rights law.[36] In upholding racial covenants, courts were perforce enabling, supporting, and reinforcing a compulsion that came not from voluntary agreement between a few self-defined individuals, as in normal private law contracts, but rather from the expectations and demands of a wider public, as those expectations and demands had crystallized into social norms or customs.

While there were any number of other indicators, violence gave the most dramatic evidence that what has been called the "taste for discrimination" behind racial covenants was not simply a bland and noncoercive preference, but rather a manifestation of a prescriptive social norm, with all the expectations and insistence that a norm entails. And violence was everywhere in the background, and long had been. As we have seen in earlier chapters, there were the threats to destroy the home of an African American schoolteacher in Boston well before the Civil War. There were the bombings of prominent African Americans' residences and businesses before and after the 1919 Chicago race riots. There were the menacing signs on the roads leading into small towns, telling African Americans not to let the sun set on them there. There were the bricks thrown through the Hansberrys' window, and the constant reviling that the Hansberry family endured on the street. There were the riots that broke out in Detroit when black war workers moved into the new Sojourner Truth housing project in 1942.[37]

There was another way too in which violence was a key link between restrictive covenants and racist norm enforcement of neighborhood segregation. The avoidance of violence had always served as a justification for the various versions of legalized residential segregation. Lawyers and academics discussing the *Buchanan* case in 1916 had defended racial zoning as a substitute for violence. When that argument failed, developers and real estate interests turned to racially restrictive covenants—which they also defended as a substitute for violence. The 1944 *Restatement of Property* too cited violence avoidance as a justification for racial covenants.

Hence both zoning and covenants were supposed to substitute for violence, using the law to let the neighbors enforce legally the social norms that might otherwise be enforced illegally, through harassment, vandalism, arson, and mob action. The tough working-class neighborhoods did not bother with covenants. They did not need them. They had bricks. Racial covenants were supposed to do what the brick throwers did, while keeping the brick throwers at bay.

Less obvious than outright violence, but a close relative in showing the forceful social norms behind racial covenants, was the all-pervasive argument of property values. Racial covenants, like racial zoning, were supposed to defend property values in white neighborhoods. And no doubt they did, over wider and wider areas, given the unfortunate circularity of the property values argument. As we have seen, by the 1940s, norm entrepreneurs had blared out the property-values message for decades, resulting in an ever-expanding self-fulfilling prophecy—a phrase that was used very soon after its coinage to describe racial fears about property values.[38] If enough people believed that minority entry caused property values to drop, then minority entry would indeed have that effect. Potential buyers would not bid; lenders would not lend; real estate agents would not bother to bring potential buyers around. The next step is easy to see: the defense of property values can powerfully motivate owners and real estate professionals to enforce norms against whatever activity might cause property values to drop. A white owner who thought that minority neighbors would diminish the value of his residence—more likely than not his main financial asset—would be highly motivated to keep out minority purchasers, by whatever means at hand.

Moreover, covenants took hold in an environment of normative practices that fell short of overt violence, but that still sounded an undertone of compulsion. There were many such normative practices: among others, the codes of "ethics" that warned real estate professionals against racial mixing in real estate, the expulsions of nonconforming brokers from professional associations, the loan approval insurance standards of the FHA, and the redlining practices of loan institutions. Some homeowners and real estate professionals undoubtedly acted on a belief in the propriety and legitimacy of these normative practices, and sometimes followed them even against their own interest—a kind of first-party compulsion through their individual consciences. Examples were the brokers who thought that it was unethical to introduce minority families into white neighborhoods, even though there was money to be made, or the white homeowner who refused to sell to minority families out of the sense that one "cannot do that to the neighbors." But if conscience was not sufficient compulsion, these normative practices created social, economic, and professional pressure to prevent any slippage from the overall goal of segregation.

Why did all these violent and not-so-violent norm-enforcement practices matter? They mattered because they showed that when judges enforced restrictive covenants, they were reinforcing and extending a social norm—not just a preference but an *enforceable* preference—that had developed over decades and spread so widely through the land to count as a customary practice. *Shelley* cited this point in passing, since custom could be analogized to state action. Indeed, the violence and violence substitutes that supported residential segregation can illustrate *why* custom might count as state action, particularly when it affects large numbers of people. Groups of people acting on their own can impose and enforce norms informally. But when such norms become pervasive, they bear down powerfully on the whole citizenry, indeed, sometimes even more powerfully than formal law.

Another factor too, and one specific to property law, links judicial enforcement of covenants to the enforcement of customary practice. Covenants running with the land are not just ordinary contracts. They involve more than an agreement between A and B. Indeed, the whole point of restrictions running with the land is that successors in interest are bound on the agreement between A and B; they are bound without renegotiation, even if they did not agree to the restriction personally. But as we have seen in earlier chapters, while property law allows people to create these ongoing restrictions on their land, it also forces these kinds of arrangements to run through a set of hoops, precisely because the restrictions extend beyond the original parties.

Among other things, standard property doctrine will not let these promises run unless they have some value to some land. That is the idea encapsulated in the seeming arcana that disfavor restraints on alienation, or that require covenants to touch and concern land in some way, or that relax covenants under changed circumstances. As we saw in earlier chapters, these limiting doctrines are loose enough to permit valuable land use arrangements to run with the land, continuing on through the inevitable transfers to new owners without requiring constant renegotiation; but they are strict enough to ensure that new owners will not be taken by surprise, and that property transactions in general will not be burdened by the merely idiosyncratic arrangements of prior owners.

The requirement that covenants must have continuing value puts judges in a special role with respect to covenant enforcement, a role that distinguishes property law from contract law. By contrast to property, when a court enforces a contract between the contracting parties, the judge need not consider whether anyone else in the world might have wanted such an arrangement. Contracting parties have said for themselves what they want. Indeed, courts explicitly reject the idea that they can second-guess the parties' evaluation of contract terms. But property covenants are an ongoing arrangement beyond the original consenting parties, and that is why they will only bind future owners when the arrangement has some continuing value. In turn, this means that when a court holds that a covenant runs to subsequent purchasers, the court implicitly assumes something about what landowners *in general,* or at least some substantial class of them, would be likely to expect and value.[39]

Would a court have been correct in assuming that as a general matter, a subsequent purchaser of residential property would be likely to value racial restrictions, and to expect that they might find them on any given property? By the 1940s, the answer for white purchasers would almost certainly have been yes, given the reinforcement of exclusionary norms over the previous decades. But to make such an assumption even about a white purchaser (while ignoring everyone else), a court would have to acknowledge and give force to a widespread attitude of racial disparagement. And as we have seen, this was an attitude that counted as more than a simple preference; it was a preference with consequences, enforceable even for persons whose preferences differed.

Because of the structure of covenant law, then, when courts held that these covenants were valid, they had to assume a background social norm of racism. For private actors, it is still not illegal to have racist attitudes, no matter how repellant they may be to others. But when parties did not specifically flag their wishes as personal, as they would in a contract, but instead tried to bind strangers to their arrangements, then the only way that those strangers could be bound was with a judicial imprimatur—a determination that the racial covenant had value. In the context of practices of residential segregation that had become widespread by the 1940s, judicial approval linked each specific agreement to a larger social norm, effectuating that norm legally and putting the force of law behind customary practice.

In such a way, one might have made sense of *Shelley*'s cryptic statement that judicial enforcement of covenants was state action. Property law always placed judges in a special relationship with covenants running with the land, and in approving racial covenants, judges were reinforcing customary practices rather than personal agreements between specific parties. For most customary practices, it would not matter that a court approved. For discriminatory customary practices, it did matter, because of the Fourteenth Amendment's prohibition on denial of equal protection.

Indeed, a seemingly minor doctrinal issue in *Shelley* itself might have highlighted the special judicial role in covenant enforcement. Legal purists will have noted that the Supreme Court in *Shelley* did not overrule *Corrigan v. Buckley*, the Court's own 1926 decision that was widely read as upholding racially restrictive covenants in Washington, D.C. One reason the cases were distinguishable, as the Court in *Shelley* correctly noted, was because *Corrigan* originated in the federally governed District of Columbia and thus did not implicate state action under the Fourteenth Amendment, unlike *Shelley* from Missouri and *Sipes* from Michigan. But this distinction was unconvincing for *Hurd v. Hodge*, the case that followed immediately on the heels of *Shelley*, because *Hurd* came from the District of Columbia too, just as *Corrigan* had. In *Hurd* the Court ruled against covenants in Washington too, but again without disavowing *Corrigan*.[40]

What else, then, made *Shelley* and especially *Hurd* distinguishable from the earlier *Corrigan* case? In both *Shelley* and *Hurd*, the Court took pains to say that, unlike *Corrigan*, the question was not whether the covenants were void even if voluntarily followed, but rather whether courts could enforce them. But a much more plausible distinction was noted earlier in this book: the earlier *Corrigan* case in fact was not about covenants running with the land at all. In *Corrigan*, the defendant was one of the original signatories to the covenants, and it was that person's direct and personal promise that was at issue. By contrast, as several of the *Shelley* briefs pointed out, the defendants in the *Shelley* cases had never signed the original restrictions, and they could only be obligated if the restrictions ran with the land.[41]

Corrigan, in short, was a case about *contract*, whereas *Shelley, Sipes*, and *Hurd* were cases about later purchasers and thus about property—even though the courts in these and most other racial covenant cases almost hypnotically overlooked the differences between these bodies of law.[42] The Supreme Court as a whole never did make much of the distinction between property and contract, but as we shall see in the next chapter, there was a whiff of it in a follow-up case to *Shelley* in 1953: *Barrows v. Jackson*. There Chief Justice Vinson, who wrote the *Shelley* opinion, dissented from his brethren in part because he drew a distinction between the enforcement of contracts and the enforcement of real estate covenants.

SUMMING UP: THE LESSONS OF *SHELLEY* AND SOCIAL NORMS

Shelley was the major case that tested racially restrictive covenants against higher level legal norms and found these covenants wanting. It has not been a successful case in the sense of breaking a path for other civil rights concerns, however, largely because of the breathtaking sweep of its seemingly unqualified assertion that judicial covenant enforcement counted as state action under the Fourteenth Amendment.

There are other routes that might have skirted the state action issue or dealt with it only obliquely—arguments from the Thirteenth Amendment's ban on slavery, or from the technical weakness of these particular covenants—but when one reconsiders more direct ways to deal with the state action conundrum, several aspects of racial covenants stand out. First, these covenants had become exceedingly pervasive in American real estate practice over the first four decades of the twentieth century, a factor that in itself strongly suggested the status of a wider norm. Second, there was much evidence—most strikingly in the concerns about violence that dominated residential segregation—

that showed that residential segregation sprang from powerful social norms that were larger than any specific set of covenants. Forceful social norms that were followed so widely could have been analogized to custom, and the enforcement of custom could already count as state action in contemporary Fourteenth Amendment law. Third, basic principles of property law required judges to assess more general social practices when they upheld covenants as "running with the land." Thus when judges enforced these covenants, they were effectively propping up and extending a set of customary practices—enough, perhaps, to say that in this instance, judicial enforcement counted as state action.

Just as important, *Shelley*'s story helps to see *why* the judicial enforcement of custom might count as state action. We know from recent scholarly explorations of social norms that norms and customs may be so powerful that they have the practical force of law—or may even override formal law. When nudged along by judicial recognition, as was the case for racial covenants, norms *become* law in the formal as well as the informal sense. If *Shelley* had focused more closely on the courts' enforcement of social norms of segregation, the decision would have been narrower, but it might have provided more effective precedent for civil rights efforts in other areas where customary practices so deeply affected the life chances of minority groups—perhaps most notably employment and public accommodations, where the state action problem dogged later legislation.[43]

What the years after *Shelley* did illustrate, however, is that the social norms supporting residential segregation—including restrictive covenants—were not about to disappear, whether these covenants were legally enforceable or not. Indeed, if more were needed, the experience of the 1950s amply illustrated the compulsory element in the social norms behind covenants, norms that had taken deep root over the previous half-century, and that would outlast the legal structures built on them.

8 After *Shelley*

Reactions, Evasions, Substitutions

The Supreme Court decided *Shelley v. Kraemer* thirty-one years after it upended racial zoning in *Buchanan v. Warley*. In both these cases the Court departed sharply from existing precedent—in *Buchanan* from the then-ruling separate but equal doctrine, and in *Shelley* from three decades of decisions holding that racial covenants were merely private matters rather than state action. But the reaction in the law reviews and press was subtly different by the time *Shelley* was decided. As we saw in Chapter 2, before and after the 1917 *Buchanan* case, law review notes in several important journals had favored racial zoning and chastised the Supreme Court for overturning it. But a quarter of a century later, the commentary suggested a considerably weaker commitment to segregation, at least in the legal community. From the end of the war up to the *Shelley* decision, many organizations pressed the Court to rule against these covenants. Legal commentators—some but not all egged on by the NAACP—added substantially to this support.[1]

After *Shelley* was decided, many law reviews, major and minor, continued on the same theme and published favorable articles and comments. Among other things, some argued that it was good policy to get the courts out of housing discrimination—that is to say, out of covenant enforcement, and beyond that, that the case might have positive implications for dismantling other kinds of racial discrimination.[2] Even an article in the *Alabama Law Review* was remarkably favorable to the decision; it gently chided the Supreme Court only for failing to make more of the United States' nondiscrimination obligations under the new United Nations Charter, an issue raised by a number of the commentators of the day.[3]

Not that the critics were silent—there were several, and they generally focused on what they regarded as the case's sweeping statements about state action and on its departure from prior precedent. One very sharp critic was lawyer and political science professor Richard Baker, writing in the *South Carolina Law Review.* He gave an extensive overview of the many judicial precedents that had uniformly supported racially restrictive covenants in the past. More than that, he recounted numerous antidiscrimination efforts in state legislatures, all of which had given a free pass to racial covenants in residential areas. From this pattern, Baker concluded that the legislatures had refrained from overturning racial covenants because that was what the voters wanted.[4]

And indeed, even those who supported the *Shelley* decision agreed to some degree with Baker's point about the voters. Whether favorably disposed to the decision or not, commentators overlapped in two forecasts of things to come: that white homeowners would try to evade the decision and keep their neighborhoods white, and that the real estate industry would try to accommodate them. Legal writers on both sides predicted a number of legal ploys that we will take up in greater detail shortly; they also predicted informal and extra-legal methods: harassment by the neighbors, steering by brokers, and lenders' refusal to lend.[5]

TESTING THE LIMITS: FROM *SHELLEY* TO *BARROWS*

A striking point about the law review articles of all stripes was the writers' implicit assumption that significant numbers of white homeowners would not accept residential racial integration. Whatever the larger legal norms, the writers assumed that the social norms of the neighborhoods, as well as those of real estate professionals, were still the same as they had been before the *Shelley* case. Some news articles of the era suggested that they were right. Washington, D.C., gave a number of examples: The *Washington Post* reported that shortly after the *Shelley* decision, eleven of twelve homeowners on a Washington block had sworn a "mutual faith covenant" not to be the first to rent or sell to "any person or persons of the Negro race or blood."[6] Moreover, Washington's Federation of Citizens' Associations (which did not permit black members) organized a large-scale racial covenant drive in the summer after the *Shelley* decision. The drive captains answered the neighbors' questions about constitutional issues with the answer that, no, they need not worry, covenants were not illegal—merely unenforceable in court. Clearly *Shelley* had opened a gap between emerging national legal norms against discrimination on the one hand and, on the other, the very common homeowner attitudes favoring segregated neighborhoods.[7]

Among real estate institutional actors, the FHA, as a federal agency, was among those most susceptible to pressure to conform to changing national norms, however reluctantly it might do so. Even before *Shelley* was decided, the 1947 version of the agency's *Underwriting Manual* had responded to civil rights protests by dropping explicit statements that promoted racially restrictive covenants. But shortly after the decision, in response to a pointed query by the NAACP's Thurgood Marshall, an FHA administrator wrote that the agency would continue to insure mortgages on houses with new racial covenants, explaining that voluntary restrictions were not illegal under the decision. To the great aggravation of Marshall and the NAACP, the FHA did not alter this position for some time. Finally, in a new policy that was publicized in 1949 but delayed until 1950, the agency announced that it would stop insuring homes with newly recorded racial covenants, although it was noticeably silent about developers' discriminatory sales practices and "gentlemen's agreements" among the neighbors.[8]

Some thought the FHA should go beyond new covenants and actively disfavor older covenants as well, but that next step would have raised serious difficulties. Once in the records, older covenants—then not illegal even if unenforceable by courts—could not have been expunged formally without the agreement of all the supposed beneficiaries, a requirement that would have presented many home sellers with an arduous task. As we shall see in the concluding chapter, similar recording issues continued for many years to dog efforts to expunge racial references from real estate transactions.

Quite aside from these formal issues about the land records, however, there were several other signals that the FHA was an unenthusiastic participant in its own policy changes well into the 1960s. When references to race dropped out of the *Underwriting Manual,* they were replaced by the euphemisms "user groups" and "incompatible groups," verbiage whose real meaning was not lost on critical contemporary commentators—or on developers. In another element of its changing policy, the agency stated that property assessments should not be altered simply because new "user groups" had entered a neighborhood, but the *Manuals* qualified this policy in various ways. The 1952 *Manual,* for example, continued to advise appraisers to take account of a neighborhood's attitudes toward the new entrants. Indeed, older racial restrictions might well have been a signal of those attitudes, and in that sense FHA policies may have continued to give some weight to older covenants in deciding the insurability of any given property. As late as 1962, in a U.S. Civil Rights Commission report on the Washington housing market, the authors complained that the FHA was simply passive about real estate professionals' measures to perpetuate neighborhood segregation.[9]

If the FHA had at best a lumbering response to *Shelley*'s shift to nondiscrimination, other real estate institutions were more overtly hostile. In August 1948, for example, the Virginia State Real Estate Association was treated to a lecture on "Suggested Plans For Avoiding the Effects of the Shelley Decision." The Los Angeles Real Estate Board went even further, proposing that NAREB sponsor a constitutional amendment to overturn the decision.[10]

Some real estate professionals thought that the best plan was simply to ignore the decision and to continue to write covenants into deeds. Over the short run, the FHA's delay in instituting its new policy against racial covenants must have powerfully encouraged developers to get racial covenants in place rapidly. No doubt the practice continued much longer, however. As late as 1966, Edmund O. Belsheim, a well-respected lawyer and legal educator, included models of the standard Caucasian-only racial covenants in the book *Modern Legal Forms,* making the familiar observation that while covenants could not be enforced in court, they were legal if voluntarily followed. Their role, evidently, was purely hortatory—a signal of the neighbors' normative commitments among themselves, along with a warning to would-be minority entrants that they were not welcome.[11]

But in the period immediately following *Shelley,* another factor prompted developers and others to include racial covenants in their transactions: many real estate professionals thought that the case was such an outlier that it would soon be overturned or at least limited—in which case, as one broker explained to a reluctant buyer, racial covenants "will protect you in case the Supreme Court ever changes its mind."[12] They must have been encouraged by the fact that three of the nine justices had recused themselves in *Shelley,* widely presumed to have occurred because at least two of the three themselves owned property with racial covenants. If *Shelley* were to be trimmed back later, wouldn't it be simpler to have the covenants already in place? Wouldn't this be preferable to the arduous process of collecting neighbor signatures after the fact? Besides, some must have thought, even if it became completely clear that the covenants were unenforceable, a new purchaser might not know that fact. As for the FHA's new policies against racial covenants, those now mattered less, since postwar state and federal banking regulations were now allowing conventional mortgages to come closer to the FHA's relaxed down payment and time terms.[13]

It was not so surprising, then, that covenants continued to be written into deeds as the legal efforts to bypass *Shelley* emerged. One potential way to get around *Shelley* was to avoid any suit against new minority residents, and instead to sue the offending white sellers for damages for breaking their covenants. This route had three points to recommend it. First, it did not appear to be aimed at minority members, thus softening the appearance of discrimination. Second, it avoided the unseemly action of the injunction, whereby a minority family might be rousted out of what family members had thought was their new home. Third, there was a legal nicety: an action for damages was merely an action at law, unlike the equitable action for an injunction. Readers may recall from Chapter 4 that equitable actions were decided by judges rather than juries and often called for considerable judicial discretion; actions at law, on the other hand, could be decided by lay persons in a jury, but their decisions were hemmed in by strict rules in order to curb the emotion and confusion to which lay persons were thought subject. The result was that a suit for damages, as an action at law, was much less likely to involve any weighing of other elements of overall fairness—unlike an action in equity, where a judge might typically engage in such considerations. *Shelley* itself had been an equitable action for an injunction; but a mere contract damage case, unlike the equitable action, might involve a judge so minimally that his or her involvement in the case would not even count as state action. Court of Appeals Judge Edgerton had made this distinction in his influential dissenting opinion in *Hurd v. Hodge*, the District of Columbia's counterpart case to *Shelley;* and Justice Frankfurter had highlighted equity jurisprudence in his own brief concurrence in *Hurd*.[14]

After *Shelley*, a handful of state courts heard damage actions against the white homeowners who had sold or rented to African Americans in violation of racial covenants. While these damage actions failed in more states than they succeeded, they did succeed in some, including Oklahoma as well as the Shelleys' home state, Missouri, where the court distinguished actions for damages from the equitable action in *Shelley*. The major test case, however, came from Los Angeles. Here a California court, citing *Shelley*, ruled that one set of white homeowners could not sue another white homeowner for damages when the latter sold a house to an African American, even though the sale violated a 1944 neighborhood covenant that the defendant white seller had actually signed.[15]

In 1953, the California case finally landed in the U.S. Supreme Court under the name *Barrows v. Jackson*. Whether judicial involvement in a damage suit against a white seller would count as state action was only a secondary matter in the case, and the Court's majority treated it only briefly, answering yes. By permitting a damage action against a seller, the Court reasoned, a court would be punishing violation of a covenant, going beyond the private party's voluntary adherence to the covenant and thus engaging in state action under the *Shelley* rule. But the Court discussed at greater length what it regarded as the major issue in the case, that is, whether the white seller could defend against the neighbors' claim by raising the issue of racial discrimination not against herself, but rather against the black person to whom she sold. The Court's majority again answered yes, because protecting the white seller also protected the minority buyer from discrimination, albeit indirectly. If faced with a damage suit, a white seller might refuse to sell, or might charge the minority purchaser more to make up for the expected cost.[16]

The *Barrows* case undoubtedly disappointed many in the real estate industry, but the response was something of a collective yawn among legal commentators, most of whom saw it simply as a logical extension of *Shelley.* After all, most observed, damage suits to intimidate white sellers would have much the same impact as direct injunctions against black buyers. Even a University of Mississippi commentator agreed somewhat sourly that the outcome was to be expected.[17]

But perhaps the most interesting aspect of the case was that Justice Vinson, who had written the Court's opinion in *Shelley,* now dissented in *Barrows.* He did not agree with the majority on the major point in contention, that a white seller could raise a discrimination issue when the discrimination was directed against someone else, namely the black purchaser. But Vinson also disagreed on the state action issue, contending that *Shelley*'s version of state action did not reach so far as to stop a state court from enforcing what he called its "contract law."[18]

In this offhand way, Justice Vinson's state action view raised an important point that may not have occurred to him: the difference between contract and property. He clearly was focused on the contractual elements of the case—and no wonder, because the defendant white seller was one of the signing parties to the original neighborhood covenant. But one of the neighbors who was suing him was *not* an original signer. That neighbor's claim for relief was implicitly based on a property theory: that the rights of his predecessor in title passed on to him, even though he himself had not been a party to the original covenant.

The real estate industry was very much aware of this factor in the case.[19] The whole idea behind the covenant form was to bind and benefit *successive* owners as a part of the *property,* so that the neighbors would not have to renegotiate the racial agreement every time a property changed hands—which they would have been forced to do, had the matter simply been one of individual contracts. The logic of Vinson's "contract" designation would have allowed all the other neighbors in the original deal to sue the seller in *Barrows*—but would have excluded the one owner who was merely a successor in interest. Sooner or later, everyone would be a successor in interest, and thus ineligible to sue anyone else for violating a racial covenant. This looming threat of impotence was exactly the result that covenant proponents had attempted to avoid: covenants were supposed to attach to the property itself, and to outlast any given owner.

To be sure, a successor owner might have tried some fancy footwork with the emergent contract theories that favored third-party beneficiaries of other parties' contracts, but in real estate, the important precedents for such theories were largely cases at equity rather than damage actions at law. And if there was anything that *Shelley* made clear, it was that courts could no longer enforce racial covenants through equitable remedies like injunctions. In any event, even proponents of third-party beneficiary remedies acknowledged that the property remedies were preferred for real estate covenants that ran with the land.[20]

The distinction between law and equity raised still another technical impediment that undoubtedly would have impeded any successor owner who tried to use a damage remedy to enforce an older racial covenant. Because a suit for damages is an action at law rather than in equity, any damage action by a successor owner would have been thrown back on some of the obscure and old-fashioned rules on covenants running with the land. As we saw in Chapter 4, those constraints had been sidelined in the decades since the 1920s, when racial covenants took advantage of the looser requirements of equity jurisprudence. But damage actions would have revived those perilous ghost doctrines that particularly haunted covenant actions at law, and the most vulnerable covenants of all would have been neighbor-generated agreements like the one in *Barrows*. These had never been enforceable with damage actions at law, but only with equitable remedies like injunctions. Civil rights lawyers such as Los Angeles's Loren Miller and St. Louis's Scovel Richardson had already figured out the technical weak spots of the covenants in their cities, and they would have been quick to call on the requirements of privity and touch and concern to send any damage action on these covenants to its doom.[21]

Thus even if the remainder of the Court had agreed with Vinson that a "simple contract enforcement" was not a matter of state action, the case need not have made a difference to the long-term durability of racial covenants. A white owner who had signed the original covenant simply would have had to find a white straw purchaser—already a much-used technique—and let that person sell to the minority buyer. In contract law, the straw could not normally be bound by a contract to which she had not agreed. The only remaining routes to enforcement would have been through equity—now impossible for a racial covenant—or through the argument that the promise ran to the new owner through property law, which it did not. Thus property law threw up major barriers to covenant enforcement, once *Shelley* had removed the possibility of an equitable remedy.

As a practical matter, then, by removing the equitable remedy, *Shelley* had turned racial covenants into arrangements that were at most individual contracts. But if the Court had left the matter at that, racial covenants that were now reduced to individual contracts would have been highly unlikely to last long. The neighbors who wanted to keep the covenants going would have had to keep up a constant round of bargaining every time an old resident left and a new one entered. The ensuing collective action problem would undoubtedly have made short work of many legally enforceable racial contracts: who would do all the work of keeping track and renegotiating?

Thus if *Shelley* or *Barrows* had simply focused on the distinction between property and contract, and especially property law's constraints on covenants running with the land, the decisions might have lost some rhetorical force, but they would have severely destabilized racially restrictive covenants. Even as a matter of rhetoric, this route would have offered a chance to illuminate the liberationist aspects of property, perhaps a useful political move during the Cold War's ideological struggles with the Soviet Union. But whatever the rhetoric, such a route would have sharply cut the durability of racial covenants, while confining the reach of the state action doctrine and making clear that ordinary contractual arrangements could remain in the realm of private law. Ordinary contracts were not much of a threat anyway, because ordinary contracts could not have effectively segregated neighborhoods over any long period. Indeed, over time, contracts themselves might have become problematic on grounds of public policy, as racial discrimination became less and less acceptable.[22] But the *Barrows* majority bypassed the property/contract distinction as a means to cabin *Shelley*, and thus *Barrows* did nothing to rein in *Shelley*'s statements about judicial action being state action—statements so vast that *Shelley* became almost unusable, because it seemed to suck in the whole array of private law.

On the other hand, there was a narrower pragmatic aspect to *Barrows*. After this case, it was clear that there was no point in trying to enforce a racial covenant in court with any kind of legal remedy. Racially restrictive covenants might have *looked* like legal documents, with all their ponderous legal verbiage, but they had now become only an empty shell of legal form. But surprisingly, residents and real estate professionals still continued to deploy covenants, sometimes in a modified form, even as they increasingly turned to other devices to maintain neighborhood segregation.

FANCY NEIGHBORHOODS DODGE THE DECISIONS

The Supreme Court's restrictive covenants cases left real estate professionals in a kind of limbo. As was widely noted at the time, after the *Shelley* and *Barrows* decisions racial covenants were not enforceable by the courts, but they were not illegal either. Indeed, they were not to become flatly illegal until some cities and states began to pass "fair housing" or "open housing" laws in the 1960s, followed by the Federal Fair Housing Act of 1968, which finally banned a variety of discriminatory housing practices, including references to racial covenants. But those statutes were still in the future. In the meantime, now that damage actions had gone the way of injunctions as means to enforce racial covenants, it was probably no surprise that real estate professionals would cast around for still other legal devices that might bypass the Supreme Court, and that might act like covenants even if they differed in form.

What devices, then, might be found to do the work that covenants had done, but under a different guise? First after *Shelley* and then after *Barrows*, legal commentators described a variety of methods that they thought might get some play. Some of the expected evasions now seem rather far-fetched, but in fact most were tried; indeed a few have had a rather extended lifespan, at least in certain segments of the housing market. One idea was that home purchasers would post a bond, to be collected if they sold to a member of the proscribed race. Another idea apparently derived from cooperative housing, especially prevalent in New York City: the neighbors could relinquish title or at least partial control to a nonprofit corporation that would say yay or nay to each proposed sale or rental—saying nay, of course, to minority entrants. Still another possibility was a covenant requiring neighborhood approval before any sale. Yet another was a requirement that all purchasers belong to a club, and the club could take over the task of excluding unwanted entrants.[23]

Nevertheless, even the writers who raised these possible evasions did not think that many homeowners would be likely to adopt them. They were costly to negotiate, and they constituted more of an intrusion on homeownership rights than most purchasers were likely to want. Furthermore, these intrusions on title could raise objections by mortgage lenders, who might be concerned that the controls could diminish the lenders' security interests in mortgaged properties.

The commentators' predictions generally played out correctly, both with respect to potential evasions and with respect to their limited usefulness. Posting bonds against sales to minorities never appeared to become a widespread practice. As for the co-op form, New York City had then (and still has) many cooperative housing arrangements, where the formal property owner is the association as a whole and the individual shareholder members are effectively tenants. Undoubtedly some co-ops did discriminate against minority entrants, and complaints about discrimination continued long after antidiscrimination laws narrowed the discretion of co-op boards to accept or reject new entrants. Indeed, such complaints continue to this day—perhaps most publicly about the celebrated but highly selective Dakota building on the upper West Side of Manhattan. But the co-op form has never taken root broadly in locations other than New York City, largely because this form of homeownership has made the individual purchase more complicated to finance.[24]

Residents might still go a further step beyond the co-op form, and give up home ownership altogether, leaving tenant selection—and segregation—to the landlord. The most spectacular example again comes from New York, in the massive Stuyvesant Town project of the late 1940s, a kind of prototype for later urban renewal projects. Stuyvesant Town was spearheaded by the Metropolitan Life Insurance Company, with considerable assistance from the state and city of New York. As Met Life Chairman Frederick Ecker notoriously remarked at the time, "Negroes and whites don't mix . . . perhaps they will in a hundred years." In the meantime, Stuyvesant Town succeeded in enforcing segregation in rentals even after *Shelley* made racial covenants in ownership arrangements unenforceable.[25]

For those who wanted to own their homes, however, two of the evasions predicted by the commentators soon appeared to be particularly promising from a legal standpoint, although in the end these too had only a limited range in practice. These were first, title arrangements conditioned on continued discrimination, and second, links between residential ownership and club membership. The first, conditional title, was a throwback to the original form in which covenants had been written, dating from the early years of the century. In those years, as we saw in Chapters 3 and 4, the covenant form was still maturing, and developers had been uncertain whether covenants could survive some of the arcane limitations on property controls, among others the Rule Against Perpetuities.

Readers of Chapter 4 will recall that by setting up their restrictions in the then more conventional form of defeasible estates, early developers could avoid the Rule Against Perpetuities—a more serious worry early in the century—as well as the somewhat looser duration constraints built into rules against restraints on alienation. According to this form of conditional ownership, if a restriction was violated, the remedy was quite draconian: the entire property title would revert back to the original owner—that is, the developer. Reversionary forms like these were less used after the early 1920s, giving way to the covenants that left enforcement with the homeowners, but after *Shelley* there was a chance that the reversionary estates could take on new life.[26]

In 1955, the Supreme Court of North Carolina heard a case that made reversionary arrangements sound promising as covenant substitutes. The case of *Charlotte Park and Recreation Commission v. Barringer* involved a situation in which several parties had donated land for a public white-only golf course in the early part of the century, with the limitation that the land revert to the original owners if the conditions of the grant could not be carried out. In the wake of several desegregation decisions, the public course could no longer be operated for whites alone, and the heirs of one of the original donors claimed that a part of the golf course should revert to them. In answer to the argument that the reversion was state action under *Shelley*, the North Carolina Court maintained that a reversionary interest of this sort did not constitute state action, because the title reverted automatically and required no judicial enforcement, thus distinguishing the judicial enforcement of the covenants in *Shelley*.[27]

The U.S. Supreme Court refused to review the case, and while this refusal did not create a binding precedent, it suggested that racial restrictions might be valid if they took the form of conditions on ownership, in which violation of the original grant terms caused the estate to revert back to the developer.[28] But although these reversionary forms later bedeviled title insurers, as we shall see in the final chapter, real estate developers never appeared to make much use of them in the 1950s and later. Perhaps this was because some courts paid no attention to the difference between racial covenants and reversionary interests and condemned them both under *Shelley*, but another important factor was undoubtedly that mortgage lenders would generally find the threat of reversion too destabilizing for home loans.[29]

Club membership was the other route that appeared to have some continuing legal viability as a basis for residential segregation. In a later case that was widely regarded as a retreat from *Shelley*, the U.S. Supreme Court decided in 1972 in *Moose Lodge No. 107 v. Irvis* that a private club could keep its state liquor license while continuing to exclude minority members on the basis of race alone, because the license did not sufficiently implicate the state in the club's activities to constitute state action in violation of the Fourteenth Amendment's equality requirement.[30] If a private club, even one with a state liquor license, could deny service without falling into the state action rubric, then a requirement that all residents belong to a club might become a viable method for excluding minorities.

But this method too does not appear to have spread widely, in spite of its legal appeal for segregationists. *Moose Lodge* to the contrary notwithstanding, state and federal antidiscrimination laws would soon sharply curtail this route to housing segregation. One interesting variation may have emerged considerably later, however, indeed within recent times. University of Chicago professor Lior Strahilevitz, writing well after the turn of the twenty-first century, noticed the unexpectedly large number of non-golf-playing residents in private communities that had golf courses. Strahilevitz surmised that golf course membership had become a surrogate method for excluding minorities, or at least many minorities, in a way that never mentions race and that could even fall outside the fair housing statutes. In today's world, of course, golf is a very crude proxy for race, and, in any event, the expense of golf course maintenance is a constraint on anyone hoping to attain residential segregation through this kind of membership requirement.[31]

In the 1950s and 1960s one area in Washington, D.C., epitomized the type of residential area that could still afford to indulge in the legal substitutes for racial covenants. Spring Valley was an older and very well-to-do community in the far northwest corner of Washington, D.C. The W.C. and A.N. Miller Company had initiated this in-town subdivision and the neighboring Wesley Heights in the 1920s, and following the model of this era's other upscale subdividers, they had developed the area over the next decades with a very tight control over landscaping, aesthetics, and occupancy—including racial restrictions.[32]

By the 1950s Spring Valley had become a favorite residential location for Washington's elite officials. But restrictions like Spring Valley's raised concerns in the State Department, which found itself embarrassed when diplomats from new African nations had difficulty finding appropriate housing in Washington. Aside from these Cold War echoes, Spring Valley's segregation methods became a fat target for domestic civil rights advocates. In a kind of belt-and-suspenders approach to maintaining the development as a white (and Christian) community, the Miller Brothers firm from the outset imposed a series of covenants on Spring Valley homes: no resident could sell or rent to a minority person, including not only African Americans but also Armenians, Persians, Syrians, or "Semitic" persons generally; owners could not sell or rent at all except with consent of either the Miller Company or the written consent of a majority of the neighbors; and all sales had to be channeled through the Miller Brothers' firm. Finally, every new purchaser was required specifically to accept the covenants as he or she signed the deed, a practice that continued into the 1960s.[33]

In order to live in this very desirable neighborhood, a number of high-profile Washingtonians did sign on, making the excuse that the racial restrictions were invalid anyway. But this step was not without risk for Washington politicians. Vice presidential candidate Richard Nixon's acceptance of the covenants got him into trouble with the press back in 1952, although his campaign manager pointed out that the Democratic vice presidential candidate, John Sparkman, had also signed the Spring Valley covenants. Nine years later, Dean Rusk, the Georgia-born secretary of state appointed by President John F. Kennedy, refused to sign; and at least for this prestigious purchaser, the Miller firm agreed to scratch the racial restrictions from the deed.[34]

Spring Valley's legal end runs around *Shelley* and *Barrows* were not really plausible outside the higher end of the housing market, however. They only could function among owners and purchasers who placed an especially high premium on controlling their neighborhoods and who had few worries about finance—as was the case with Spring Valley, where purchasers could take advantage of the Miller Brothers' long-standing relationship with Washington's Riggs National Bank. In a sense, after the Supreme Court's racial covenant cases, the exclusionary tweaks on covenants returned these legal devices to the kinds of very well-to-do residential developments in which they had originated, back in the first decades of the century.[35]

Legal commentators on *Shelley* and *Barrows* had predicted that the relevant players further down the class scale would use other methods, without attempting to re-legalize devices resembling covenants. As we shall discuss in the next section, all of these less formal and nonlegal methods did come into use. White homeowners would harass minority entrants, banks would not extend credit to minority purchasers in white neighborhoods, and real estate professionals would work to steer minorities away from white neighborhoods. But covenants continued to play a role here too, even though their legal enforceability was gone.

MORE EVASIONS FURTHER DOWNSCALE

While real estate professionals in upscale developments cast about for legal substitutes for covenants, the professionals' motivations were more ambivalent in older and less well-to-do parts of town. In the 1950s, racial covenants were still on the books for houses in many of these less wealthy neighborhoods. While some covenants were time limited and would expire on their own terms within some set number of years, others had a long duration or no termination date at all. Lower-end FHA finance was still possible for properties with racial covenants in these older areas, since the FHA still insured properties with covenants that preceded its policy changes of 1950. On the other side of the covenant equation, however, FHA financing would not be available for properties with new covenants, a constraint that continued to carry weight in mid- to lower-end residential transactions.[36] Moreover, with accelerating white flight to the suburbs, real estate professionals came to regard many urban neighborhoods as "transitional" anyway, in which case racial covenants would not be helpful at all.

Afloat on these crosscurrents, real estate professionals in fact often continued to reconfirm preexisting racial covenants. Supporting this pattern was a kind of scrivener's mentality that was closely related to issues of finance, whether FHA or conventional. In a survey released several months after the *Shelley* decision, bankers across the country asserted that anyone who removed covenants on his own—even unenforceable ones—risked creating a "cloud" on the title, and there was nothing a financing institution wanted less than a cloudy title. Some conceded that the cloudy title warning was an excuse to refuse minority loans, so as to protect white neighborhood values; but whatever the lenders' motivations, real estate professionals simply rewrote the title documents and deeds, references to covenants and all, so as not to create any questions for mortgage finance reviewers.[37]

In some instances, rote rewritings of racial covenants ran against the real estate industry's own interests, particularly when brokers steered minorities toward neighborhoods that they regarded as "in transition." Historian Phyllis Palmer has studied Washington, D.C.'s Shepherd Park neighborhood, whose residents in the 1950s and 1960s attempted to maintain it as an intentionally integrated neighborhood. Real estate brokers viewed Shepherd Park differently, and they generally only brought black customers around to see properties, on the view that any integrated neighborhood would soon be all black anyway. Nevertheless, they insisted that some reference to racial restrictions had to be maintained in the title documents, even over the objections of white purchasers, and no doubt of black purchasers even more.[38]

Even if it was contrary to their interests at some times, at other times it certainly appeared to be in the brokers' interest to continue to write covenant references into deeds in white neighborhoods. Although these restrictions could not be enforced, they still carried a signaling function, albeit a weakened one. As Rose Helper's 1969 book illustrated, real estate brokers through the 1950s and 1960s were almost universally convinced that minority entrance into a previously white neighborhood would lower property values. As usual, there was something of the well-known self-fulfilling prophecy to this phenomenon: a chief reason for a drop in property values, at least initially, appeared to be panic sales by white owners, fed by the very fear of loss of property value.[39]

Given the sharp concerns of white owners about minority entrance, real estate professionals undoubtedly thought that even a weak signal of mutual commitment would be useful to shore up white neighborhoods against minority entrance. Nevertheless, the influence of covenants had declined in the late 1950s and 1960s, and not only because of their loss of direct legal enforceability. Indeed, the loss of legal force was only part of a larger shift in attitude about covenants. The tepid response to *Barrows* among legal commentators and news reporters was a sign that attitudes were changing. No one seemed surprised by the case, or even particularly resentful of it. Covenants had seemingly lost not only their legal status but also the outward approval of the larger community; at a minimum, no one expected that the larger community would uphold racial covenants in any formal or public way. It was a straw in the wind that even before *Barrows,* NAREB's 1951 revised Code of Ethics dropped references to race in admonishing its members to avoid introducing "incompatible" elements into residential areas. Even the mainstream real estate industry had changed its tune, or perhaps, to put it more accurately, its public tune.[40]

All the same, the NAREB membership continued to have race very much in mind as an important "incompatible" element. If brokers and finance agents now relied less on racial covenants, they still found other means to perpetuate residential segregation. Racial steering was still very much a part of standard broker practice through the 1950s and into the 1960s. In St. Louis, the city real estate board continued to steer, requiring that a minimum of three black families move to any given block before they would show properties to other African Americans. It was generally not illegal to steer racially until the later 1960s, and many brokers appeared to believe sincerely that it was their ethical obligation to do so. Even a major spokesman of Washington's Shepherd Park, Marvin Caplan, who staunchly opposed steering at the time, remarked that many brokers who steered racially were just trying to settle their customers into neighborhoods that the customers themselves would prefer.[41]

Perhaps most importantly, it made business sense for brokers as a group to steer their customers by race. Decades of racial covenants and segregationist real estate practices had reinforced the view that racial mixing undermined property values, at least for white purchasers. If white buyers would pay a premium for a home in a segregated neighborhood, many brokers stood to do well over the long run by giving them what they wanted.

Developers in the new suburbs operated on a similar presumption. Given the income and wealth disparities between the races in this era, the primary purchasers of new suburban homes were white. Taking the view that white purchasers would prefer not to have minority neighbors, developers sold only to white persons. In 1954, a reporter asked William Levitt about his firm's refusal to sell to African Americans in his huge new suburban tracts. But for Levitt, it was a business matter, no matter how regrettable; as he saw the issue, so long as white buyers preferred all-white neighborhoods, they would not buy the Levitt company's houses if the company failed to meet those preferences. According to Levitt's memorable statement, the position of the firm was that "we can solve the housing problem, or we can try to solve a racial problem. But we cannot combine the two." Almost a decade later, the Levitt firm maintained this same stance. As the company's general counsel later explained to the U.S. Civil Rights Commission in 1962, the firm complied with the law, but where no law applied, "as a business enterprise our company cannot defy or offend the customs and traditions of the locality in which our company operates."[42]

Meanwhile, as many white urban residents left for the newly developed suburbs, African Americans moved into areas of cities that had previously been closed to them legally through racial covenants. The expansion of urban minority residential areas raises a question about the effectiveness of racially restrictive covenants all along. Historian Arnold Hirsch noted that covenants collapsed as the suburbs opened up to whites, and he argued that this fact tended to show that covenants had never been very effective in the first place; rather, the dominating factor was that whites had had nowhere to escape. Nevertheless, new research on Chicago and St. Louis, two cities with relatively good information about the location of racial covenants, argues persuasively that the demise of legally enforceable covenants significantly influenced the demographic profiles of these cities, as African Americans moved in large numbers into now-open covenanted areas.[43]

Certainly that was the opinion of contemporary real estate professionals, if the Chicago brokers that Rose Helper interviewed were at all typical. One of those brokers stated bluntly that the Supreme Court's racial covenant decisions meant that African Americans could now "pile in" to formerly white neighborhoods all over Chicago—and presumably other cities as well.[44] Moreover, the new housing opportunities in the white suburbs could not show a great deal about the effectiveness of covenants in the pre-*Shelley* era. When the postwar period opened up new white suburbs, the old urban neighborhoods became at least somewhat less important to their white residents, because people who wanted to live in segregated areas now had other options. It was not that legally enforceable covenants had been an insignificant line of defense, but rather that the suburbs made the defense itself matter less.

One way to sort out these issues is to think of the players' motivations and strategies in the light of the game-theoretic interactions described in the introductory chapter. In the next chapter, we undertake this task, to inquire how and why the relevant parties might continue to play some variants on covenant games even where legal enforceability had evaporated.

Changing Games in the Twilight of Covenants

Signals, Tipping Points, and Quotas

9

As we saw in the last chapter, in the years immediately after *Shelley*, white neighbors faced a legal universe in which they could no longer count on legal enforcement of racial covenants, and they cast about for substitutes. In this chapter, we analyze some of the situations they faced by analogy to games and strategic interactions. Since we have stressed the signaling function of racial covenants throughout their history, we continue the motif in this chapter, focusing particularly on the interactions between signals and neighborhood "games."

We will begin with the residual power that covenants retained as signals of neighborhood intent to remain all white. However, as covenants lost their ability to reassure white residents about one another's actions, and as the suburbs grew more attractive to those who would move out, white urban neighborhoods faced what came to be known as "tipping points" of white flight and rapid racial transition. In reaction, the neighbors attempted to find new forms of reassurance to counter the tipping phenomenon. We consider both the tipping phenomenon and two of the antitipping efforts that ultimately failed—failed among other reasons because they were held to violate constitutional legal norms. The first antitipping effort focused explicitly on information: a series of moves to calm white residents by using and controlling a different and rather cruder form of signal, namely For Sale and Not for Sale signs. The second type of antitipping effort was in effect a harder-edged form of reassurance: a set of programs to establish stable integrated communities, all of which entailed some form of benevolent racial quotas—oddly reminiscent of racial covenants themselves. The chapter concludes with what was supposed to be an endgame for housing discrimination more generally, among other things banning racial covenants along with other signals of discrimination: the federal Fair Housing Act of 1968.

COVENANTS WITHOUT LAW

Prior to 1948, the most obvious participants in racial covenant activities had been the parties arrayed opposite each other: on the one side were homeowners in white neighborhoods who deployed covenants to keep their neighborhoods white, and on the other were the minority members who were excluded by those very same covenants. There were of course supporting players on both sides: notable on the side of the white homeowners were real estate professionals and neighborhood improvement associations who backed covenant enforcement; but notable on the side of the minorities were civil rights advocates as well as those more shadowy figures, the profit-seeking blockbusters and panic peddlers. As between these two sides, the central game theory category was Hawk/Dove, with covenants acting as legal fortifications for the white homeowners, who hoped to defend their hawk role. Covenants gave off the signal that minority entrants should back away—play dove—or face an expensive fight from the white hawks who asserted ownership of the entire neighborhood. They also gave out a signal of respectability and entitlement—that the white homeowners had the law on their side, and that the rest of the community officially recognized their entitlement.

Shelley and *Barrows* unquestionably caused racial covenants to lose force in the hawk/dove context and undermined their credibility as effective barriers to minority entrance to a covenanted neighborhood. Those persons who had been reluctantly playing the dove role now knew that at a minimum, they would no longer bear legal costs if they turned into hawks themselves. The cases also undermined any implicit moral approbation that legality may have imparted; immediately after *Shelley*, racial covenants would be tolerated, but they no longer put legal force behind white residents who claimed not only ownership of their houses individually, but also of the entire neighborhood collectively.

This is not to say, however, that the loss of legal enforceability removed all the deterrent effects that covenants had for minority entrants. As signals of the neighborhood's commitment to be hawkish toward minorities, covenants were effectively "cheap talk," as economists say, and they still retained some of their capacity to guide new entrants' decisions. For one thing, not every potential buyer realized that the covenants had become unenforceable. And even where the new entrant understood the legal situation, there were still costs associated with knowing that one was moving to an area where the residents had recently attempted to keep one out by legal means, and where some might now resort to harassment or even violence.

These kinds of costs would most seriously affect the first minority entrants, the so-called pioneers. Indeed, many African Americans in the 1950s and 1960s reported that while they wanted good housing, they had no wish to be pioneers. Overcoming these first-mover impediments could slow entrance until someone thought it worth the cost. Besides, even if minority members were willing to take these risks of pioneering, they might find it difficult to locate agents who would show them the properties they wanted, or lenders who would finance a purchase. Real estate professionals, especially those with substantial business in a white neighborhood, continued to feel that it was "unethical" to introduce the first minority family into a white neighborhood.[1]

The second-line players were important in this now-attenuated Hawk/Dove game as well, but perhaps none so important as the blockbusting broker, who was now freed from binding legal restraints. As we shall see, blockbusting, or panic peddling,—in the form of statements about racial entry aimed at inducing panic sales—later became illegal under the federal Fair Housing Act of 1968, as did racial covenants. But between the Supreme Court's *Shelley* decision in 1948, and the passage of that statute in the late 1960s, the legal costs of blockbusting had effectively dropped to zero—a fact that undoubtedly induced more brokers to bring minority buyers to formerly covenanted areas during the 1950s and 1960s. Indeed, it was during this time that the "blockbusting" label became widespread as a shorthand phrase for these activities.[2]

Once blockbusting practices had no major legal obstacles, the main constraints were a matter of social norms. Conventional local brokers purported to despise blockbusting on moral and professional grounds, shunning the blockbusters and asserting that these brokers were putting money ahead of their professional ethics. Indeed, although many blockbusters cited principles of equal treatment, they often had a defensive tone when describing their practices. It is significant that according to Rose Helper's study of Chicago brokers in the 1950s, the blockbuster seldom had an office in the sales community. Instead, it was located downtown or elsewhere in the city. Because of his outsider status, the blockbuster broker could be impervious to retaliation from local brokers or to hostile neighborhood attitudes toward him, and he did not face risks to his person or his family's well-being if the white neighbors resisted minority entrance "informally," since he did not live in the neighborhood personally.[3]

The blockbuster did have to convince minority entrants, especially the pioneers, to take the risks entailed in moving into a potentially hostile neighborhood. But the blockbuster could play a critical role in overcoming first mover problems. One typical method was to arrange a house sale to a minority buyer, at a price that might be adjusted downward to overcome the hostility that would face the first pioneer. Blockbusting brokers often arranged for financing as well when the black buyers could not arrange financing with more conventional lenders; this was often the case both because the usual home finance offices would not lend to anyone "breaking" a neighborhood, and also because the new buyers often could not afford more than a very modest down payment. Introducing the first pioneers would have the added payoff of frightening the neighborhood's existing white residents. If those residents panicked and fled, the blockbusters had more houses to buy on the cheap. They had more potential minority purchasers as well—that larger group who wanted better housing but did not want to pioneer, and who now had less to fear from hostile and resistant whites.[4]

In short, as a result of *Shelley* and *Barrows,* the blockbuster was the external player most likely to cause the old hawk/dove status to erode, and to start playing hawk instead of hanging back. When he took these entrepreneurial moves, he could induce minority entrants to play hawk as well, leaving the white neighbors with the unpleasant choice of continuing their own hawk role or taking wing for the suburbs.

Turning to the white neighbors: racial covenants had been a tool to leverage the relationships among the white neighbors themselves as well, but now that these covenants were no longer enforceable, there were still several games in play. One was the classic Prisoner's Dilemma, or PD, game described in the Introduction, in which each neighbor would be in the best position if he or she could defect while everyone else cooperated. For a close relative to the PD, consider the neighbor who had already decided to move out, and whose best option was to sell before panic sales hit the neighborhood. Law professors Abraham Bell and Gideon Parchomovsky have described the dynamic between this person and the other neighbors, which they call the "Resegregation Game," but which other writers have more colorfully dubbed the "Boxed Pigs" game. In a simple version, this game might be played between two neighbors: the first neighbor finds it better to defect no matter what the other does, while the second would stay if the other were staying and only defect otherwise. Since the first will defect come what may, the game produces the same result as the Prisoner's Dilemma game: both leave, presumably selling to the new minority entrants.[5] Against either of these types of defectors, the post-*Shelley* loss of legally enforceable covenants obviously made a difference; the remaining neighbors could no longer threaten either one with legal consequences.

But legal norms and direct legal consequences had never been the only matters at stake. Social norms had mattered as well among the neighbors. Even unenforceable covenants continued to signal the neighbors' preferences and past commitments, and white residents were often reluctant to "sell out" on one another, making the familiar statement that "I couldn't do that to my neighbors." It is significant that the first sellers to minority entrants often did so indirectly and perhaps inadvertently, first selling to a white broker or straw purchaser. Other early sellers were themselves outsiders to the community, such as adult children who were settling the estates of deceased parents. These were doubtless among the persons most likely to trigger Bell and Parchomovsky's Resegregation Game, because they were likely to sell under any circumstances, no matter what the other neighbors did. In her searing autobiographical account, Beryl Satter's observed that some of the neighbors also looked at Jews as potentially defecting outsiders, because they thought Jews were more willing to sell to African Americans, some simply for profit, but—more interestingly as a sign of changing norms—some out of egalitarian principle.[6]

Putting to one side such "outsiders," at least some of the white neighbors wanted to stay in the neighborhood but only as long as it stayed white. For these persons, the game was a rather more subtle one than the Prisoner's Dilemma; it was the Stag Hunt or Assurance Game discussed in the Introduction, and also described by Bell and Parchomovsky.[7] In this game, the preference of each of these white neighbors was to remain so long as the others did—together capturing the stag—but once the other white neighbors started to leave, each would think that the lesser choice of moving elsewhere individually—taking the hare's part—would be preferable to remaining in a neighborhood in racial transition.

In this more subtle game, covenants too had always played a more subtle role: they had acted not so much as an enforcement threat against defectors, but rather as a reassuring signal among the white neighbors—that is, a signal of commitment to the common strategy of staying in place. One of Rose Helper's 1955 interviewees, broker N, described how covenants had influenced even those who had not signed them in the pre-*Shelley* days. He remarked, "With the restrictive agreement we were able to control this [sales to black buyers], . . . there was a little opening [for owners who had not signed the covenants], but very little of that was done." That is to say, when covenants were in force, they influenced even those who were not legally bound by them—unlike the later period, when white sellers began to sell in much greater numbers.[8]

After *Shelley* and *Barrows* made racial covenants legally unenforceable, these covenants lost credibility among the white neighbors as commitment devices, and the weakening sign of each neighbor's commitment would tend to weaken the commitment of others as well. As Helper observed, even among the many residents of white neighborhoods who really would have preferred to remain, the resolve of some disintegrated with just one sale to an African American. Broker N described the matter this way: "Perhaps it is a high-class colored person," he said, referring to a new minority buyer in a formerly all-white neighborhood. "But it's just the idea about selectivity. I'd want to sell my property too and get out."[9] It did not help, according to another broker in the survey, that white owners feared that "high-class" minority purchasers were bound to be followed by others who were not so high-class, presumably causing neighborhood relationships, schools, and public safety to deteriorate—all of which would diminish the all-important measure of property values.[10]

To return to the Stag Hunt, still further undermining their common commitment was the very powerful factor of suburban development, which made the hare option comparatively more attractive. Why hang on in the city when one could have one's own backyard and picket fence and good schools in the suburbs? And if A was not so sure B would hang on, might it not be better to go it alone in the suburbs? Might not B think the same of A and decide to leave too? And might not C and D think the same?

The previous chapter remarked on historian Arnold Hirsch's view that the collapse of so many covenants during the postwar white flight showed that covenants had never really had much effect at all, melting away as soon as the suburbs opened up.[11] But as we mentioned there, Hirsch's view appeared to overstate the case substantially, and we can now see why. The later growth of the suburbs did not mean that legal enforceability had not mattered in the earlier era. Rather, legal enforceability had played a much more variegated and subtle role than a simple threat to take interlopers and defectors to court. Much more significant was the signaling function performed by legally enforceable racial covenants. They signaled both to outsiders and to insiders that the white residents were committed to staying and to keeping the neighborhood white; they signaled where brokers should steer and lenders should redline; and they signaled as well that the larger community approved of these means. Once enforceability was gone, those signals all weakoned, while of course the attractions of the suburbs sapped them even further. As we shall see, covenant signals did not yet lose all force, but as urban neighborhoods began to change, some of the white neighbors turned to other and more direct kinds of signals.

TIPPING POINTS AND THE QUEST FOR ASSURANCE

When one observes the post-*Shelley* period through the lens of various strategic games, and when one notes the role of racial covenants as signals, a particular feature of the story commands attention: not all the white neighbors were committed to 100 percent segregation. After the legal defanging of racial covenants, there were a number of stories about urban white residents who posted signs saying Not for Sale when the first minority residents moved in or appeared to be about to do so. These neighbors too were playing an Assurance or Stag Hunt game. Covenants had been replaced by signs in the front yard, but the neighbors were still attempting to signal their preference for staying where they were.

After *Shelley* and *Barrows*, racial covenants in the record books gave a signal of past neighborhood preferences that might or might not continue; but signs in the front yard gave a much more direct and intense signal to anyone who was looking.[12] It should be noted that signs like these were not necessarily benevolent, and they were commonly organized in an attempt to stave off the march of racial transition. But one striking feature about such signs, especially when they postdated the arrival of the first minority residents, is that those who posted the signs made clear that they wanted to remain even after some new neighbors of a different color had arrived.[13]

Indeed, those signs should cause a certain reconsideration of racial covenants themselves in their heyday, particularly the after-the-fact neighborhood covenants that started in the 1920s and that continued over the next decades in older urban neighborhoods. As we have seen, the organizers of after-the-fact neighborhood covenant drives had rarely been able to garner 100 percent of the property owners' signatures. During the drives, many neighbors had pledged to abide by the racial covenants as soon as some percentage of the neighborhood signed on, even knowing that the remaining percentage of the neighborhood homes might be occupied by minorities.

The motivations behind covenant drives and pledges had certainly not been attractive, and the covenants themselves had curtailed minority members' ability to move where they pleased, but even with those formidable objections, covenants had not necessarily signaled a commitment to 100 percent segregation. As in the case of the *Shelley* neighborhood, it is certainly possible to think that racial covenants helped to maintain a neighborhood that was in fact integrated, however much one may reject the racial fears that underlay the covenants themselves.

From the perspective of an Assurance Game, the most interesting point is that white urban neighbors, even those with the neighborhood covenants, had been willing to countenance some limited number of minority neighbors all along, even if far too few to meet the larger minority demand. In the 1950s, the white neighbors who put out the Not for Sale signs signaled even more overtly that they did not intend to let a threat of minority entrance force them out. Nevertheless, the Not for Sale signs suggested that a neighborhood was already moving toward integration, and, in the meantime, the suburbs beckoned. In the end, in great part, those owners did sell after all, as integration turned into transition and ended in resegregation.

The question is why this happened. Studies from the late 1950s and early 1960s found that substantial numbers of white persons nationwide—as many as 50 percent—claimed that they would be willing to live in integrated neighborhoods.[14] Given those findings, why did the white neighbors' Stag Hunt turn into a hare rout? A standard answer emerged in those same years: integration meant different things to different people, and many neighborhoods reached what University of Chicago political scientist Morton Grodzins in 1958 called a "tip point"—later to be called a "tipping point." That is, minority entrance had reached some point at which the white neighbors felt that too many other white neighbors had left, too many minority neighbors had arrived, and that they themselves could no longer comfortably remain.[15]

The next question, of course, is what the tipping point was. It is easy to understand a tipping point with an extremely simple formulation: suppose that members of two groups, A and B, would be happy to live in a neighborhood that had some members of the other group—so long as the neighborhood had a majority of one's own group. Obviously both A and B groups cannot be in a majority, and in short order one would expect all the As and Bs to live in entirely separate areas, despite the willingness or even desire of all to live in an integrated setting. But the tipping point may actually come much earlier in the integration process. In a famous thought experiment, Nobel Prize–winning economist Thomas Schelling demonstrated that persons with fairly weak preferences for segregation—"I will stay as long as a third of my neighbors are of my race"—will nevertheless gradually separate completely.[16] And, of course, as Schelling noted, different persons might tip at different points, so that each new minority resident could create a swelling cascade of white departures.

Indeed, a closer consideration of the tipping phenomenon reveals several important patterns not only about the urban demographics of the 1950s, but about earlier patterns of neighborhood covenants. One can see this more subtle pattern by imagining ten white neighbors—or even a hundred—in an Assurance or Stag Hunt game, in which each had to decide between following the cooperative stag strategy of staying in place, or the individualist hare strategy of selling and leaving. From each neighbor's position, it would obviously have been better to stay if all the others were staying, but to leave if the others were leaving. But aside from these all-or-nothing decisions, there could be some more intermediate situations; after all, to be reassured, one does not necessarily need everyone to hunt a stag, just a sufficient number. And so, even if some neighbors were hesitant about committing to stay, it might be better to cooperate and stay so long as a sufficient number of other neighbors were on board. On the other side of the issue, any given owner might not want to wait for everyone else to sell before selling and leaving himself or herself. Thus there were ranges of expectations that could support either the stag or the hare strategy.

In earlier decades, similar thinking must have affected the neighbors' decisions to sign or not sign onto the neighborhood covenant agreements that became so prevalent in older cities. Seeking 100 percent agreement to keep a neighborhood segregated would have carried considerable dangers: if the assenting neighbors had to wait for the last few doubters or holdouts to sign on, the whole effort could be put in jeopardy. But at the same time, no one had wanted to be locked into an agreement that would restrict his or her ability to sell while most others in the neighborhood were free to do as they pleased. The solution had been to insert a condition into the agreement, requiring that some minimum number of neighbors—but less than 100 percent—would sign the covenant before anyone was legally committed. Rose Helper's Chicago broker N may have said, "we never got one hundred percent," but in fact, the threshold often ranged from 75 percent all the way to 95 percent of the property frontage (sometimes including churches and commercial buildings). Those figures suggest that the covenant signers had put up with a risk that 5 to 25 percent of the neighboring properties might be sold to minorities.[17]

In the era when covenants were legally enforceable, those thresholds served as an outer limit on minority entry, beyond which the white neighbors could not sustain an agreement to stay in place. But below those thresholds—say, with only 5 or 10 percent of the neighbors implicitly signaling that they might sell to minorities—many white neighbors could and did still resolve to stay. After all, social norms against selling to minorities reinforced the legal ones. Indeed, the signing owners might stay even with an unexpected sale or two to minority families, given a high expectation that the other white households would remain in place. But for each neighbor there would be a critical point of expectations—a point of indifference between sticking it out and selling. At that point the homeowner and the other neighbors could in effect flip a coin or randomize between the two "pure" strategies—an option known as a mixed strategy.

Without taking up some of the less obvious game-theoretic aspects of mixed strategies, one can observe an underlying instability of mixed strategies that provides a useful perspective on tipping points. Mixed strategies can produce stable outcomes, where the neighbors are happy to continue mixing their strategies, given what each believes the others will do in a more or less random pattern of leaving and staying. All the same, such equilibrating outcomes cannot withstand small changes in expectations about the behavior of others. As game theorists say, these equilibrium outcomes are not robust to subtle changes in beliefs. A sale, a threatened sale, or even some lesser event might cause a white neighbor to update his or her beliefs about what others are going to do, and if such an event predictably causes him or her to change behavior, others will follow in an increasing flood of departures. All this would cause a rapid shift in the neighborhood, as the white neighbors' strategies tip from the mix and pour into what game theorists call the "basin of attraction": in this case, the hare strategy of selling and leaving.

Thus the neighbors' beliefs and expectations play a critical role in tipping point situations. While it may well appear that the white owners sold and fled because black residents moved into the neighborhood, in fact the causal direction could have been largely the reverse. After all, black residents could only move in if white owners were selling. To be convinced to sell, white owners only needed to believe that black families—or rather, *too many* black families—would be moving into the neighborhood.

Manipulating these beliefs became a central focus of several actors, particularly after *Shelley*, as white homeowners attempted to counter the panic-spreading messages of blockbusting brokers. Sometimes they did so to prevent black families from entering, but sometimes—in a striking example of changing social norms—they did so to give assurances that an area could be both integrated and stable. As we shall see, however, good motives were not enough to save some of these efforts from contrary legal norms.

THE BATTLE OF THE SIGNS

In neighborhoods that had had racial covenants, the demise of legal enforceability, taken together with the new construction of the suburbs, undoubtedly made homeowners' expectations about one another much more volatile than they had been in earlier years. The continued existence of racial covenants did signal a moral commitment to stay in place, but by the later 1950s and 1960s, a homeowner knew that a neighboring seller could find a new home in the all-white suburbs and was very likely to know that no irate neighbor could step in to enforce racial covenants—and neither could a third-party enforcer like the St. Louis Real Estate Exchange.

Meanwhile, the blockbusting brokers were not lawbreakers any more. And from all reports, the blockbusters in this post-*Shelley* era were relentless, working every possible angle to manipulate beliefs about neighborhood change. One reported technique was to move in tenants who would most closely match the worst racial stereotypes of the white neighbors. Another was to make a great show of bringing a black family to see a house in the target neighborhood. Brokers hired African Americans to walk and drive on certain streets, ostensibly showing an interest in the neighborhood. One broker reportedly hired an African American woman simply to walk down the street with her baby, so as to spread panic among the white residents. Meanwhile, brokers flooded the target neighborhood with leaflets and telephone calls, all conveying open or veiled threats of racial transition and falling property values.[18]

The white residents' Not for Sale signs represented one effort to send a countersignal, but those flickered out in many neighborhoods that tried to use them. Instead, the Not for Sale signs came to be replaced by forests of For Sale signs. The For Sale and Sold signs pushed neighborly expectations in exactly the opposite direction from the steadfast, stay-calm rhetoric that characterized the earlier stage of Not for Sale signs. Now passersby and the neighbors themselves could see the new message delivered by the accumulation of signs: they implicitly informed the viewer that panic had already set in, and that racial transition was underway.

To stem the tide of departures and to stabilize existing neighborhoods, a number of communities took aim at the signs in the front lawns. One that did so was Shaker Heights, a well-to-do Cleveland suburb. Readers may recall Shaker Heights from Chapter 5; it began as one of the high-end new housing areas of the early twentieth century. The initial Shaker Heights subdivision was developed before racial deed restrictions had become standard practice in such suburbs, but the developers themselves kept a tight rein on sales, among other things excluding African Americans.[19] In the ensuing years, Shaker Heights had become a municipality, but when one black family became the first to purchase a home on one Shaker Heights street in 1960, a dozen For Sale signs sprouted up among the approximately fifty homes on the street. By April 1964, the town had decided to silence the implicit message, banning For Sale signs in residential areas.[20]

Oak Park, Michigan, was another municipality that banned such signs, though it banned other signs too. Indeed, Oak Park's antisign ordinance prohibited any kind of sign at all on properties or buildings that served as one- or two-family residences. To contain the sweep of such a prohibition, however, the ordinance provided for some exceptions, and the range of exceptions suggested that the primary target was For Sale signs. Signs posted by municipal order were allowed, as were signs with street names and occupants' names, along with signs announcing garage sales, and signs indicating a number of not-to-do's: No Soliciting, No Dumping, No Walking on the Grass, and No Picking the Flowers all survived the ordinance, as did Beware of Dog and some other signs so long as they did not exceed one square foot in size.[21] But For Sale signs for the houses were still taboo.

It was a highly contested matter whether ordinances like this actually shifted any residents' expectations about one another—or the behavior based on such expectations—but that detail did not stop the ordinances' growth. At least that was the case until 1977, when these sign ordinances fell afoul of the U.S. Constitution's First Amendment protections for free speech. The case that brought the sign ordinances to the Supreme Court came from the Township of Willingboro, New Jersey, after a New Jersey corporation, Linmark Associates, sued the township in order to post a For Sale sign on property that it owned in the township.

Willingboro's ordinance presented a considerably more interesting case than something like a sheer effort to maintain an all-white or mostly white community. Willingboro had started as a Levitt & Sons development in the late 1950s, and like the typical Levitt projects, it was planned for middle-income buyers. Middle-income *white* buyers, that is, because as we have seen with other Levitt developments, these developers in that earlier era had refused to sell to minority buyers. The New Jersey Supreme Court had intervened, however, and put a halt to this race-based discrimination in sales. In 1960 there had been a mere six black people living in Willingboro, out of a population of about 12,000. By 1970, the town population had grown to about 43,000, with about 38,000 whites and 5,000 nonwhites. Although population leveled off at about 44,000 in the early 1970s, there was a decline of about 2,000 white residents and an increase in the nonwhite population by 3,000. Rumors of tipping and panic sales swept through the community. In 1973, a town meeting was called, pointedly titled "Willingboro: to Sell or Not to Sell." The meeting itself could have been enough to coordinate expectations that invested neighbors would not sell, but Willingboro had always been a more loose-knit community. It was close to several military installations, most notably Fort Dix, and, consequently, at least some of its population had been transient from the start.[22]

When Willingboro's ordinance was challenged, the mayor at the time of the meeting, William Kearns, had remarkably specific memories of Willingboro's attitudes about tipping. He recalled that an increase in minority population up to 20 percent, "or even somewhere in a range of 20 to 25 percent," would not have concerned "anyone," presumably, although not necessarily, meaning the white residents when he said "anyone." Nor, he said, would it bother anyone that some white residents were selling and moving, so long as they were motivated by job transfers or the wish to get a larger house or some similarly neutral factor. But what would have been alarming would be the belief that they were moving "because what they sensed was the reaction of the community," and that "we would wind up with Willingboro hitting beyond the point of minority group population that would turn it into an isolated pocket of minority groups in Burlington County." In that case, he added, "it would no longer reflect an integrated community, but would become a ghetto." To reduce the possibility of such cascading beliefs, he said, a community member had suggested a ban on real estate signs, and the township duly prohibited For Sale or Sold signs by an ordinance in March 1974.[23]

But in spite of the segregated origins of both towns, Willingboro was not the more exclusive Shaker Heights community. Interestingly enough, the NAACP filed a friend of the court petition on behalf of the Willingboro, observing that "the ordinance was *not* passed in response to the entry of the first black family . . . into the community," and supporting its "effort to preserve integration and stability." The brief went on to state that local authorities' early intervention "may be the best and perhaps only effective remedy for blockbusting; it may be impossible to reverse the process of panic and resegregation once underway."[24]

Nevertheless, Willingboro's ordinance met resistance in the courts, where the initial district court took a less favorable view of it. And so did Thurgood Marshall, the former star of the NAACP's national litigation team, who had successfully argued against racially restrictive covenants before the Supreme Court in 1948. By this time Marshall was himself a justice on the Court—indeed, the Court's first black justice—and it was he who delivered the unanimous opinion that Willingboro's ordinance was an unconstitutional restraint on free speech.[25] By way of consolation, he observed that in invalidating the ordinance, the Court "by no means leave[s] Willingboro defenseless in its effort to promote integrated housing. . . . It can give widespread publicity—through 'Not For Sale' signs or other methods—to the number of whites remaining in Willingboro."[26] One wonders what Justice Marshall might have thought of the new black residents in Lakeview, Long Island, who cooperated with their neighbors by putting signs in their own windows, exhorting other African Americans to do their part for integration by buying somewhere else.[27]

Marshall's opinion vindicated the point that all these For Sale and Not for Sale signs conveyed important information—considerably more than what was on the face of the signs themselves. The signs supplied information that would lead neighbors to update their expectation about one another's behavior. It was precisely because Willingboro wanted to impede this information and updating, and the behavior that would follow, that the township's ordinance was a free speech violation.[28] The town's benign motivations give a quite poignant reminder that legal norms can still police even a favorable turn in social norms. An encouraging fact, though, and also a sign of changing social norms, was that even after the case was decided many white residents stayed on in Willingboro.

INTENTIONAL INTEGRATION, BENEVOLENT QUOTAS

A significant factor in the tipping phenomenon in the post-*Shelley* era was home *ownership.* A 1960 study detailed surveys of white people's newfound willingness to live in integrated neighborhoods, but it also noted that white purchasers did not wish to buy a house immediately next to a nonwhite owner—leading the authors to comment dryly that this pattern might explain why so many people thought that the first nonwhite purchase inevitably led to a complete neighborhood transition. On the other hand, white *renters* were considerably more willing to remain or even move into mixed neighborhoods, apparently because they had less at stake.[29]

These findings bolstered the view that the white owners did not tip entirely because of personal preferences, but rather because of their expectations about the preferences of others—or more specifically, because of their assessment of the market value of homes in all-white as compared to integrated neighborhoods. The years of racial covenants echoed through this reasoning, with their ever-repeated mantra that segregation maintained property values, and the reinforcement of that mantra by brokers, lenders, and government officials over the decades past. That mantra had the effect of tipping homeowners particularly precipitously, reinforcing what even then was known as the self-fulfilling prophecy about race and property values.[30]

Real estate brokers of the 1950s clearly understood both how low the opening tipping point was for homeowners, and how quickly the first sale could create a cascade. Those patterns emerged in an especially poignant fashion in connection with the efforts of some urban groups to swim against the tide, and to encourage integration in their own residential areas. Historian Phyllis Palmer was mentioned in an earlier chapter, along with her study of one such effort in the Shepherd Park area of Washington, D.C. In Shepherd Park, white and black residents formed the "Neighbors Inc." organization in the 1950s, in an attempt to maintain an integrated neighborhood over the next decade. Real estate brokers did not make this effort easy. Their view was that there was no such thing as a stable, integrated community. If the neighborhood was integrated now, for the brokers it was in transition—and that meant it was moving inexorably from white to black.[31]

Indeed, even nonblockbusting real estate professionals helped to make this happen through their steering practices, bringing only African American buyers to see any houses for sale in integrated neighborhoods. When the Shepherd Park neighborhood association tried to get the brokers to change their practices, the neighbors received, in Palmer's words, "a lesson in housing economics."[32] The brokers explained that they could sell houses on Shepherd Park's tree-lined streets much more easily to middle-class black purchasers, both because those buyers had fewer opportunities for such housing, and because potential white purchasers would be nervous about moving into a mixed neighborhood. In an ironic twist, the Shepherd Park neighborhood organization found itself hunting for potential white buyers, in a kind of through-the-looking-glass image of the brokers' own steering practices. Indeed, the neighbors' strategy in Shepherd Park would have closed off housing opportunities for some African American purchasers, even if the latter would have paid more than white purchasers. The brokers had a more businesslike attitude: they took note of pent up African American demand, and they took the money.[33]

When the Shepherd Park neighbors particularly sought out white buyers to keep the neighborhood mixed, they were acting out an informal version of an integration method more formally known as a benevolent quota. The idea of a benevolent quota was that housing opportunities could be opened up to minority buyers in an integrated project or area, but only in a measure that would not cause the area to tip. Thus benevolent quotas would give residents a more hardened assurance—considerably harder than mere Not for Sale signs—that nonwhite residents could enter a community without threatening to flood it. More precisely, the quotas would undercut white residents' panicky assumptions about one another, and stave off the white reactions that contributed to sudden and total racial transition.

What the tipping or quota measure should be, of course, was indeterminate. Morton Grodzins noted in his 1958 study that two Quaker communities outside Philadelphia had imposed restrictions to limit the proportions of minority to white residents at 45–55 percent. But he also observed that few aside from "confirmed, egalitarian Quakers" were likely to accept a minority ratio this high.[34]

Grodzins's remark conjures up pictures of unseemly community debates about acceptable percentages, and more recent demographic patterns in the United States—particularly the entry of substantial numbers of new minority groups—suggest that these kinds of debates might have had to be renewed periodically. Moreover, as Rose Helper pointed out in 1969, the very use of the term *quota* called forth complaints of antidemocratic meddling. Nevertheless, Helper herself was sympathetic to the benevolent quota approach, and others who offered some support for them included the eminent housing discrimination specialist Charles Abrams, the Antidefamation League's Oscar Cohen, and community activist Saul Alinsky. These and other commentators noted that benevolent quotas raised both dignitary and practical problems, but they explicitly described the function of these quotas as one of reassurance. As one put it, when a white person thought that the entire neighborhood would become nonwhite, that person would move; but "[t]he exception, housing experts say, is where there is an 'element of management.'"[35]

While these discussions went on during the 1950s and 1960s, a handful of law review articles pointed that benevolent racial quotas also raised legal issues. These devices, after all, looked a great deal like racially restrictive covenants. The hope of the proponents of benevolent quotas was that their pro-integration purpose would save them from ineffectiveness under *Shelley* or, by the 1960s, from outright condemnation under the increasing numbers of local, state, and finally federal fair housing laws. We shall return to those laws shortly, but where legislation was not so clear, many found the legal issues highly ambiguous. One of the great legal scholars of the day, Yale's Alexander Bickel, used benevolent quotas as an example of a thorny issue whose legality the Supreme Court should leave undecided, in order to give the political branches of government room to experiment.[36]

Like the ordinances banning For Sale signs, however, benevolent quotas were to meet their demise some years later, falling afoul of a higher-level legal norm. The chief case that closed the door on benevolent quotas was *United States v. Starrett City* in 1988, based on the 1968 federal Fair Housing Act. Starrett City was a very large Brooklyn housing development that received state and federal support. It was also intentionally integrated and had used benevolent quotas since the mid-1970s, designating 64 percent of the units for white residents, 22 percent for black, and 8 percent for Latinos—a formula designed to prevent the development from tipping. But the Reagan administration's Justice Department brought a housing discrimination suit against the development, on the ground that the quota put a ceiling on the number of black residents on racial grounds alone. The defense that these quotas helped to prevent white flight prevailed only with one judge—Judge Jon Newman—on the three-judge panel that heard the case on appeal. The Supreme Court refused to review the *Starrett City* decision, and while that refusal was not absolutely dispositive, for all practical purposes it settled the point that benevolent quotas in housing cannot withstand a Fair Housing Act challenge so long as the statute remains in its current form.[37]

The trouble with benevolent quotas, among other matters, was that they did have something of the flavor of racially restrictive covenants, despite their very different motivations. Oddly enough, at least some of the older racially restrictive covenants had acted as de facto benevolent quotas in the 1920s, '30 s and '40s, even though they were certainly not so intended. This was because, as we have noted earlier, the neighbor-driven covenants had generally taken effect when some supermajority of the neighbors had signed, while potentially leaving the remaining residences open to minority members. Obviously the older neighborhood racial covenants had not aimed at integration—quite the contrary, the signatories would have been happy to have 100 percent if they could have gotten it. But the neighbors generally could not get unanimity, leading to the phenomenon noted above, that racial covenants in fact existed in some integrated neighborhoods like the Shelleys', and they might possibly have had the effect of stabilizing those neighborhoods racially by cabining the white residents' worries about other white neighbors' potential defections.

This is not to make excuses for the older racial restrictions, but only to point out that their existence had many twists and turns, and that some of their techniques might have been used for more sympathetic purposes. Clearly the traditional racial covenants—including the neighbor-driven ones—had enormous down sides, most directly in closing off minority housing opportunities, and even more importantly and perniciously, solidifying the idea that racial mixing caused housing values to decline.

That latter view has been hard to shake, and it lies behind the phenomenon of tipping itself—no doubt more than offsetting any effect that the older racial covenants may have played in reassuring white residents and stemming urban white flight. But the striking feature of the benevolent quota debate is that some of the methods of racial restrictions might have been deployed for a very different purpose: to overturn the same pervasive and counterproductive beliefs that covenants had helped to instill. For all their many dangers, benevolent quotas aimed to show that housing values can thrive in an integrated setting. Indeed, the debate about them is not yet entirely over, as we shall see in the concluding chapter.

TURNING OFF THE SIGNALS? THE FEDERAL FAIR HOUSING ACT

Linmark and *Starrett City* called a halt to the two major efforts to counteract racial tipping by manipulating signals: after those cases, neither For Sale sign ordinances nor benevolent quotas were available tools for Assurance Games. But those cases were decided, respectively, in 1977 and 1988, and much had changed in the preceding decades. In 1954, the Supreme Court's *Brown v. Board of Education* case had pointedly introduced the issue of schools into the housing segregation question.[38] The civil rights movements of the 1960s impressed many with the need to end discrimination in housing, often seen as the key issue in addressing the many other inequalities that flowed from segregated neighborhoods—notably in education, poverty, and public services.

Back in the early 1950s, as mentioned in the previous chapter, political scientist Richard Baker had sharply criticized the *Shelley* decision for upending state and local legislators' well-nigh universal toleration of residential racial restrictions.[39] But by the 1960s, many of those legislatures—if not necessarily all the voters—had changed their minds. A number of municipalities and states began to pass fair housing, or open housing, laws that invalidated racial discrimination in real estate transactions. California was among the first and most prominent of these with two fair housing statutes enacted in 1959 and 1963, although the sailing was not smooth. In 1964 California voters repudiated those acts in a referendum that altered the state constitution, barring any state legislation that interfered with owners' "absolute discretion" in selling—or refusing to sell—their property. Thereafter the California Supreme Court invalidated the referendum-induced amendment, finding that it constituted discriminatory state action in violation of the Fourteenth Amendment. The U.S. Supreme Court affirmed, although the justices were divided on the issue.[40]

Meanwhile, the U.S. Congress followed up the state and local measures with the federal Fair Housing Act of 1968, which banned housing discrimination on several fronts, notably race but also religion, gender, and national origin. Like earlier state and local legislation, the Fair Housing Act outlawed outright discrimination in sales, as well as brokers' practices of racial steering and most discriminatory advertising.

Several parts of the Fair Housing Act took aim at signaling behavior and the dissemination of information. Not only did the act outlaw discrimination in the conditions of almost all sales and rentals, but it went so far as to curtail references to racial preferences in advertisements and professional home sales and showings. In that measure, the act finally took the definitive step that the *Shelley* and *Barrows* cases had not: it made it illegal to create racial covenants or even to let existing racial restrictions be mentioned so as to influence real estate transactions.[41]

The ostensible constitutional basis for the Fair Housing Act was congressional authority under the commerce clause as well as the Fourteenth Amendment, and the latter basis once again raised the state action issue so central in the earlier race covenant cases. Could Congress actually legislate against private individuals' discriminatory practices, when the Fourteenth Amendment referred only to discrimination through state action? *Shelley* obviously had not settled the issue definitively for Congress, but just as the act was passed, the Supreme Court weighed in once again on a St. Louis housing discrimination case. This time the Court helpfully decided that the dusty old 1866 civil rights legislation, which bars racial discrimination in contractual matters—by individuals—could be supported under the Thirteenth Amendment's ban on slavery and "badges" of slavery.[42]

As we have noted earlier, the Thirteenth Amendment has no state action predicate, and under its newfound authority, Congress presumably could have revisited the housing act and barred all racially discriminatory practices in residential real estate transactions, right down to the individual level. Congress did not do so, however, and the Fair Housing Act of 1968 continued to include minor exceptions that allowed "Mrs. Murphy" type discrimination in small owner-occupied buildings, along with a few other exceptions.[43]

A rather different kind of hesitation appeared in the act's treatment of those most ambiguous of players in the politics of neighborhood segregation, the blockbusters. Here again the key feature was information: the act made it illegal to promote panic sales through references to racial entry to a neighborhood. In this antiblockbusting section, one might hear the last eerie echo of the conventional brokers' "ethics" favoring racial steering and eschewing the introduction of nonwhite persons into white neighborhoods. Blockbusters had defied the conventional brokers' steering ethic in the past, and in so doing they had expanded residential opportunities for minority buyers and renters in cities. But particularly in the years after *Shelley* had removed the threat of legal retaliation, blockbusting practices of sowing fear had also very much inflamed racial anxieties and animosities. At least indirectly, the blockbusters' practices may even have exacerbated discriminatory practices in the suburbs, where brokers and bankers routinely denied service to minorities.[44]

Evidently, the act's congressional creators regarded the blockbusters' fanning of the flames as sufficiently objectionable and dangerous to outweigh any benefit they might have provided in opening up previously segregated neighborhoods. Certainly the blockbusters were instrumental players in tipping formerly white neighborhoods; sending out frightening signals was one of their central tactics.

Nevertheless, the blockbusters had their defenders. African Americans who acquired housing through blockbusters were less negative about their activities, even though the blockbusters' high housing finance charges undoubtedly undermined goodwill toward them. A few years after the Fair Housing Act passed, when a new Illinois statute threatened panic-peddling brokers with the loss of their licenses, African American columnist Vernon Jarrett complained in the *Chicago Tribune* that the "hidden intent" of the measure was to prevent black purchasers from buying in white neighborhoods.[45]

The Fair Housing Act generally approached housing discrimination from what economists call the supply side. The act especially focused on discriminatory practices of real estate professionals, outlawing racial steering and the withholding of information and services to buyers and renters because of their ethnicity, and of course outlawing references to racial restrictions—including covenants. Once *Starrett City* ruled out the use of benevolent quotas, the Fair Housing Act basically was a measure based on neutrality—no favoritism on racial or ethnic grounds, no matter that the purpose might be benign promotion of integration. Housing supply should be open to all on an equal basis.

This supply-side approach has made a difference. While some assert that real estate professionals still engage in discriminatory practices to this day, nevertheless, in the wake of the act, total minority housing opportunities increased. Minority buyers and renters have moved to areas that were once closed off to them, including not only to neighborhoods beyond the adjacent "rings of steel" of covenants around former ghettos, but also to suburbs that were once all white. But stable, integrated neighborhoods remain the exception.[46]

This pattern suggests that the supply-side approach has not been sufficient to achieve residential integration, and it raises the question whether residential integration is indeed what Americans want. Yet Americans do seem to want integration. The demand side too has shifted substantially over the last half-century, with most people of all ethnicities now describing themselves as favoring housing integration, at least in the abstract. Willingboro and Shepherd Park are by no means so exceptional nowadays, in their interest in maintaining stably integrated communities.[47]

And there is the rub: concrete moves toward housing integration have been very slow, not to say glacial. How, then, did racial restrictions interact with the desire or at least willingness of white residents to live in integrated communities? In our conclusion, we will consider the role of racial covenants over the long run in limiting and weakening that ostensible demand side for more integrated communities.

Conclusion

Covenants' Legacy

10

Racially restrictive covenants did many things, but they did not initiate or create the antipathy to residential integration among white Americans. That antipathy long predated racial covenants, as we saw in Chapter 2. Racial covenants did make it possible for this antipathy to harden into action, among many people who would otherwise have been unable to effectuate their antipathies. Violence was always an option in the background, but racial covenants made it possible to mark out neighborhoods as white without resorting to violence—a matter especially important for the urban residents who were not so tightly connected among themselves, and who lacked the taste or commitment that violence would have entailed. Because racial covenants were framed as property rights, neighborhoods that used them could hold any newcomers to the same obligations that their predecessors had taken on, over long periods of time, mimicking the results that stronger informal norms had in more close-knit neighborhoods.

As legal instruments, existing in official records, racial covenants took on the mantle of civic acceptability. In this respectable legal form, racial covenants could be deployed by a variety of professional institutions, becoming tools for real estate developers, brokers, financial agents, and insurance institutions—including those of the U.S. government. In many new urban and suburban residential developments, these institutional players helped to initiate racial covenants as part of the private law governing home purchases. In older, already-settled neighborhoods, real estate professionals campaigned to make racial covenants become an openly available rallying point for "neighborhood improvement associations" and "property owners' associations," many of which focused principally or entirely on staving off minority entrance.

Legality also affected wider norms. The dominating normative ideas in neighborhood segregation were first that minority neighbors would undermine white property values, and second that white residents owed it to their neighbors to keep that from happening. Legal acceptability undoubtedly enhanced the widespread attitude among real estate professionals—even formalized in professional codes—that maintaining segregation was a part of their professional ethical responsibility. As for the norms among the white neighbors themselves, as we saw in the last chapter, covenants signaled a commitment that drew in even those who had not personally signed on to the covenants and whose own property was not subject to the covenants. Moreover, when confronted with would-be minority purchasers or renters, covenants enabled the white neighbors to enforce the color line as a legal matter, without resorting to violence and even without reference to personal hostility. As to the minority buyers and renters who were kept out, the legal character of covenants caused hardship and insult, but it also made exclusion much more difficult to challenge. Not only white neighborhood norms but also the weight of the law was against the pioneers, and it took unusual boldness and tenacity to try to lift that weight.

In short, legality allowed racially restrictive covenants to become institutionalized and internalized. Legal racial covenants turned neighborhood segregation into a pattern that was durable, open, expected, normal, and not often challenged even by those who disagreed or who found themselves victimized by it.

The legal basis of covenants did make them vulnerable, however. They were vulnerable first to the formalities of older property law. As we saw in the early chapters, these formalities were shot through with rhetorical commitments to free alienability, even though these commitments had bent in favor of covenants of all kinds by the 1920s. Later, however, racial covenants were vulnerable to a major shift in constitutional law, itself influenced by a larger shift in public attitudes about equal citizenship. Legal support for covenants crumbled with *Shelley,*

Barrows, and the Fair Housing Act, and might well have decayed in the more conventional common law of property as well over time, as the nation's sense of equity began to shift against racial restrictions.

In an important way, however, much normative damage had already been done, on what the economists call the demand side. If racially restrictive covenants did not initiate white antipathy to residential integration, they certainly helped to solidify and normalize that antipathy. They did so by reinforcing the idea that the property values in white neighborhoods depended on residential segregation, and that white neighbors, and all those who dealt with them, had an obligation to maintain neighborhood segregation.

When racial covenants first appeared in wealthy new suburbs in the early part of the twentieth century, the covenants' very association with opulence sent a message that segregation would help to maintain property values in white neighborhoods. In only a little over a decade, racial covenants became a desired feature in new middle-class developments as well, and older and more established urban neighborhoods were soon to follow. By the 1920s and 1930s, real estate professionals, financial institutions, and governmental agencies had all publicly stated that property values depended on segregation, and they had acted on that basis, as had the residents of covenanted neighborhoods. Post-*Shelley* revisions of real estate professional ethics codes and mortgage insurance standards could hardly unsay what had already been said for decades.

Moreover, precisely because covenants helped to squeeze minority groups into overcrowded urban neighborhoods, they added to the pressure-cooker character of minority housing, in a way that sharpened fears about property values once the Supreme Court's decisions made covenants unenforceable. Both before and especially after *Shelley* and *Barrows,* blockbusting brokers could see the gains to be made from arbitrage in relieving minority housing pressures. They picked away at the weaker covenants and border areas, looking for cracks in the "iron rings" surrounding minority areas. But when any neighborhood that had once been covenanted was breached, minority families poured through the gap, white families fled, and the resulting rapid march to a tipping point only reinforced fears in other white neighborhoods that the first minority residents spelled a total transition.[1]

If they had not had the cover of legal covenants from the 1910s through the 1940s, many urban neighborhoods could not have entirely withstood some minority entrance. That would have particularly been the case for those neighborhoods that were largely middle class and loosely knit, many of whose residents were reluctant to turn to more violent "informal" means to maintain all-white ownership of the neighborhood. Had there been less pressure from covenants on urban minorities, those white neighborhoods might have offered opportunities for an education in the possibility of integration, however reluctantly the white homeowners might have participated in the opening stages. As it was, racial covenants reduced the possibilities for experiments in integration, and thus the opportunities for learning.

On the other hand, as we noted in the previous chapter, there were some instances in which covenants may have actually promoted integration, albeit uneasily, particularly in border areas between white and minority neighborhoods—like the mixed neighborhood where the Shelleys moved in St. Louis. As we saw in that chapter, there is an intriguing lesson in the fact that the post hoc neighborhood covenant agreements were often structured to go into effect at 75 or 80 percent agreement among the white neighbors. Those percentages suggest that the white residents had varying views of a tipping point, or at least that many set the tipping point at a more lenient level than the mere possibility of a single minority neighbor.

Could it be possible that, after the legal demise of racially restrictive covenants, some other covenant-like devices might have calmed the white panic about property values? By the later 1960s, of course, with the rise of charismatic black nationalist leaders like Malcolm X, one might wonder whether it was worth the effort: why bother to calm down white people when their flight opened up whole neighborhoods to minority families? Separation was not a problem, Malcolm asserted, but rather a solution: just give us a state of our own. Less provocatively, new, largely black suburbs like Prince George's County outside Washington, D.C., proved that minority families could indeed get along perfectly well by themselves. Still, for many citizens, integrated neighborhoods remained a public policy goal, since stable residential integration had so many implications for integration in other aspects of public life, notably education.

So, to return to the question: might some different form of covenants have been useful to alter the demand side for integration? As we saw in the last chapter, commentators from the 1950s through the 1970s pursued this possibility in the discussion of benevolent quotas that might reassure white residents about neighborhood change. But those efforts were controversial: they seemed to coddle panicky white people, and they had the practical effect of closing the door to minority residents precisely because of their race. For the latter reason, they were ultimately quashed as a violation of the Fair Housing Act in the *Starrett City* case in 1988.[2]

A different kind of covenant might have required the neighbors to approve new purchasers; such covenants might possibly have had a calming effect and might have allowed for experimentation. But the neighbor-consent idea too had dignitary and exclusionary issues that were even more obvious than the benevolent quotas. In any event, neighbor-consent covenants very probably would have suffered the same fate as benevolent quotas under the Fair Housing Act. Moreover, quite aside from the implicit threat of discrimination, neighbor-consent requirements would have intruded substantially on the sale potential of any given property; as such, they would be likely to raise objections from mortgage institutions, always suspicious of restrictions that could undermine the value of their security interests.[3]

Perhaps the most intriguing covenant idea—considering its source—was floated in late 1945 by Robert Weaver, a well-known champion of integrated housing and foe of racially restrictive covenants. Weaver proposed to the American Council on Race Relations that, instead of racial restrictions, neighborhoods might substitute restrictions limiting housing to single family occupancy and restricting the numbers and types of occupants. The idea was to protect neighborhood character while allowing more affluent minority buyers to find housing in attractive areas. Implicit in Weaver's suggestion—as with other similar ideas at the time—was the idea that the source of the white neighbors' fear was not the first well-to-do minority purchaser, who would merely be looking for a generally better neighborhood ambience, but rather the lower-class types who might follow—and who no doubt would indeed follow, if the white neighbors panicked and all sold out in a rush. The *Chicago Defender* published an article about Weaver's suggestion, only to jump all over it, condemning it as a classist restriction that the *Defender* thought would ignore the conditions of most urban black people, and if anything divide cities even more. But something like Weaver's idea for maintenance covenants was actually adopted in the Oakland/Kenwood area in Chicago, now a well-to-do and largely African American neighborhood just north of Hyde Park—the area was to become the home base for Elijah Muhammed's Nation of Islam temple, and later the actual home of Senator and then President Barack Obama.[4]

For better or worse, Weaver's trial balloon and ideas like it have had a long afterlife. While Weaver and others hoped that neighborhood-upkeep covenants would give a boost to racial integration, motives have been more mixed in other instances. In much exaggerated form, similar ideas have appeared in subdivision covenants that require expensive lots and high association fees, and that still generally keep low-income residents out of planned developments. They have appeared as well in public regulations in the so-called exclusionary zoning ordinances, through which municipalities limit apartment construction, require large lots, or impose other requirements that generally make housing too expensive for less affluent residents.[5] Some states and localities have tried to limit these exclusionary measures, at least the public ones, but in a society that values free enterprise and the ability to spend your buck where you please, it is difficult entirely to constrain limitations that are based on willingness to pay, whatever the classist consequences. Milder versions of Weaver's suggestion continue to have appeal in the ongoing effort to maintain urban neighborhoods—covenants that police for poor maintenance, for example, or that call for dues to support block-level patrols and sprucing-up activities.[6]

Of all the devices for reassurance and education that have spun off from the idea of benevolent quotas, one stands out as having the greatest chance for political and constitutional acceptability—although it too has been controversial. After pondering antitipping quotas in the early 1970s, the earnestly progressive Chicago suburb of Oak Park instituted a plan in 1978 for "home equity assurance." This was an insurance pool, funded by a tax on homeowners, that would pay out to individual homeowners in the case of a sudden drop in the value of their homes. The hope was that this insurance plan, by addressing homeowners' property value concerns, would substantially raise the tipping point as this suburban city integrated. In turn, by reducing the white flight that itself deflated home prices, the insurance would never have to be collected at all—which indeed turned out to be the case in Oak Park.[7]

Ten years later, however, when the Illinois state legislature considered a bill to make the Oak Park scheme generally available, some black political figures objected sharply. They described the plan as racist "black insurance," and as a new iteration of the old saw that integration causes property values to drop. Nevertheless, the legislature did pass enabling legislation for other areas to institute the Oak Park model, and a number of Chicago precincts did so. Meanwhile, since that time, other states and localities have debated and sometimes adopted similar models as a means to stave off white panic sales, and legal scholars continue to take an interest in Oak Park's equity insurance as a means to lower the stakes in homeownership, and thus to reduce the ill effects of some property-value-driven decisions by homeowners—notably white flight.[8]

Housing law scholar Sheryll Cashin has suggested that none of these intentional solutions, however well-meaning, is likely to make a great deal of difference in people's attitudes about housing integration. She thinks that an education in integration is more likely to come from edgy, thoroughly mixed "multicultural island" neighborhoods like Adams-Morgan in Washington, D.C., or the Uptown area of Chicago. She may be right, particularly for younger people, although one has to wonder whether conventional middle-class homeowners would take many lessons from the youths that wander around such neighborhoods, bedecked with Mohawks, tattoos, and navel rings, or whatever their equivalent may be in years to come. But any beginning is a good one.[9]

Yet other scholars have proposed measures that might attack the problem of residential segregation from a rather different angle. Whereas Oak Park offered insurance to lessen homeowners' anxieties about housing value, these other proposals would lower anxieties by weaning residents from home ownership altogether. On their prescription, we should reexamine tax breaks and other subsidies for homeowners, among other reasons because all these subsidies make people far too heavily invested in their home's value. While a main target of this scholarship is the lack of homeowners' financial diversification, a closely related issue could be the problem that overinvestment in homes makes owners resist integration in large measure because of their assessment of the housing market. With lower stakes in the places they live, everyone might be more willing to experiment with integration and learn some valuable lessons about the value of diverse neighbors.[10]

Even without dramatic changes in the laws that encourage home ownership, however, it is encouraging that some of the middle-class people who fled urban areas in years past are thinking of moving back. It has taken a long time to loosen the attitudes that racial covenants helped to solidify, but some of those attitudes have begun to relax.[11]

A constant reminder of a racially covenanted past, however, lies in the middle of town: in the halls of the Recorder of Deeds. As a conclusion to this chapter, and to the book as a whole, we arrive at this coda on the role of the written records.

CODA: ANNOUNCING THE PAST, REPUDIATING THE PAST: COVENANTS IN THE LAND RECORDS

Readers will recall from earlier chapters that the critical issue in the *Shelley* case was state action. What factor could make an ostensibly private property arrangement among white homeowners turn into something akin to legislation or an official act? What factor made these arrangements look like an act or practice or directive that was limited by the Fourteenth Amendment's constraints on state action? *Shelley*'s answer was that judicial enforcement of racial covenants constituted state action, but as we saw in earlier chapters, many commentators—even sympathetic ones—thought that this formulation swept too far. To call judicial enforcement state action threatened to turn the whole area of private law into state action, potentially choking off vast numbers of individual arrangements that citizens routinely make among themselves. Some commentators argued, however, that there was another and perhaps even better candidate than the courts for the state action rubric. That candidate was the recorder of deeds.

In the years prior to *Shelley,* recordation of racial covenants in the official land records was the essential component that made covenants stick. Their recorded status turned covenants into *real* covenants—that is, real estate obligations. Through recording, covenants could become durable *property* as opposed to shorter-term contractual arrangements between individually agreeing parties. Once in the record system, a racially restrictive covenant bound the future purchasers of a given property, even though those purchasers had never personally agreed, or indeed even though they did not personally know of the covenant. Their obligation derived from the fact of ownership itself, because the property that they purchased came with the racial covenant attached. And what attached it was the recording system.

The recording system gave "record notice" even to unwitting purchasers like the Shelleys. But it also conveyed information to anyone who had a serious eye toward claiming some interest in the property, including lenders or insurers, without whose participation most houses could not be sold. The routines and requirements leading up to the title closing on any given property assured that all the relevant actors would normally acquire information contained in the recording system. Even though the real estate professionals were the ones most familiar with the recording system and its contents, their professional obligations generally required them to inform their nonprofessional clients what they found there—the Shelleys' experience to the contrary notwithstanding. What is more, each of those actors would know that all the others had access to the same information, so that it could become common knowledge among them. But as a result of this normal information exchange, everyone involved in a purchase would know that a neighborhood with racial covenants had resisted minority acquisition of the property in the past, and perhaps was still resisting, even if the neighbors could no longer resort to the courts.

It is not surprising, then, that the stodgy old recording system became a kind of battle ground in the fight against racial covenants, even after the *Shelley* and *Barrows* decisions made racial covenants unenforceable in courts. Until the passage of the Fair Housing Act in 1968, the leftover problem from the cases was that they did not make racial covenants illegal; if the covenants were recorded, they could continue to signal the racial preferences of a neighborhood long into the future.

Some commentators thus took aim at the recording system as another public institution that could fill the bill for state action. If recording counted as state action, then the recorders of deeds could no longer accept new racial covenants, or possibly even retain references to older ones. Indeed, the position seems plausible on first glance: the recorder of deeds is a public official, and his or her stamp is needed for inclusion in the public records. Besides that, the public records themselves are located in governmental offices, often rather imposing ones at that. Why not, then, consider the act of recording, or even the very presence of a document in the public records, as state action?[12]

The usual answer is somewhat reminiscent of the general answer about judicial enforcement of most private arrangements (aside from the enforcement of racial covenants): the recorder of deeds does not create the documents, but merely notes their presence. On this account, the recorder's office is a kind of empty pipe through which information about private transactions flows into a publicized condition. The recorder adds and subtracts nothing to the documents recorded; he or she judges nothing, insures nothing, and plays no part other than to note their presence and to file them in the appropriate binders. The recorder is not likely even to read the documents. How could this purely ministerial role count as state action when, for the most part, even judicial actions do not?

Of course, after *Shelley,* judicial action *did* count as state action, at least with respect to racial covenants, though perhaps not much else. But on the issue of race, there is at least a plausible case that recorders of deeds performed functions akin to those performed by judges. Judicial actions themselves display a range of public exposure. A court may make a ruling, which orders the relationship between the parties, but it may go on to issue an opinion on which the ruling is based. This is a very public pronouncement indeed, which helps others to coordinate their future relationships. Similarly, by aggregating otherwise private information and making it publicly and broadly available, the recorder's task, mechanical though it is, helps buyers, lenders, insurers, and others to coordinate their transactions.

This coordinating function applies to all recorded claims, racial covenants included. When a potential buyer, white or black, learns of the recorded racial covenant, he or she learns something of the neighbors' expectations. The neighbors know this too, and the potential buyer knows that they know (and so on) because the covenants are cross-referenced in their own deeds. In this way, the recorder's office may not have created the racial covenant, but its coordinating function at least arguably turns its record keeping into an institution for creating common knowledge of the covenant—state action in the same way that a published judicial opinion can generate common knowledge of points of law.

It bears noting that recorded information about racial covenants may have had substantial consequences. The postwar years saw many incidents of violence when African Americans moved into previously all-white neighborhoods. In this context, recorded information about the neighbors' long-held sentiments toward black entrants may well have influenced the financial costs born by pioneers. Readers will recall from Chapter 6 that even after explicit racial directives were dropped, FHA appraisers were still told to look for neighborhood attitudes toward new entrants; recorded racial covenants could help to supply that information, which could in turn affect FHA insurance decisions. Other lenders and insurers were quite concerned about bearing the costs of bombings and less dramatic but still significant forms of property destruction—like the mean-spirited stink bombs, with their long-lasting and malodorous effects.[13]

In spite of the judicial analogy and the practical effects of the record system, the mechanical and nonjudgmental character of recording insulated the recorder's office from the state action rubric in the decade after the *Shelly* case, during which racial covenants were unenforceable but still legal. But with the passage of the Fair Housing Act in 1968, Congress added some statutory flesh to the skeletal constitutional arguments about state action. Section 3604 (c) of the Fair Housing Act made it illegal "to make, print, or publish . . . any notice, statement or advertisement, with respect to the sale or rental of a dwelling that indicates any preference, limitation, or discrimination based on race, color, religion, or national origin. . . ."[14] Might this language about making, printing, or publishing include the recording of a deed with a racial covenant—or even include maintaining such covenants in older recorded deeds? One very interesting federal case in Washington, D.C., batted this issue about, ultimately concluding that, yes, the statutory language did include those functions.

The case was *Mayers v. Ridley,* first brought in the early 1970s. At the outset, things did not go well for the plaintiffs, a group of white home purchasers who objected to racial covenants in their own deeds. They came to court complaining that the recorder of deeds refused to strike covenant language in these deeds, language that prohibited sale to or use by a whole panoply of unwanted persons, including not only African Americans but also "Armenians, Jews, Hebrews, Persians and Syrians," or anyone else of the "Semitic race." Trial judge Howard Corcoran was openly contemptuous of these provisions, but he was more swayed by the mechanical character of the recorder's job. He suggested instead that the plaintiffs direct their attack to "the real estate brokers and/or Title Insurance Companies which perpetuate such covenants in deeds despite full knowledge as to their unenforceability."[15]

The case was appealed, and the appeal was first decided by the usual three-judge panel, where the majority agreed with the trial judge. But the matter was sufficiently contested to come back before the entire District of Columbia Court of Appeals, and this time the plaintiffs prevailed. The reversal was "per curiam," a kind of summary order normally reserved for noncontroversial matters, but this time the order was accompanied by four separate and quite impassioned opinions, two speaking for the seven judges who agreed that recording racial covenants violated the Fair Housing Act, and two for the three judges who dissented.[16]

One reason why the *Mayers* majority opinions found the recordation of racial covenants to be a "publication" under the statute was their ability to signal discriminatory intent; even an unenforceable signal could have had what Judge Wilkie called "a discouraging psychological effect." Judge Wright was even more emphatic, stating that "the official recording of these documents is likely to give them a legitimacy and effectiveness in the eyes of laymen which they do not have in law." Indeed, it was possible that "a black person might be reluctant to buy a home in a white neighborhood when government itself implicitly recognizes racially restrictive covenants as 'affecting the title or ownership of real estate.'"[17]

The *Mayers* majority's view of recording racial covenants has not garnered universal assent, however. In another case almost fifteen years later, *Woodward v. Bowers*, a federal court in Pennsylvania distanced itself from the *Mayers* majority and took the conventional view that at least as far as Pennsylvania law was concerned, the recorder of deeds was simply a neutral transmitter of documents, taking no part in the information recorded and hence not a "publisher" of racially discriminatory real estate preferences. Implicitly, the only actors involved were private ones, even if the recording system passively broadcast their preferences.[18]

Private actors on their own, of course, can also act in ways that create common knowledge and coordinate the actions of others, even without official authorization. Thomas Schelling made this point with his illustration of the bystander who directs traffic at an impromptu traffic jam. Interestingly enough, the *Mayers* debate over racial information has had a more recent revival in connection with craigslist, the Internet posting site that has no connection with the recorder of deeds' office at all. The Chicago Lawyers Committee for Civil Rights sued craigslist for posting blatantly racist housing advertisements—for example, "NO MINORITIES." The defense for craigslist echoed that of the recorders of deeds: the site is merely a neutral transmitter of other people's messages. In 2008, a federal court of appeals agreed with the defense, and, echoing *Mayers* trial court Judge Corcoran, Judge Frank Easterbrook suggested that the Lawyers' Committee sue those posting the message instead.[19]

As for those who were still "posting" racial covenants in the recorders' official records in the early 1970s, an interesting fact emerged in the *Mayers* opinion: that the Justice Department had been pressuring the title companies to remove offending racial language from their documents. In late 1969, the Civil Rights Division had written to major title insurance companies, apprising them of the Fair Housing Act section on publication as well as the Justice Department's view that this section prohibited reference to racial restrictions in such documents as deeds and title insurance. The letters urged the companies to eliminate these references in future policies, and to instruct their staffs in the ways to eliminate the effects of racial covenants in current policies, and to do all this "voluntarily . . . and without the necessity for resort to the judicial process."[20]

The major companies apparently agreed, but in practice they continued for some time to report the existence of older recorded racial covenants even if they annotated their illegality. A 1972 school desegregation case in Richmond, Virginia, noted the prevalence of racial covenants in the area—as well as the references to those covenants in title insurance documents. Northwestern University law professor Leonard Rubinowitz worked on another school desegregation case in the Milwaukee area in the mid-1980s; in investigating patterns of housing discrimination in the area, he and his research team uncovered many title documents from the previous decade referring to older subdivision "restrictions of record." Upon perusal, those restrictions of record often included older racial exclusions. But of course, few of those exclusionary documents were created later than the early 1950s, and they were rather unlikely to be seen by ordinary home purchasers. Perhaps that explains why, as late as 2005, an attorney in Seattle remarked that there was "no consistency" in real estate professionals' title reporting practices with respect to old racial covenants. "Some blank it out," he said, "some make an attachment showing it as invalid or amended; some simply show it."[21]

Indeed, while the official recorders of deeds may have had a plausible defense against the charge of publication, given the mechanical character of their record keeping, one could not say the same of those real estate professionals and title companies who continued to reference recorded racial and religious restrictions in the title documents they prepared for home purchasers. One might wonder what ever possessed them to do so, after the Fair Housing Act so plainly prohibited references to discriminatory restrictions or even preferences. The answer comes again from property law: formally, a real estate covenant cannot be released without the unanimous consent of the beneficiaries. Without such a release, a real estate professional's omission of a covenant that appears in the records would appear to be misstating the condition of the title. In a 2010 interview, a past president of the American Land and Title Association (ALTA), an attorney who had worked with one of the major titling companies from the early 1950s through the 1990s, recalled both the Justice Department's 1969 letter, as well as his firm's great concern about Justice's pressure to eliminate references to racial restrictions in title documents. "Leaving out a patent defect in a title," he said, "—we couldn't do that."[22]

Indeed, title insurers had a special reason to be concerned: title insurance policies insure the title against any claim other than those listed as exceptions from the policy's coverage—which means that title insurers could be liable, at least in theory, if they failed to mention a racial covenant in the records as an exception. But what of it? If no one any longer has a legal claim under a racial covenant, what risk would there be to the title insurer? In an intriguing echo of past practices, one worry for title insurers apparently derived from one of the old property law ghosts, legal concerns that were reflected in the very earliest schemes of racial covenants.

Readers will recall from Chapter 4 that the early community-builder developers had structured their restrictions in the form of defeasible estates, according to which any violation of a restriction would cause a property to revert to the original developer or his firm. Back in those early years, these reversionary forms of ownership seemed a safer way to lock lasting restrictions into a new development, among other reasons because they would not violate the old-fashioned Rule Against Perpetuities. But as readers will also recall from Chapter 4, these reversionary arrangements were extremely awkward for developers. Many developers had no wish to remain on the scene as enforcers of subdivision restrictions, particularly if their only enforcement method was the bombshell of reverter—that is, homeowner forfeiture of an entire property, even for a minor violation. The reversionary forms largely fell out of fashion by the late 1920s for private land use restrictions of any kind, but there were still some on the books from the earlier era, as well as some others that had been created later.

More to the point in the 1970s, as we saw in Chapter 8, these kinds of reversionary limitations had never been definitively ruled to fall under the *Shelley* rule that judicial enforcement constituted state action. In contrast to the more conventional covenants, reversions appeared to occur automatically, without requiring judicial participation at all. This distinction created a frightening scenario for a title insurance firm. The Fair Housing Act forbade such a firm from referring to any racial preferences in documents relating to real estate sales; but if the firm failed to list a racial reversionary interest, it might be held liable to an insured homeowner who sold to a member of the forbidden minority. In that nightmare scenario, the sale would cause the homeowner's property to revert back to the long-ago original seller (or more likely, the subdivision company). The next step would be that the title insurance firm—which, following the Fair Housing Act, had not listed the race-based reversion as an exception to insurance coverage—would be obliged to pay the insured homeowner for the value of the entire property. The title insurance lawyer mentioned above recalled very well that what he called the "automatic reversions" had been a special headache. The industry had no problem with flagging the ordinary racial covenants as illegal, but insurance companies bridled at the reversionary interests, and they continued to report those clauses.[23]

What happened next? Apparently, over time and in the face of Justice Department pressures, the major title insurers for the most part just decided to take a chance and treat racial reversionary interests in the same way that they treat more conventional racial covenants, omitting references to them or annotating them as illegal. They may have taken heart from the Colorado Supreme Court, which had already deemed racial reversionary interests to be the equivalent of covenants and illegal under *Shelley;* and other courts might take the same path if confronted with the issue.[24] State legislation too must have emboldened them somewhat. In 1951, the Florida legislature limited the duration of conditional reversionary interests to twenty-one years, although the state's courts subsequently ruled that the limitation could only apply to interests created after the legislation was passed. A number of other states have imposed time limits on some reversionary interests, usually ranging from thirty to sixty years, but those limitations also do not necessarily apply to older applications.[25]

Aside from these instances, however, to the best of the authors' knowledge the reversionary issue has never been entirely resolved. The U.S. Supreme Court has been reluctant to touch the states' trust and estate law on which these issues depend, no doubt because so many charitable institutions depend on bequests, however idiosyncratic those may be. Indeed, as some otherwise critical commentators have acknowledged, by leaving estates and trusts alone, the courts and legislatures still permit some breathing room for *benevolent* racial preferences by private parties.[26]

As a more practical matter, because reversionary interests are so awkward in their draconian remedies—and hence so unappetizing to most purchasers, developers, and lending institutions—even their most offensive incarnations are deployed too infrequently to have much impact on public policy. In turn, if these devices are too rare to affect public policy, their legal enforceability loses significance. As we saw in

Chapter 7, it was the *widespread* use and impact of racial covenants that gave a kind of underlying rationale for treating them as constitutionally comparable to state action.

Is it enough that racial restrictions are now crossed out or flagged as illegal or omitted altogether in new deeds? Some think not. Our past of racial residential discrimination is still with us, but some would like to repudiate its most durable signaling form: the racial covenant that is still buried in the land records. To be sure, as Judge Corcoran pointed out in 1971 in the trial phase of the *Mayers* case against the Washington recorder of deeds, owners could disavow any claims for themselves under racial covenants.[27] But disavowal might not entirely solve the matter. Under standard covenant law, one owner's covenant renunciation cannot affect the other neighbors' covenant entitlements unless those others consent to the change. True, the neighbors have had no legally enforceable claim since the *Shelley* case in 1948, but that might not stop them from trying to convince gullible newcomers that the covenants still carry some weight, if only as signals of a tacit agreement to keep the neighborhood white.

In answer to the wish absolutely and publicly to eliminate all claims under racial covenants, in the early twenty-first century several states have passed legislation making it possible for racial restrictions to be eliminated from title documents—or at least flagged as illegal—whether all the supposedly "benefited" neighbors give their consent or not. As in many legal issues, California led the way beginning in 1999. California's legislation provides property owners a procedure through which they may request that the county recorder's office determine whether their property contains an illegal discriminatory restriction, and, if so, to record a statement repudiating it. Given the procedural steps, however, an owner acting under this measure has to be reasonably dedicated to the project of finding and rooting out all racial claims against a given property. No doubt some are only moderately interested and do not bother. But at least the option is there for one's own deed.[28]

Planned communities—the kinds of urban and suburban developments in which racial restrictions were born—present a special problem. In these communities, every deed refers to the the "Covenants, Conditions, and Restrictions," the CC&Rs," that act as a kind of master plan for the community's physical character and governance. Unlike the formal deeds themselves, these CC&Rs are actually rather likely to be perused by a purchaser upon buying into the community. This is because the CC&Rs often contain provisions that delineate homeowners' dues and other responsibilities, or limit their options in such matters as parking places or landscaping. But many older CC&Rs also include racial or religious restrictions. The result is that, while prospective buyers read about on-street parking or setback lines, they also may note that, at least according to the old provisions, they are not permitted to rent or sell to an African American—or in some cases, to a Jew, Asian, Latino, Persian, or "Mongolian" either.

Many homebuyers, no matter what their race or religion, are likely to find these kinds of clauses distressing. But what is one to do? Even though most CC&Rs do not require the unanimous consent of all the owners for amendment or alternation, the amendment process nonetheless can be arduous, often requiring some kind of supermajority along with legally acknowledged signatures of the participating members. Needless to say, these kinds of procedures create substantial collective action problems.[29]

California's legislation cuts the knot by simply requiring homeowners' associations to delete discriminatory restrictions from their CC&Rs, without the need for homeowner assent, and the law also gives individual homeowners a right of action to force the association to do so. Like California, several other states have begun to loosen the consent requirements for amending discriminatory CC&R restrictions, though some are less forceful than California. The state of Washington, for example, permits (but does not require) a homeowners' association to repudiate racial covenants simply through the vote of an association board's majority; Colorado, more cautiously, also permits homeowners' associations to change their CC&Rs in this way without universal or supermajority agreement, but still requires a majority of homeowners to assent. More encouragingly, Missouri, the state whose enforcement of racial covenants was overturned in *Shelley v. Kraemer*, has followed California in requiring homeowners' associations to renounce racial covenants, and in providing a private right of action through which individual owners can pressure them to do so.[30]

Does any of this matter? In the case *Mayers v. Ridley* discussed above, the trial judge made an interesting observation when he asserted that the recorder of deeds was not publicizing racial preferences when he or she recorded deeds with racial covenants. These documents really do not make a bit of difference to sale negotiations, he said. "It is stretching too far to say that the presence of the offensive language in a deed in the custody of the Recorder is going to frighten a would-be buyer." No home buyer really pays any attention to these things at the outset, he said, but rather leaves the search to "brokers, attorneys, and title insurance companies," who know perfectly well that they cannot be enforced.[31] Just as Justice Rehnquist was to say years later, everyone knows that racial covenants are illegal, so why should it matter if they show up in the chain of title, or even in a current deed? Or for that matter, in the CC&Rs, even if the buyer reads them?

Although the majority of the appeals court in *Mayers* disagreed, in fact, Judge Corcoran and Justice Rehnquist were probably right about most people. But not about everyone. In 2002, an incident occurred in the Richmond suburbs in which a fairly elderly white man refused to sell to an African American woman because, he said, he was not permitted to do so by the racial covenants on the property. She knew better, and she took the incident to an equal housing organization, which sent the usual mix of successive black and white testers, finding that he told the same story to the black testers. She thereupon sued him for violating the state's fair housing law, making the rather imposing damage claim of $100,000, which was cut back to $4,500 when she won the case. The man's neighbors said that he had simply not known that the covenants had no legal force: "He comes from a time and a place that, thank God, has gone by the wayside," said one. In addition to the fines, the judge in the case required the man to take a three-hour course at the state Fair Housing Office. What stands out about the incident, though, is that even as late as 2002, not everyone knew that racial covenants had become illegal; but what also stands out is that most people did know.[32]

This book began with a story about racial covenants—that concerning Justice Rehnquist, who in fairness was only one of many famous figures, across the political spectrum, whose titles included references to racial covenants long after the covenants had lost legal force. It is only fitting to end with another story about another person, not this time a famous person but simply an ordinary home purchaser. An African American acquaintance of one of this book's authors related the experience that her sister had a few years ago, but well into the twenty-first century. The sister had signed a contract to buy a house in a neighborhood in a large city in the Pacific Northwest. Within a few days, her realtor told her that the property had once been subject to a racially restrictive covenant. But not to worry, the realtor added hastily, those things had been illegal for years, and there was no way that anyone could possibly make anything of them.

That night the sister had a nightmare: she had moved into her new house, but the police had come to the door, entered the house, and dragged her out of what she had thought would be her new home. It was just a bad dream, of course, because the realtor basically was right: racially restrictive covenants are a thing of an older era, an unpleasant reminder of a more racist past that cannot quite be forgotten. It cannot be forgotten in part because our method for establishing property rights in real estate depends on history—but in part because the past is still inscribed on our racially divided cities and neighborhoods.

Still, would it matter to this home buyer to be able to repudiate racial restrictions in the records? Yes, probably, it would be a gratifying way to punctuate the point that times have changed. Would it matter to her if a predecessor owner of the house—perhaps even a white owner—had already repudiated them? Again, probably yes, gratifying in a different way, a symbol of social support. Repudiating racial covenants is a way of remembering the past but refusing to accept its constraints, sending a different signal to those to come. After all, racially restrictive covenants had a legal life, but they had an even more important life as signals, acting as rallying points for coordinating the segregation of neighborhoods. In their primary official life as legal requirements, but even more in the secondary life as signals, covenants did much damage. Changing the signals is a step toward repairing the damage.

Notes

Acknowledgments

Index

Notes

1. Introduction

1. "Unenforceable Covenants Are in Many Deeds," *New York Times*, August 1, 1986, A9; "Senator Biden Linked to a Restrictive Deed," *NewYork Times*, August 8, 1986, A7; "William Rehnquist on Trial," *U.S. News and World Report*, August 11, 1986, 18.
2. "Justice's Deed Excludes Jews," *Boston Globe*, July 31, 1986, 8 ("meaningless" quote); see also "Justice Knew of Deed in '74," *New York Times*, August 6, 1986, A13; "Opponents Quiz Rehnquist on Race Covenants," *Los Angeles Times*, August 1, 1986, 1.
3. "Rehnquist Hearing Turns Town to Deed Pondering," *New York Times*, August 2, 1986, 112 (neighbor); Bob Herbert, "The Real Disgrace," *New York Times*, January 10, 1999, sec. 4, 421.
4. Racial covenants in the major litigated cases generally excluded African Americans, either by name or as "non-Caucasians," but some covenants (primarily in the West) named Asians, and some (primarily in the southwest) named persons of Mexican origin. See, e.g., Foster v. Stewart, 25 P. 2d 497 (Cal. App. 1933) (covenant excluding persons of "Negro, African, or Asiatic race"); Austin v. Richardson, 278 S.W. 513 (Tex. Civ. App. 1925) (covenant excluding "Mexicans and negroes").
5. 334 U.S. 1 (1948)
6. See, e.g., William A. Fischel, "Why Are There NIMBYs?" *Land Economics* 77 (2001):144–152, 148; Lee Anne Fennell, *The Unbounded Home: Property Values Beyond Property Lines* (New Haven: Yale University Press, 2009), 184–186, 191–193.

7. For disfavor to group property, see Carol M. Rose, "Left Brain, Right Brain and History in the New Law and Economics of Property," *Oregon Law Review* 79 (2000): 479–492, 483–87.
8. See generally James W. Loewen, *Sundown Towns: A Hidden Dimension of American Racism* (New York: New Press [distributed by W.W. Norton], 2005).
9. For some of the norm entrepreneurial activities, see Herman H. Long & Charles S. Johnson, *People vs. Property* (Nashville: Fisk University Press, 1947), 17–19, 29–31, 69; Colin Gordon, *Mapping Decline: St. Louis and the Fate of the American City* (Philadelphia: University of Pennsylvania Press, 2008), 78–79.
10. For some leading examples, see Robert C. Ellickson, *Order Without Law: How Neighbors Settle Disputes* (Cambridge, Mass.: Harvard University Press, 1991); Elinor Ostrom, *Governing the Commons: The Evolution of Institutions for Collective Action* (Cambridge: Cambridge University Press,1990); Eric A. Posner, *Law and Social Norms* (Cambridge, Mass.: Harvard University Press, 2000).
11. See, e.g. Ellickson, *Order Without Law,* 225–29 (describing gossip and other informal norm enforcements).
12. For law as a focal point, see Richard H. McAdams, "Beyond the Prisoner's Dilemma: Coordination, Game Theory and the Law," *Southern California Law Review* 82 (2009): 209–258, 233–34.
13. Ellickson, *Order Without Law* (ranchers); James M. Acheson, *The Lobster Gangs of Maine* (Lebonon, N.H. : University Press of New England, 1988) (fishing communities).
14. Others have also noted the PD character of neighborhood transition issues; see, e.g., Alex M. Johnson, Jr., "How Race and Poverty Intersect to Prevent Integration: Destabilizing Race as a Vehicle to Integrate Neighborhoods," *University of Pennsylvania Law Review* 143 (1995):1595–1658, 1618–1622; and for a variant that we will discuss in Chapter 9, Abraham Bell & Gideon Parchomovsky, "The Integration Game," *Columbia Law Review* 100 (2000): 1965–2029. For a typology of norm-enforcement methods, from first-party guilt through second-party refusal to deal to third-party pressure, see Robert C. Ellickson, "A Critique of Economic and Sociological Theories of Social Control," *Journal of Legal Studies* 16 (1987): 67–99, 71–72.
15. Notably Robert Sugden, *The Economics of Rights, Co-operation and Welfare* (2d ed.; Houndmills, Basingstoke, Hampshire: Palgrave Macmillan, 2004), 61–65, 91–107.
16. See, e.g., Robert C. Weaver, *The Negro Ghetto* (New York: Russell & Russell, 1948), 250 (quoting from report of a Chicago property owners' association describing covenant drive as response in most "threatened" areas).
17. In focusing principally on the developments in racial covenants over time, the

approach of this book differs from that of Dennis Chong's very interesting study *Collective Action and the Civil Rights Movement* (Chicago and London: University of Chicago Press, 1991). Chong's primary focus is on collective action and game theory, using the civil rights movement as a source of examples—some very telling indeed.

18. "Northeast Journal," *New York Times,* Nov. 16, 1986, 150.

2. Before Covenants

1. For these incidents see Leon Litwak, *North of Slavery: The Negro in the Free States, 1790–1860* (Chicago: University of Chicago Press, 1961), 169–170.
2. For the pre–Civil War era demographics, see U.S. Dept. of Commerce, Bureau of the Census, *The Social and Economic Status of the Black Population in the United States: An Historical View, 1790–1978,* (Washington, D.C.: Government Printing Office, 1979), ix, 6–7, 11 (Table 3); Jane Riblett Wilkie, "The United States Population by Race and Urban-Rural Residence 1790–1860," *Demography* 13 (1976): 139–148, 145. Free African Americans were consistently more urbanized than the general population through all the censuses from 1800 through 1860, e.g., at 19.5 percent in 1830 (to the general U.S. figure of 8.8 percent), and 33.1 percent in 1860 (to the general figure of 19.8 percent). See also Richard H. Steckel, "The African American Population of the United States, 1790–1920," in *A Population History of North America,* ed. Michael R. Haines & Richard H. Steckel (Cambridge: Cambridge University Press, 2000), 433–481, at table 10.5, 454–55. For living conditions of northern free African Americans, see Litwak, *North of Slavery,* 168–70.
3. Litwak, *North of Slavery,* 168 (New York); see also Gilbert Osofsky, *Harlem: The Making of a Ghetto* 9–12 (2d ed.; New York: Harper & Row, 1971), 9–12. Five Points was the area in Lower Manhattan where Park, Worth, and Baxter Streets intersected. For interracial contacts in New Orleans and other southern areas, Loren Schweninger, "Prosperous Blacks in the South, 1790–1880," *American Historical Review* 95 (1990): 31–56, 34–35, 44–47. For more on New Orleans's white gentlemen's *placage* or contractual liaisons with free black or mixed race women, see <http://www.frenchcreoles.com/CreoleCulture/quadroons/quadroons.htm>.
4. Schweninger, "Prosperous Blacks in the South," 40.
5. See, e.g., Michael Vorenberg, "Abraham Lincoln and the Politics of Black Colonization," *Journal of the Abraham Lincoln Association* 14 (1993): 22–45, and the numerous sources cited therein.
6. Of the many studies of this era, the classic history is Eric Foner, *Reconstruction: America's Unfinished Revolution: 1863–1877* (New York: Harper Collins, 1988) 128–142, 198–216, 251–280, 516–601.

7. For jailhouse contracts and employee intimidation, Pete Daniel, *The Shadow of Slavery: Peonage in the South, 1901–1969* (Urbana: University of Illinois Press, 1990), particularly 26–30; for early evolution of convict leasing and jailhouse contracts, Douglas A. Blackmon, *Slavery by Another Name* (New York: Anchor Books [Random House], 2008), 53–57, 65–69 and passim; for major cases, see Peonage Cases, 123 F. 671 (D.C. Alabama, 1903); Bailey v. Alabama 219 U.S. 219 (1911).
8. Jennifer Roback, "Southern Labor in the Jim Crow Era: Exploitative or Competitive?" *University of Chicago Law Review* 51 (1984): 1161–1192; David E. Bernstein, "The Law and Economics of Post–Civil War Restrictions on Interstate Migration by African Americans," *Texas Law Review* 76 (1998): 781–823. For the ongoing use of vagrancy and other petty offences to incarcerate African Americans, Blackmon, *Slavery by Another Name,* 7, 53, 375; for the policing of intimate relationships, see Katherine M. Franke, "Becoming a Citizen: Reconstruction Era Regulation of African American Marriages," *Yale Journal of Law and the Humanities* 11(1999): 251–310, 305–307. Even newer wildlife laws favoring "sporting" methods of hunting suppressed rural African Americans' hunting for food; see Thomas Lund, "Nineteenth Century Wildlife Law: A Study of Elite Influence," *Arizona State Law Journal* 33 (2001): 935–984, 962 and footnote 161 (2001).
9. Roback, "Southern Labor in the Jim Crow Era," 1192. For land ownership patterns, see Claude F. Oubre, *Forty Acres and a Mule: The Freedman's Bureau and Black Land Ownership* (Baton Rouge: Louisiana State University Press, 1978), 179 (Table 2), showing black farmers' ownership in seven Deep South states in 1900, ranging from high of 30.8 percent (Texas) to low of 13.7 percent (Georgia), with overall farm operators' ownership at 19.1 percent for the seven states. For land sales to black farmers in spite of white norms to the contrary, see Loren Schweninger, *Black Property Owners in the South 1790–1915* (Urbana: University of Illinois Press, 1990), 145–53.
10. Schweninger, *Black Property Owners,* 154–55, 166–70, 177–83 (greater urban property ownership and economic possibilities); Howard N. Rabinowitz, "More Than the Woodward Thesis: Assessing the Strange Career of Jim Crow," *Journal of American History* 75 (1988) 842–856, 848 (some urban political influence).
11. For a capsule history and references, see Ira Berlin, *The Making of African America: The Four Great Migrations* (New York: Penguin, 2010), particularly Chap. 4, "The Passage to the North," 152–200, and sources cited therein, 272–281. See also Steven Grant Meyer, *As Long as They Don't Move Next Door: Segregation and Racial Conflict in American Neighborhoods* (Lanham, Md.: Rowman & Littlefield, 2000) 13–23. Southern black urbanization in this era is especially stressed by Howard N. Rabinowitz; see, e.g., his *Race, Ethnicity, and*

Urbanization 209–211 (1994). For growing urban percentages, see Steckel, "African American Population," 465–66. For Washington, D.C., and the civil service, see Schweninger, "Prosperous Blacks," 51–52; Nicholas Patler, *Jim Crow and the Wilson Administration: Protesting Federal Segregation in the Early Twentieth Century* (Boulder: University Press of Colorado, 2004) 3, 10. For Harlem's growth, see Osofsky, *Harlem*, 105. For a series of personal accounts, largely drawn from the later years of the Great Migration, see Isabel Wilkerson, *The Warmth of Other Suns: The Epic Story of America's Great Migration* (New York: Random House, 2010).

12. See generally Meyer, *As Long As They Don't Move Next Door*, 16. For Baltimore, see also Garrett Power, "Apartheid Baltimore Style: The Residential Segregation Ordinances of 1910–1913," *Maryland Law Review* 42 (1983): 289–328, 290. For Kansas City, Kevin Fox Gotham, "Urban Space, Restrictive Covenants, and the Origins of Racial Residential Segregation in an American City, 1900–1950," *International Journal of Urban and Regional Research* 24 (2000): 616–633, 619–20.

13. Two well-known European commentators on the weakened social ties of urban areas were Emile Durkheim, *De la Division du Travail Social: Etude sur l'Organsation des Societes Superieres* (Paris: Germer Bailliere, 1893), and Ferdinand Toennies, *Gemeinschaft und Gesellschaft* (Leipzig: Fues's Verlag 1887). For southern ubanization and "uppityness" see David Delaney, *Race, Place and the Law 1836–1948* (Austin: University of Texas Press, 1998), 100–101. For several early twentieth century lynchings for trivial offenses to white sensibilities in the South, see Leon Litwak, *Trouble in Mind: Black Southerners in the Age of Jim Crow* (New York: Alfred A. Knopf, 1998), 306–311.

14. Gunner Myrdahl referred to the social distance/physical distance trade-off in his classic work, *An American Dilemma: The Negro Problem and Modern Democracy* (New York, London: Harper & Bros. 1944), 621. "Pigtown" was a name given to the first major black slum in Baltimore; Power, "Apartheid Baltimore Style," 290.

15. Rose Helper, *Racial Policies and Practices of Real Estate Brokers* (Minneapolis: University of Minnesota Press, 1969), 98.

16. For crosscurrents of race, class and gender in railroad segregation laws, see Kenneth W. Mack, "Law, Society, Identity, and the Making of the Jim Crow South: Travel and Segregation on Tennessee Railroads, 1875–1905," *Law and Social Inquiry* 24 (1999): 377–408; Barbara Y. Welke, "When All the Women Were White, All the Blacks Were Men: Gender, Race, Class, and the Road to Plessy," *Law and History Review* 13 (1995): 261–316; see also Welke's "Beyond Plessy: Space, Status, and Race in the Era of Jim Crow," *Utah Law Review* 2000: 267–299, 270–271, 273–274, describing railroad companies' resistance to legal segregation.

17. Plessy v. Ferguson, 163 U.S. 537 (1896). The Louisiana statute at issue required "equal but separate" facilities; 163 U.S. 540, a phrase that the Court repeated with respect to a Mississippi statute, id. at 547. Only Justice Harlan's dissent used the phrase "separate but equal" for which the case came to be known. Id., at 552.
18. *Plessy,* 551–52. See also Jack M. Balkin, "Plessy, Brown and Grutter: A Play in Three Acts," *Cardozo Law Review* 26 (2005): 1689–1730, 1693–1704. This division of types of rights continues in some modern thinking; see, e.g., Amrita Basu, "Who Secures Women's Capabilities in Martha Nussbaum's Quest for Social Justice?" 19 *Columbia Journal of Gender and the Law* 19 (2010) 201–218, 202, noting that modern philosopher Nussbaum rejects the sequencing of political and civil rights before social and economic rights.
19. For a slightly later example, see Guinn v. United States, 238 U.S. 347 (1915), which invalidated Louisiana's grandfather clause exception to a literacy requirement, on grounds that it was applied discriminatorily, but finding no fault with a literacy requirement itself.
20. *Plessy,* 550–51.
21. Jim Crow laws have been much studied; a classic is C. Vann Woodward, *The Strange Career of Jim Crow* (New York: Oxford University Press,1951); some other perspectives include Jack Temple Kirby, *Darkness at the Dawning: Race and Reform in the Progressive South* (Philadelphia: J. B. Lippencott, 1972), and, more recently, Leon Litwak, *Trouble in Mind.* See also Howard Rabinowitz, "From Exclusion to Segregation: Southern Race Relations 1865–1890," *Journal of American History* 63 (1976): 325–350, arguing that Jim Crow segregation laws replaced outright exclusion of African Americans. Gunnar Myrdahl's classic study of race relations in America also discussed Jim Crow laws at a time when they were still in force: *American Dilemma,* 578–82, 628–30. For private discrimination in otherwise public facilities, see, e.g., Charlotte Park and Recreation Assn. v. Barringer, 88 S.E.2d 114 (N.C. 1955), cert. den. 350 U.S. 983 (1956) (describing private donation in 1929 to public body for white-only golf course).
22. People ex rel Gaskill v. Forest Home Cemetery Co., 101 N.E.219 (1913).
23. Patler, *Jim Crow and the Wilson Administration,* 19–20, 54–67; Judson MacLaurey, "The Federal Government and Negro Workers Under President Wilson," speech delivered at Annual Meeting, Society for History in the Federal Government, Washington, D.C., Mar. 16, 2000, available at http://www.dol.gov/asp/programs/history/shfgproo.htm
24. Patler, *Jim Crow and the Wilson Administration,* 56–67, 90–112, 154–171.
25. Harry Golden, "The Vertical Negro Plan," in *Only in America* (Cleveland, Ohio: World Publishing Company,1958), 121–123; also reprinted in Jack Claiborne and William Price, eds., *Discovering North Carolina: A Tarheel*

Reader (Chapel Hill: University of North Carolina Press, 1991), 340–342. The commentary originally appeared in Golden's newsletter *The Carolina Israelite* in 1956, in response to several bills by the North Carolina legislature to avoid school desegregation.

26. "Bessie and Sadie: The Delany Sisters Relive a Century," *Smithsonian Magazine*, October, 1993, 144 (adapted from their book, Sarah Louise Delany, Annie Elizabeth Delany, with Amy Hill Hearth, *Having Our Say: The Delany Sisters' First 100 Years* (New York: Bantam Books, 1993).
27. For diversity's short-term negative effect on social capital, see Robert D. Putnam, "*E Pluribus Unum:* Diversity and Community in the Twenty-First Century," *Scandinavian Political Studies* 30 (2007): 137–174, 148–150.
28. For the older treatises, see for example H. G. Wood, *A Practical Treatise on the Law of Nuisances* (3rd ed., San Francisco: Bancroft-Whitney, 1893); Joseph A. Joyce & Howard C. Joyce, *Treatise on the Law Governing Nuisances* (Albany: M. Bender, 1906).
29. Hertle v. Riddle, 106 S.W. 282, 286 (Ky. 1907).
30. U.S. v. Coulter 25 F. Cas. 675 (D.C. Cir. 1805) (affirming fine against establishment as a common nuisance for selling liquor to "negroes and slaves, assembled in considerable numbers" on the Sabbath).
31. Sanders v. Ward, 25 Ga. 109 (1858) (allowing a will that emancipated slaves outside the state, describing freed slaves within the state as a "great nuisance").
32. 29 Kan. 292 (1883).
33. Joyce and Joyce, *Treatise on . . . Nuisances*, at 49, n. 22. For similar cases in this era, see Rachel D. Godsil, "Race Nuisance: The Politics of Law in the Jim Crow Era," 105 *Michigan Law Review* 105 (2006): 505–558, 516–519.
34. See for example Boyd v. Bd. of Councilmen of Frankfort, 77 S.W. 669 (Ky. 1903).
35. Diggs v. Morgan College, 105 A. 157 (Md. 1918).
36. For mixture of race-and-conduct cases, see Godsil, "Race Nuisance," 519–529. For contractual element, see, e.g., Wyatt v. Adair, 110 A. 801 (Alab. 1926). In this case the state supreme court ruled that a landlord breached a lease to a white family when he rented a second unit to a black family that would share toilet facilities, noting with approval that the "customary" practice against interracial sharing was an implicit part of landlord's and tenant's contractual arrangement. Thanks to Marilyn Drees for alerting the authors to this case.
37. Fox v. Corbitt, 194 S.W. 88 (Tenn. 1917).
38. Stratton v. Conway, 301 S.W.2d 332 (Tenn. 1957).
39. Ernst Freund, *The Police Power: Public Policy and Constitutional Rights* (Chicago: Callaghan, 1904), sec. 616, at 639. Freund was discussing such matters as floods and weeds, but he took a chary view of racial segregation, e.g., sec 700, at 720–21, where he argued that laws distinguishing between the races were in practice discriminatory.

40. On the externalizing of enforcement costs, see David E. Bernstein, "Philip Sober Controlling Philip Drunk: *Buchanan v. Warley* in Historical Perspective," *Vanderbilt Law Review* 54 (1998): 797–880, 803, 859.
41. For zoning history, M. T. Van Hecke, "Zoning Ordinances and Restrictions in Deeds," *Yale Law Journal* 37 (1928) 407–425. For history and the influence of the Fair, Anthony Sutcliffe, *Towards the Planned City: Germany, Britain, the United States, and France, 1780–1914* (New York: St. Martin's Press,1981), 32–33, 97–98, 102–110, 184–185. However, William H. Wilson, *The City Beautiful Movement* (Baltimore: Johns Hopkins University Press, 1989), 53–74, downplays the influence of the World's Fair on the City Beautiful movement.
42. Sutcliffe, *Towards the Planned City,* 116–125.
43. Ibid., 115. For other critical views of early zoning, particularly as status-quo oriented, see Eric R. Claeys, "*Euclid* Lives? The Uneasy Legacy of Progressivism in Zoning," *Fordham Law Review* 73 (2004), 731–770 (2004); Martha A. Lees, "Preserving Property Values? Preserving Proper Homes? Preserving Privilege? The Pre-Euclid Debate over Zoning for Exclusively Private Residential Areas, 1916–1926," 56 *University of Pittsburgh* 56 (1994): 367–440; Raphael Fischler, "The Metropolitan Dimension of Early Zoning: Revisiting the 1916 New York City Ordinance," *Journal of the American Planning Association* 64 (1998): 170–188, 173–178. For later association with corruption, see, e.g., John A. Gardner and Theodore R. Lyman, *Decisions For Sale: Corruption and Reform in Land-Use and Building Regulation* (New York: Praeger, 1978).
44. Village of Euclid v. Ambler Realty Co., 272 U.S. 365 (1926); for the more modern turn to mixed uses, see Brian W. Ohm and Robert J. Sitkowski, "The Influence of New Urbanism on Local Ordinances: The Twilight of Zoning?" *Urban Lawyer* 35 (2003), 783–794, 784–85.
45. David M.P. Freund, *Colored Property: State Policy and White Racial Politics in Suburban America* (Chicago and London: University of Chicago Press, 2007), 54–66.
46. John F. Dillon, *Treatise on the Law of Municipal Corporations* (Chicago: J. Cockcroft, 1872), sec. 55, at 101–102.
47. One particularly famous constitutional law case involved such regulations: Slaughter-house Cases, 83 U.S. 36 (1873), 62–63.
48. New York City began to regulate tenement housing in 1867, amending its ordinance in 1887; see Health Dept. of the City of New York v. Rector of Trinity Church, 39 N.E. 833 (N.Y. 1895). New York State passed its own tenement law in 1901, upheld in Tenement House Dept. v. Moeschen, 72 N.E. 231 (N.Y. 1904) For a turn-of-the-century description of New York's and some other states' and cities' tenement legislation, see Robert W. DeForest, "A Brief History of the Housing Movement in America," 51 *Annals of the American Academy of*

Political and Social Science 51 (1914): 8–16. DeForest, 16, particularly mentions the influence of Jacob Riis's 1903 book, *How the Other Half Lives,* in generating support for tenement legislation.

49. For a chary view of aesthetic regulation, Welch v. Swasey, 214 U.S. 91, 106–107 (1908) (citing Commonwealth v. Boston Advertising Co., 74 N.E. 601 (Mass. 1905); *Welch,* however, approved height limitations on safety grounds, citing fire protection.
50. Welch v. Swasey, 107–108. For billboard regulation based on both fire and crime prevention, see Thomas Cusack Co. v. City of Chicago 242 U.S. 526 (1916).
51. Fischler, *Metropolitan Dimension of Early Zoning,* 171–72, cites New York's 1916 ordinance as the first to regulate both bulk and uses citywide.
52. Power, "Apartheid Baltimore Style," 289–300.
53. Ibid., 310; Bernstein, "Philip Sober," 834–36; Richard Sterner, *The Negro's Share: A Study of Income, Consumption, Housing and Public Assistance* (New York, London: Harper & Brothers, 1943), 206 (cities with racial zoning); Clarence Lang, *Grassroots at the Gateway: Class Politics and Black Freedom Struggle in St. Louis, 1936–75* (Ann Arbor: University of Michigan Press, 2009), 12 (St. Louis ordinance).
54. Power, "Apartheid Baltimore Style," 300; Bernstein, "Philip Sober," 844–45.
55. Osofsky, *Harlem,* 46–52; David Godschalk, *Veiled Visions: The 1906 Atlanta Race Riot and the Reshaping of American Race Relations* (Chapel Hill: Univ. of North Carolina Press, 2005); Roberta Senechal, *The Sociogenesis of a Race Riot: Springfield, Illinois* (Urbana: University of Illinois Press, 1990). Disturbances after the Johnson-Jeffries fight gave a number of cities a reason to ban the movie of the fight; Barak Y. Orbach "The Johnson-Jeffries Fight and the Censorship of Black Supremacy," *New York University Journal of Law and Liberty* 5 (2010): 270–346.
56. See Power, "Apartheid Baltimore Style," 299–300.
57. The first ordinance was overturned without a written opinion; a second version was then enacted, then reenacted with amendments. See Power, "Apartheid Baltimore Style," 303–305. This amended version was overturned in State v. Gurry, 88 A. 546 (Md. 1913), in an opinion that stressed the intrusion on vested rights.
58. Carey v. City of Atlanta, 84 S.E. 456 (Ga. 1915); State v. Darnell 81 S.E. 338 (N.C., 1914).
59. 245 U.S. 60 (1917). For the early NAACP legal tactic of the "test case" in general and the Buchanan case specifically, see Susan D. Carle, "Race, Class and Legal Ethics in the Early NAACP (1910–20)," *Law and History Review* 20 (2002): 97–146, 124–28.
60. Buchanan v. Warley, 80–81.

61. The most famous of these cases was Lochner v. New York, 198 U.S. 45 (1905), invalidating, as a violation of freedom of contract, a New York labor law setting a maximum hour limitation. The literature on this case and its successors is voluminous and generally unfavorable. For a review and an effort to rescue the case, see David E. Bernstein, *Rehabilitating Lochner: Defending Individual Rights Against Progressive Reform* (Chicago: University of Chicago Press, 2011).
62. The Chinese laundry case was Yick Wo v. Hopkins, 118 U.S. 356 (1886); cf. Soon Hing v. Crowley, 113 U.S. 703 (1885).
63. For a variant on this theme, see Buchanan v. Warley, Brief for the Plaintiff in Error (Clayton B. Blakey) 42–44, in a concluding section entitled "What America Owes to the Negro."
64. A much-discussed modern variation on this idea is the emphasis on promoting economic development by securing formal land titles to informal squatters, championed by the Peruvian Hernando DeSoto in influential book, *The Mystery of Capital: Why Capitalism Triumphs in the West and Fails Everywhere Else* (New York: Basic Books, 2000).
65. Buchanan v. Warley, Brief for the Plaintiff in Error (Blakey), at 8–15, 16, 41–42; Brief for the Plaintiff in Error 12, 14–17, 25 (Moorfield Storey and Harold S. Davis); Brief for the Plaintiff in Error on Rehearing 23–27 (Clayton B. Blakey and Moorfield Storey); Amicus Curiae Brief of the Baltimore Branch, NAACP (W. Ashbie Hawkins), 20. Blakey was the Louisville attorney hired by the NAACP, and Storey was national NAACP president; see Roger L. Rice, "Residential Segregation by Law, 1910–1917," *Journal of Southern History* 34 (1968) 179–199, 188. Despite these arguments in the *Buchanan* case, Kenneth W. Mack argues that African American civil rights lawyers of the era distrusted common law freedom of contract prescriptions: Mack, "Rethinking Civil Rights Lawyering and Politics in the Era Before *Brown*," *Yale Law Journal* 115 (2005): 256–354, 276, note 54.
66. For Louisville's arguments, see Buchanan v. Warley, Brief for the Defendant in Error (Stuart Chevalier and Pendleton Beckley, attorneys for City of Louisville, March 27, 1916), 3, 11, 20, 25, 47–48, 79, 81–91; Supplemental and Reply Brief for the Defendant in Error on Rehearing 142–45 (Stuart Chevalier and Pendleton Beckley). For Bernstein's comments, "Philip Sober," 799–803, 836–60. Power, "Apartheid Baltimore Style," 300–302, also comments on the "progressive" character of the arguments for Baltimore's racial zoning.
67. Louisville's lawyers made much of the dangers of "amalgamation," citing antimiscegenation laws and adding an Appendix with an array of racist theories of the day. Reply Brief, 123, 142–45. For the Court's treatment of this argument, Buchanan v. Warley, 81. For commentary on property values and violence, Bernstein, "Philip Sober," 836–60.

68. For a contemporary account of adverse neighborhood reaction, including whites' actions due to property value fears, see Louise Venable Kennedy, *The Negro Peasant Turns Cityward: Effects of Recent Migrations to Northern Cities* (New York: AMS Press, 1930), 146–150.
69. For riots, Thomas Lee Philpott, *The Slum and the Ghetto: Neighborhood Deterioration and Middle-Class Reform, Chicago 1880–1930,* at 170–77 (New York: Oxford University Press, 1978).
70. Tyler v. Harmon, 104 So. 200 (La. 1925) (describing and upholding New Orleans's ordinance); reversed per curiam Harmon v. Tyler, 273 U.S. 668 (1927). For Richmond's initial ordinance, Irvine v. City of Clifton Forge, 97 S.E. 310 (Va. 1918); for the follow-up, City of Richmond v. Deans, 37 F. Supp. 712 (1930) (briefly describing ordinance that it invalidated), aff'd per curiam, 281 U.S. 704 (1930).
71. For Atlanta, Bowen v City of Atlanta, 125 S.E. 199 (Ga. 1924); see also Smith v. City of Atlanta, 132 S.E. 66 (Ga. 1926), discussed in Bernstein, "Philip Sober," 862. For Oklahoma City, Allen v. Oklahoma City, 52 P. 2d 1054 (Okla. 1935) (ruling ordinance unconstitutional under Buchanan); see also Jones v. Oklahoma City, 78 F.2d 860 (10th Cir. 1935) (dismissing federal case against ordinance for want of federal jurisdiction).
72. For the drain on the NAACP, Bernstein, "Philip Sober," 868; Meyer, *As Long As They Don't Move Next Door,* 27.

3. The Big Guns Silenced

1. For an extensive description of the role of restrictive covenants in the early suburban development in the United States, see Robert M. Fogelson, *Bourgeois Nightmares: Suburbia, 1870–1930* (New Haven: Yale University Press, 2005).
2. Ibid., 32–34. Fogelson notes that the very wealthy did buy huge estates, but even some of them disliked the isolation.
3. For the classic theory of regulatory competition among localities, see Charles Tiebout, "A Pure Theory of Public Expenditures," *Journal of Political Economy* 64 (1956): 416–424. Private covenants should allow even greater tailoring in local residential markets.
4. Gerald Korngold, "The Emergence of Private Land Use Controls in Large-Scale Subdivisions: The Companion Story *Village of Euclid v. Ambler Realty Co.,*" *Case Western Law Review* 51 (2001) 617–644, 617–20; Evan McKenzie, *Privatopia: Homeowners Associations and the Rise of Private Government* 36–38 (New Haven: Yale University Press, 1994); for a critical analysis of specific types of restriction, Fogelson, *Bourgeoise Nightmares,* at 118–200.
5. See Helen Monchow, *The Use of Deed Restrictions in Subdivision Development* (Chicago: Institute for Research in Land Economics and Public Utilities, 1928),

47–50, describing racial deed restrictions in forty of eighty-four planned subdivisions; Fogelson, *Bourgeoise Nightmares,* 95–103; see also Korngold, "Emergence of Private Land Use Controls," 638–39, noting the possibility of indirect racial restraints in the Shaker Heights subdivision outside Cleveland.

6. Kathan v. Stevenson, 12 N.W.2d 332, 334 (Mich. 1943).
7. For the bank run analogy to illustrate assurance or Stag Hunt games, see Richard H. McAdams, "Beyond the Prisoner's Dilemma: Coordination, Game Theory and the Law," *Southern California Law Review* 82 (2009): 209–258, 221.
8. Gandolfo v. Hartman, 49 F. 181, 182 (Cir. Ct., S.D. Cal. 1892).
9. For a more extensive discussion, see Chapter 7. The distinction was a key issue in the racial covenant case, Shelley v. Kraemer, 334 U.S. 1 (1948), to be discussed in that chapter.
10. Nathan William MacChesney, *The Principles of Real Estate Law* (New York: MacMillan, 1927), 586–587.
11. See, e.g., Title Guarantee & Trust Co. v. Garrott, 183 P. 470, 471 (Cal. App. 1919) (upholding constitutionality of racial covenant without mentioning *Gandolfo*); Parmalee v. Morris, 188 N.W. 330, 331 (MI 1922) (distinguishing *Gandolfo*); Kraemer v. Shelley, 198 S.W. 679, 683 (Mo. 1946) (describing *Gandolfo* as invalid); Hurd v. Hodge, 162 F.2d 233, 240 (1947) (Edgerton, diss.) (majority not mentioning *Gandolfo* despite dissent's prominent citation). As will be discussed in Chapter 8, the Missouri case was reversed in 1948 in Shelley v. Kraemer, 334 U.S. 1, and the D.C. case was reversed at the same time in Hurd v. Hodge, 334 U.S. 24. For the reference to *Gandolfo* as a "stray," see the quotation in D. O. McGovney, "Racial Residential Segregation by State Court Enforcement of Restrictive Agreements, Covenants or Conditions in Deeds is Unconstitutional," *California Law Review* 33 (1945): 5–39, 7.
12. The major case from Michigan was Parmalee v. Morris in 1922; that from Missouri was Koehler v. Rowland, 205 S.W. 217 (Mo. 1918). Other much-cited early cases upholding racially restrictive covenants were California's Title Guarantee and Trust v. Garrott in 1919, and Louisiana's Queensborough Land Co. v. Cazeaux, 68 So. 641 (La. 1915). *Queensborough* predated *Buchanan* and hence could not cite it, but it was cited in later state cases that also ignored *Buchanan;* see, e.g., *Title Guarantee,* 471; *Parmalee,* at 331.
13. Corrigan v. Buckley, 271 U.S. 323, 330 (1926).
14. See, e.g., Eckhart v. Irons, 20 N.E. 687, 692 (Ill. 1889), stating that all doubts about a land restriction were to be resolved in favor of "natural rights, and against restrictions thereon," quoted favorably in another subdivision restriction case, Hutchinson v. Ulrich, 34 N.E. 556, 557 (Ill. App. 1893); Boyden v. Roberts, 111 N.W. 701 (Wis. 1907), enforcing restrictions between subsequent purchasers in high-end Forest Glen summer community, over a strong dissent that would have treated the covenants as merely personal contracts.

15. For a comprehensive historical account of the alienability of land in the colonial era and early republic, see Claire Priest, "Creating an American Property Law: Alienability and Its Limits in American History," *Harvard Law Review* 120 (2006): 385–458, 441–47. Priest argues, however, that whatever the rhetoric, a key factor in early American anti-entailment measures was assistance to creditors rather than anti-aristocratic sentiment.
16. See, e.g., Cowell v. Colo. Springs Co., 100 U.S. 55, 57 (1879); White v. White, 150 S.E. 531, 532 (W. Va. 1929)
17. Cowell v. Colo. Springs Co., 57. Fogelson, *Bourgeoise Nightmares*, 62, describes the advice of lawyers against racial restrictions for mid-1890s Baltimore suburban development; see also White v. White, 539, a 1929 case that explicitly distinguished restraints on uses from restraints on the race of the owner.
18. The phrase derives from Gary Becker, *The Economics of Discrimination* (2d ed.; Chicago: University of Chicago Press, 1971) (originally published in 1957).
19. Cazeaux, 643; Koehler, 220; see also Kemp v. Rubin, 69 N.Y. Supp. 680, 685 (N.Y. Sup. 1947). Some other courts, for example those of Washington, D.C., permitted racial covenants to prohibit sales to minorities without discussing the specific issue of restraints on alienation; see, e.g., Torrey v. Wolfes, 6 F.2d 702 (1925).
20. The main cases for California and Michigan were, respectively, Los Angeles Investment Co. v. Gary, 186 P. 2d 596 (Cal. 1919); Porter v. Barrett, 206 N.W. 532 (Mich. 1925).
21. Title Guarantee and Trust v. Garrott, 473.
22. Los Angeles Investment v. Gary, 597; Porter v. Barrett, 534; see also Title Guarantee v. Garrott, 474. West Virginia's supreme court appeared to take a similar position in White v. White, although only sale and not lease was at issue in that case.
23. Arthur T. Martin, "Segregation of Residences of Negroes," *Michigan Law Review* 32 (1934): 721–42, 737. The case was Stratton v. Cornelius, 277 P. 893 (Cal. App. 1929); a similar result occurred in Littlejohns v. Henderson, 295 P. 95 (Cal. App. 1931), where the black purchasers were prohibited from residing in the residences they had bought. Aside from Martin, another sharp contemporary critique of the sale/use distinction appeared in Merrill I. Schnebley, "Restraints Upon the Alienation of Legal Interests II," *Yale Law Journal* 44 (1935): 1186–1215.
24. L.A. Investment Co. v. Gary, at 598. Chapter Nine will discuss some more recent criticism of policies promoting home ownership.
25. 17 U.S. 518, 667.
26. For some of the traits ascribed (or not ascribed) to corporations, see Arthur W. Machen, "Corporate Personality," *Harvard Law Review* 24 (1910–1911): 347–65, 348 (attributions like fraud and malice); Felix S. Cohen, "Transcendental Nonsense and the Functional Approach," *Columbia Law Review* 35 (1935):

809–849, 811–812 (characteristics of corporate "presence"); Sanford A. Schane, "The Corporation is a Person: The Language of a Legal Fiction," *Tulane Law Review* 61 (1986–1987): 563–610, 595, 607 (no physical presence). Much discussion of corporate "personhood" has been generated by the U.S. Supreme Court's decision in Citizens United v. Federal Election Commission, 130 S. Ct. 876 (2010) that corporations are comparable to individual persons for purposes of laws regulating "speech" through political donations.

27. Leon Fink, *Workingmen's Democracy: The Knights of Labor and American Politics* (Urbana: University of Illinois Press, 1983), 150 (schoolchildren); Howard N. Rabinowitz, "From Exclusion to Segregation: Southern Race Relations 1865–1890," *Journal of American History* 63 (1976): 325–50, 337 (prostitutes), 327–28, 331–32 (parks, other public places and facilities, recreational locations). For a comprehensive list of segregation statutes with respect to hospitals, schools, prisons, hotels, public facilities, and more, see Pauli Murray, ed., *States' Laws on Race and Color* (Cincinnati: Women's Division of Christian Service, Board of Missions and Church Extension, Methodist Church, 1950), 17.
28. People's Pleasure Park v. Rohleder, 61 S.E. 794 (Va. 1908). For a fuller description of the background to the case, see Richard R. W. Brooks, "Incorporating Race," *Columbia Law Review* 106 (2006): 2023–2094, 2047–2056.
29. People's Pleasure Park v. Rohleder, 795–96.
30. Brooks, "Incorporating Race," 2024, 2057, citing complaints of formalism by early twentieth-century legal scholar I. Maurice Wormser; for similar doubts two decades later, see M. T. Van Hecke, "Zoning Ordinances and Restrictions in Deeds," *Yale Law Journal* 37 (1928): 407–425, 412
31. Cf. Morton J. Horwitz, "Santa Clara Revisited: The Development of Corporate Theory," *West Virginia Law Review* (1985)173–224, 182, asserting that some courts treated corporations similarly to partnership until sometime before World War I.
32. For an interesting sidelight on these issues, see the brief remarks of Justice Powell in Village of Arlington Heights v. Metropolitan Housing Development Corporation, 429 U.S. 252, 263 (1977), to the effect that a low income housing corporation had no race and thus could not bring a charge of racial discrimination; but see Hudson Valley Freedom Theater, Inc., v. Heimbach, 671 F.2d 702, 707 (2d cir. 1982), certiorari denied 459 U.S. 857 (1982), in which respected judge Henry Friendly allowed that he hoped the Supreme Court would not follow Justice Powell's remark "slavishly."
33. For Virginia, A. Leon Higginbotham, Jr., and Barbara Kopytoff, "Racial Purity and Interracial Sex in the Law of Colonial and Antebellum Virginia," *Georgetown Law Journal* 77 (1989): 1967–2030, 1975–81; for Virginia and other states, Daniel J. Sharfstein, "The Secret History of Race in the United States," *Yale Law Journal* 112 (2003) 1473–1509; Michael A. Elliott, "Telling the Difference:

Nineteenth Century Narratives of Legal Taxonomy," *Law and Social Inquiry* 24 (1999): 611–636; Ariela J. Gross, "Litigating Whiteness: Trials of Racial Determination in the Nineteenth-Century South," *Yale Law Journal* 108 (1998): 109–188. Some modern corporate owners turned the older "common knowledge" approach on its head, asserting that widespread race-baiting comments made their corporation an appropriate claimant against racial discrimination. See Bains LLC v. Arco Products Co., 220 F. Supp. 2d 1193, 1196 (W.D. Wash. 2002); the corporate claim was affirmed though other parts of the case were overruled in Bains LLC v. Arco Products Co. 405 F.3d 764 (9th Cir. 2005).

34. Van Hecke, "Zoning Ordinances and Restrictions in Deeds," 412 (citing Frick v Webb, 281 Fed. 487 (N.D. Cal. 1922)).
35. Dadoo, Ltd., and Others v. Krugersdorp Municipal Council, 1919 (1920) A.D. 530 (A) (S. Africa), 540–541.
36. Ibid., 549–550.
37. Edward E. Mansur, "The Work of the Missouri Supreme Court for the Year 1939," *Missouri Law Review* 5 (1940) 377–510, 407 (disapproving); Elvin R. Latty, "The Corporate Entity as a Solvent of Legal Problems," *Michigan Law Review* 34 (1936) 597–636, 609–610 (disapproving but more ambiguously); Isaac N. Groner and David M. Helfeld, "Race Discrimination in Housing," *Yale Law Journal* 57 (1948) 426–458, 446, note 97 (apparently approving). *Rohleder* was cited in a number of other notes and comments, but generally only for the proposition that a corporation is separate from the identity of its shareholders.
38. Perkins v. Trustees of Monroe Ave. Church of Christ, 70 N.E.2d 487, 489 (Ohio Ct. App. 1946).
39. Brief for the Defendants-Appellants at 48–49, App. A, 70 N.E. 2d 487 (No. 30931).
40. Perkins v. Trustees of Monroe Ave. Church of Christ, 490.
41. Ibid., 492–93.
42. Perkins v. Trustees. of Monroe Ave. Church of Christ, 72 N.E.2d 97 (Ohio 1947) (per curiam); Brooks, "Incorporating Race," 2060–2061.
43. Trustees of the Monroe Ave. Church of Christ v. Perkins, 334 U.S. 813 (1948) (per curiam).

4. Pushing Down the Ghosts

1. Robert M. Fogelson, *Bourgeois Nightmares: Suburbia, 1870–1930* (New Haven: Yale Univ. Press, 2005), 56–59 (developers' and purchasers' motivations), 78–80 (purchasers' strong preference for racial restrictions).
2. *Body Heat* (Warner Brothers 1981). Putting the movies to one side, sophisticated lawyers have made errors about the RAP in real cases; see, e.g., Symphony

Space, Inc. v. Pergola Properties, Inc., 669 N.E. 799 (N.Y. 1996) (option contract failed for violation of RAP).

3. See Chapter 3. The externality of added search costs for all land purchasers is explored at length in Thomas W. Merrill and Henry E. Smith, "Optimal Standardization in the Law of Property: the *Numerus Clausus* Principle," *Yale Law Journal* 110 (2000): 1–70.
4. *Restatement of the Law Third–Property (Servitudes),* Sec. 3.3, in *A Concise Restatement of Property* (St. Paul: American Law Institute Publishers, 2001), stating that the RAP is inapplicable to "servitudes," i.e., deed restrictions, covenants, easements. This was the general view by the 1930s; see Note, "Enforcement of Affirmative Covenants Running With the Land," *Yale Law Journal* 47 (1938): 821–827, 826, stating that the strict RAP was not applicable to covenants but the antiperpetuity policy still applied. Some doubts about the applicability of the RAP to covenants persisted for decades, however; see, e.g., Olin L. Browder, "Running Covenants and Public Policy," *Michigan Law Review* 77 (1978): 12–46, 30, citing ambiguous cases from the 1960s.
5. For an early case with a relatively short duration, see, e.g., Title Guarantee and Trust v. Garrott, 183 P. 2d 470 (Cal. App. 1919). For the later survey, see Helen Monchow, *The Use of Deed Restrictions in Subdivision Development* (Chicago: Institute for Research in Land Economics and Public Utilities, 1928) 56. Fogelson, *Bourgeois Nightmares,* 106–109, discusses developers' struggles with various aspects of covenant duration.
6. See Arthur T. Martin, "Segregation of Residences of Negroes," *Michigan Law Review* 32 (1934): 721–42, 731–732, noting the RAP's inapplicability to reversionary covenants. Martin's article as a whole sharply criticizes the courts' formalism and inattentiveness to African Americans' social conditions in decisions on racial restrictions.
7. See, e.g., Los Angeles Investment Co. v. Gary, 186 P. 2d 596 (Cal. 1919); Queensborough Land Co. v. Cazeaux, 68 So. 641 (La. 1915) (restrictions structured as reversionary interests); see also Koehler v. Rowland, 205 S.W. 217, 221 (Mo. 1918) (same, and noting that RAP does not apply to conditional estate/reversionary structure). Technically, this property form is called a "possibility of reverter," reflecting the fact that the triggering event may never occur. For ease of exposition we will refer to this kind of estate as "conditional" and "reversionary" as well as being a "possibility of reverter," although readers may wish to note that there are some technical differences. These are described in standard texts, for example Thomas W. Merrill and Henry E. Smith, *Property: Principles and Policies* (New York: Foundation Press, 2007), 548–561.
8. Fogelson, *Bourgeois Nightmares,* 103–106.
9. Los Angeles Investment Co. v. Gary, 597.
10. Wayt v. Patee, 269 P. 660 (Cal. 1928).

11. For more on these developments, see Carol M. Rose, "Servitudes," in *Research Handbook on the Economics of Property Law,* ed. Keith Michael Ayotte and Henry E. Smith (Cheltenham, UK, and Northampton, Mass.: Edgar Elgar, 2011), 296–325.
12. A handful of cases did refer obliquely to the horizontal privity problem. For example, in Littlejohns v. Henderson, 295 P. 95, 96 (Cal. App. 1931), the appellate court corrected the trial court's view that a neighborhood racial covenant was "merely personal" and would not run with the land. A similar admonition that a racial covenant was enforceable even though "not created by deed but . . . [by] contract" occurred in Swain v. Maxwell, 196 S.W. 2d 780, 782 (Mo. 1946). Shortly before the *Shelley* case, an important dissent in a Washington, D.C., case also referred to the privity issue, but here arguing that the doctrine created problems for enforceability: Mays v. Burgess, 147 F.2d 869, 876, note 11 (1945) (Edgerton, dissenting), certiorari denied 328 U.S. 868, rehearing denied 328 U.S. 896. For more on *Mays,* see Chapter 6.
13. Another technical constraint has been called "vertical privity": covenant obligations would only bind one who had the same type of interest as the original promissor. For example, a short-term renter would not normally be held to account for the covenant obligations of the owner, but a new owner would be, presumably because a new owner would inquire about such obligations.
14. Gilbert Osofsky, *Harlem: The Making of a Ghetto: Negro New York, 1890–1930* (2d ed. New York: Harper & Row 1971), 71–110.
15. Ibid., 106–109.
16. Meade v. Dennistone, 196 A. 330 (Md. 1938), 332–333.
17. See, e.g., Porter v. Johnson, 115 S.W.2d 529 (Mo.App. 1938) (upholding 1921 neighbor agreement adopted when African American purchased nearby); Wendy Plotkin, "Deeds of Mistrust: Race, Housing and Restrictive Covenants in Chicago, 1900–1950" (Ph.D. diss., University of Illinois, Chicago, 1999) (describing most covenants in neighborhoods adjacent to "black belt"); Colin Gordon, *Mapping Decline: St. Louis and the Fate of the American City* (Philadelphia: University of Pennsylvania Press, 2008), 80 (quoting St. Louis attorney Scovel Richardson on the "ring of steel").
18. For Harlem covenants, Osofsky, *Harlem,* 106. For Washington, Mara Cherkasky, "'For Sale to Colored': Racial Change on S Street, N.W.," *Washington History* 8 (1996/97): 40–57, 46–47. For covenants requiring future explicit inclusion, see, e.g., Wayt v. Patee. For the more formalistic versions of covenants, see for example the 1925 neighborhood covenant quoted in Mays v. Burgess, 870; for more on model covenants, see Chap. 6.
19. See for example Du Ross v. Trainor 10 P. 2d 763 (Cal. App. 1932); Oberwise v. Poulos, 12 P. 2d 156 (Cal. App. 1932); Russell v. Wallace, 30 F. 2d 981 (D.C. Cir. 1929). St. Louis civil rights lawyer Scovel Richardson later wrote a primer on

these vulnerabilities: "Notes and Comments: Some of the Defenses Available in Restrictive Covenant Suits Against Colored American Citizens in St. Louis," *National Bar Journal* 3 (1945): 50–56.

20. For developers' early turn to equitable jurisprudence, see, e.g., Korn v. Campbell, 85 N.E. 687 (N.Y. 1908) (describing types of covenants that would run to future purchasers, though denying injunction in this case). For the special importance of equity to neighborhood covenants see, e.g., Meade v. Dennistone, 333–334, upholding an injunction based on a neighborhood racial covenant in spite of lack of privity, stating that privity was not required for equitable enforcement.
21. Mays v. Burgess, 147 F.2d 869, 876–77 (D.C. Cir. 1945) (Edgerton, diss.). See also Fairchild v. Raines, 151 P. 2d 260, 267 (1944) (Traynor, conc.). Even the Missouri Supreme Court was uneasy about this pattern when it decided the *Shelly* case in favor of covenant enforcement, in the decision that was ultimately reversed by the U.S. Supreme Court; see Kraemer v. Shelley, 198 S.W. 2d 679, 683 (Mo. 1946).
22. See, e.g. Wayt v. Patee, 662–63, holding that courts can enforce neighborhood agreements in equity to a purchaser with notice, even if not enforceable as running with the land at law; Meade v. Dennistone, 332 (same); Thornhill v. Herdt, 130 S.W.2d 175, 177 (Mo App. 1939) (same).
23. Osofsky, *Harlem*, 106
24. A frequently cited case for the "wild deed" doctrine is Board of Education of City of Minneapolis v. Hughes, 136 N.W. 1095 (Minn. 1912).
25. Cherkasky, "For Sale to Colored," 46–49. See also Sherry Lamb Shirmer, *A City Divided: The Racial Landscape of Kansas City, 1900–19* (Columbia and London: University of Missouri Press, 2002), 111–12, describing some white homeowners who agreed to waive neighborhood covenants in the 1920s, shortly after the covenants had been instituted.
26. Clement E. Vose, *Caucasians Only: The Supreme Court, the NAACP, and the Restrictive Covenant Cases* (Berkeley and Los Angeles: University of California Press, 1959), 58–59. The attorney was Spottswood Robinson III of Richmond, later to become a distinguished federal judge.
27. Ibid.; the lawyer citing litigation costs was Loren Miller, later to become a judge in California.
28. See also Arnold R. Hirsch, *Making the Second Ghetto: Race and Housing in Chicago, 1940–1960* (2d ed. 1998), 30, describing the collapse of many Chicago racial covenants in the 1940s.
29. 15 N.E.2d 793 (N.Y. 1938).
30. This idea has been particularly developed in Merrill and Smith, "Optimal Standardization." For a briefer account, see Carol M. Rose, "What Government Can Do for Property (and Vice Versa)," in *The Fundamental Interrelations*

Between Government and Property, ed. Nicholas Mercuro and Warren J. Samuels (Stamford, Conn.: JAI Press, 1999) 209–222, 213–15.

31. Queensborough Land Co. v. Cazeaux, 643; Monchow, *Use of Deed Restrictions*, 17, 20.
32. Fogelson, *Bourgeois Nightmares*, 77, 80, noted that by the 1920s, buyers in more modest Los Angeles housing developments in 1920s wanted restrictions on race but little else.
33. Parmalee v. Morris, 188 N.W. 330, 332 (Mich. 1922). See also Shelley v. Kraemer, 334 U.S. 1 (1948), Brief for the Petitioners, McGhee v. Sipes 1947 WL [Westlaw] 30427, 15–18, noting the anomaly in covenant law of restricting occupants as opposed to activities.
34. For one version of the extremely common opinion on property values, see Stanley L. McMichael, *McMichael's Appraising Manual: A Real Estate Appraising Handbook for Use in Field Work and Advanced Study Courses* (3rd ed.; New York: Prentice Hall, 1944), 51–54. For the other actors and institutions, see discussion in Chapters 5 and 6.
35. Schulte v. Starks, 213 N.W. 102 (Mich. 1927); Fairchild v. Raines, 151 P. 2d 260, 263 (Cal. 1944).
36. Neponsit Property Owners' Association v. Emigrant Industrial Savings Bank; Rose, "Servitudes."

5. The Calculus of Covenants

1. Kevin Fox Gotham, "Urban Space, Restrictive Covenants, and the Origins of Racial Residential Segregation in an American City, 1900–1950," *International Journal of Urban and Regional Research* 24 (2000), 616–633, 621–22 (2000) (early twentieth-century social agencies and other concerned parties inadvertently raised racial fears).
2. We will consider in Chapter 9 the phenomenon of tipping points and similar choices that lead to unexpectedly high levels of segregation.
3. For the benefits of a "reputation for ferocity," see David M. Kreps, Paul Milgrom, John Roberts, and Robert Wilson, "Rational Cooperation in the Finitely Repeated Prisoners' Dilemma," *Journal of Economic Theory* 27 (1982). For the value of sending costly signals in showing commitment, see also Eric Posner, *Law and Social Norms* (Cambridge, Mass.: Harvard University Press, 2000), 5, 18–22. For surreptitious reprisals, see, e.g., James M. Acheson, *The Lobster Gangs of Maine* (Lebanon, N.H.: : University Press of New England, 1988), 73–77.
4. See Chapter 3. For new subdivisions, an early example was the practice of the real estate development firm Middaugh and Shannon, which used racial covenants in a series of in-town subdivisions in Washington, D.C., in the early

1900s; some of these were later involved in litigation. See, e.g., Torrey v. Wolfes, 6 F.2d 702 (D.C. Cir. 1925); Cornish v. O'Donoghue, 30 F.2d 983 (1929). See also Robert M. Fogelson, *Bourgeois Nightmares: Suburbia, 1870–1930* (New Haven: Yale University Press, 2005), 95–103. For older areas, see the experience of Carl Hansberry in the Washington Park/Woodlawn area of Chicago, described in the Chapter 6.

5. David E. Bernstein, "Philip Sober Controlling Philip Drunk: *Buchanan v. Warley* in Historical Perspective," *Vanderbilt Law Review* 54 (1998) 797–880, 803, 864–67, 870–71.
6. For developers' attentiveness to zoning, see Marc A. Weiss, *The Rise of the Community Builders: The American Real Estate Industry and Urban Planning* (Washington, D.C.: Beard Books 1987), 71–72, citing 1916 speech of J. C. Nichol, a prominent Kansas City developer. The best-known modern litigation on "exclusionary zoning" began with S. Burlington NAACP v. Twp. of Mt. Laurel 336 A.2d 713 (N.J. 1975), a case that generated extensive further litigation and enormous academic commentary.
7. Stephen Grant Meyer, *As Long As They Don't Move Next Door: Segregation and Racial Conflict in American Neighborhoods,* 17–20 (Lanham, Md., Oxford: Rowman & Littlefield, 2000), 17–20, describing Baltimore ordinance and its changes, as well as copycat ordinances in other locations.
8. See, e.g., Carol M. Rose, "Planning and Dealing: Piecemeal Land Controls as a Problem of Local Legitimacy," *California Law Review* 71 (1983): 837–912, 841–42.
9. "Mongolians" appeared from time to time in racial covenants, including those in the *Shelley* case; see Shelley v. Kraemer, 334 U.S. 1, 4 (1948); see also Helen Monchow, *The Use of Deed Restrictions in Subdivision Development* (Chicago: Institute for Research in Land Economics and Public Utilities, 1928), 47–49, noting ban on Africans as well as Mongolians in the Allegheny Furnace and Locust Hills developments in Altoona, Pennsylvania, as well as the Fernside development in Oakland, California.
10. For early developers' concerns over covenant duration and shift to longer-lasting covenants, and for the courts' increasing acceptance of longer-lasting covenants, see Chapter 3 and especially Chapter 4.
11. For the constraints on aesthetic regulation, see Chapter 2. Housing researcher Helen Monchow at the time cited the greater "intensity" of subdividers' restrictive covenants by comparison with zoning; Monchow, *Use of Deed Restrictions,* 6; Fogelson, *Bourgeoise Nightmares,* 13–19, gives an example with the extensive deed restrictions on Palos Verdes Estates, developed in early 1920s. The geographically unbounded character of neighbor-driven racial covenants would later raise concern in the influential dissent in Mays v. Burgess, 147 F.2d 869, 876 (1945) (Edgerton, diss.)

12. Fogelson, *Bourgeois Nightmares,* 103–106; see also William S. Worley, *J. C. Nichols and the Shaping of Kansas City* (Columbia and London: University of Missouri Press, 1990), 148, describing the 1917 and 1919 High Class Developers' Conferences.
13. Monchow, *Use of Deed Restrictions,* 62–63; Fogelson, *Bourgeois Nightmares,* 105–106; Worley, *J. C. Nichols,* 166–177. An important case that solidified the powers of the homeowners' associations arrived somewhat later with Neponsit Property Owners' Association, Inc., v. Emigrant Industrial Savings Bank, 15 N.E.2d 793 (N.Y. 1938). For modern homeowner complaints, Goodenough v. Hidden Hills Homeowners' Assn., 121 Wash. App. 1013 (2004) gives interesting examples: a homeowner who had been reprimanded by the association for violating a rule against home business operations then sued (unsuccessfully) to force the association to enforce rules against storage of boats, trailers, and recreational vehicles.
14. Two cases that were to be much cited later in civil rights suits concerned Asians: Gandolfo v. Hartman, 49 F. 181 (Cir. Ct., S.D. Cal. 1892), invalidating an anti-Chinese covenant; and Yick Wo v. Hopkins, 118 U.S. 356 (1886), invalidating an ordinance aimed at Chinese small enterprises.
15. Longer-term black resident blacks' fear of status drop from new migrants is described in Louise Venable Kennedy, *The Negro Peasant Turns Cityward: Effects of Recent Migrations to Northern Centers* (New York: AMS Press, 1930), 222–223, and more recently in Isabel Wilkerson, *The Warmth of Other Suns: The Epic Story of America's Great Migration* (New York: Random House, 2010), 287, 289–90.
16. Fogelson, *Bourgeois Nightmares,* 61–63, 99 (Roland Park); Garrett Power, "The Residential Segregation of Baltimore's Jews: Restrictive Covenants or Gentlemen's Agreements?" *Generations,* Fall 1996, 6 (same); Gerald Korngold, "The Emergence of Private Land Use Controls in Large-Scale Subdivisions: The Companion Story to *Village of Euclid v. Ambler Realty Co.,*" *Case Western Law Review* 51 (2001): 617–644, 621, 638–39 (Van Swearningens); Worley, *J. C. Nichols,* 32–33, 147–53.
17. Fogelson, *Bourgeois Nightmares,* 15 ("usual restrictions"); Monchow, *Use of Deed Restrictions,* 50.
18. See, e.g., Sherry Lamb Shirmer, *A City Divided: The Racial Landscape of Kansas City, 1900–19* (Columbia and London: University of Missouri Press, 2002), 107–109, describes J. C. Nichols' development of middle-class Armour Hills. See also Monchow, *Use of Deed Restrictions,* p. 63, 69–71; Fogelson, *Bourgeois Nightmares,* 65, 77–80, 136. The Albuquerque deeds are both available at http://www.krqe.com/generic/news/larry_barker/larry_barker_albuquerque_covenants_deeds—; the former deed is in the New Harwood subdivision, and the latter for a transaction in the Lavaland subdivision.

19. Weiss, *Community Builders,* 15, 19, 22, 24, 169 note 13. The organization has the exclusive right to use the term "realtor." It changed its name in 1974 to the National Association of Realtors or NAR, and, interestingly enough, the NAREB name now belongs to the National Association of Real Estate Brokers, a minority-dominated organization whose members refer to themselves as "realtists." This book will refer to the original organization as NAREB in any reference to its activities up to 1974.
20. Weiss, *Community Builders,* 24–25; see also Rose Helper, *Racial Policies and Practices of Real Estate Brokers* (Minneapolis: University of Minnesota Press, 1969), 221.
21. Helper, *Racial Policies,* 201.
22. Ibid., 227.
23. Ibid., 222–229.
24. Ibid., 224; Herman H. Long & Charles S. Johnson, *People vs. Property: Race Restrictive Covenants in Housing* (Nashville, Tenn.: Fisk University Press, 1947), 39–55, 57, 67 ("strategic relationship"); Thomas J. Sugrue, "Crabgrass-Roots Politics: Race, Rights, and the Reaction against Liberalism in the Urban North, 1940–1964," 82 *Journal of American History* (1995): 551–578, 557–558; see also Joe T. Darden, Richard Child Hill, June Thomas, and Richard Thomas, *Detroit: Race and Uneven Development* (Philadelphia: Temple University Press, 1987), 111.
25. Helper, *Racial Policies,* 228–230
26. Ibid., 229 ("color question"); 230 (emergent "norm").
27. Weiss, *Community Builders,* 16, 24–25, 68–76, 141–58.
28. Ibid., 146.
29. For HOLC, see Michael H. and Susan M. Wachter, "The Spatial Bias of Federal Housing Law and Policy: Concentrated Poverty in Urban America," *University of Pennsylvania Law Review* 143 (1995): 1285–1342, 1309–1310 (1995). Among the best-known modern critiques of FHA racial policies is Kenneth T. Jackson, *The Crabgrass Frontier: The Suburbanization of the United States* (New York: Oxford University Press,1985), 195–203. There were many more contemporary critiques, however, notably Robert C. Weaver, *The Negro Ghetto* (New York: Russell & Russell, 1948).
30. See Jackson, *Crabgrass Frontier,* 196–97, 204–205; see also Adam Gordon, "The Creation of Homeownership: How New Deal Changes in Banking Regulation Simultaneously Made Homeownership Available to Whites and Out of Reach to Blacks," *Yale Law Journal* 115 (2005): 186–226, 191–95.
31. Gordon, "Creation of Homeownership," 194–206; Weiss, *Community Builders,* 154.
32. Weiss, *Community Builders,* 146, 152; Jackson, *Crabgrass Frontier,* 207–209, 213.

33. *Valuation Procedure under Title II of the National Housing Act* (1936). Race and class mixing in schools supposedly also made neighborhoods "far less stable" (par. 266). For extensive critiques of the FHA manual and policies favoring segregation, see John Kimble, "Insuring Inequality: The Role of the Federal Housing Authority in the Urban Ghettoization of African Americans," *Law and Social Inquiry* 32 (2007): 399–434; David M.P. Freund, *Colored Property: State Policy and White Racial Politics in Suburban America* (Chicago and London: University of Chicago Press, 2007), 118–213.
34. See, e.g., David M. Cutler, Edward L. Glaeser, and Jacob Vigdor, "The Rise and Decline of the American Ghetto," *Journal of Political Economy* 107 (1999): 455–506, 463–69 (cities highly ghettoized by 1940).
35. Sugrue, "Crabgrass-Roots Politics," 564.
36. See, for example, the tract housing of the late 1930s and early 1940s described in Jackson, *Crabgrass Frontier*, 205–206, and Weiss, *Community Builders*, 156.
37. For the influence on developers of the FHA directives, racial and otherwise, Weiss, *Community Builders* 133–49; Jackson, *Crabgrass Frontier*, 204–209; Leonard S. Rubinowitz and Elizabeth Trosman, Affirmative Action and the American Dream: Implementing Fair Housing Policies in Federal Homeownership Programs," *Northwestern University Law Review*, 74:491–616 (1979), 511–514. Documents concerning the race restrictions in the Milwaukee suburb, Assessment Subdivision No. 94, Town of Lake, Milwaukee County, Document No. 2272322, July 18, 1940, were provided to the authors by Leonard Rubinowitz. For similar references to the FHA, see John P. Dean, "Only Caucasian: A Study of Race Covenants," *Journal of Land and Public Utility Economics* 23 (1947): 428–432, 430–431.
38. Rubinowitz and Trosman, "Affirmative Action and the American Dream," 491; Jackson, *Crabgrass Frontier*, 209, 212–14; Gordon, "Creation of Homeownership," 209; Schill and Wachter, "Spatial Bias of Federal Housing Law," 1310.
39. Weiss, *Community Builders*, 41–45, 156. For the wartime hiatus in new housing, see, e.g. Arnold R. Hirsch, *Making the Second Ghetto: Race and Housing in Chicago, 1940–1960* (Cambridge: Cambridge University Press, 1983), 17–20; see also Jackson, *Crabgrass Frontier*, 231–33.
40. Kimble, "Insuring Inequality," 403–405; see also Charles Abrams, "Race Bias in Housing I: The Great Hypocrisy," *The Nation*, July 19, 1947, 67–69, at 69. For the FHA's role in perpetuating the view that minority entry adversely affected property values, see Gordon, "Creation of Homeownership," 210–211; Freund, *Colored Property*, 155–162; Rubinowitz and Trosman, "Affirmative Action and the American Dream," 511–12. For an extended critique, see Charles Abrams, *Forbidden Neighbors: A Study of Prejudice in Housing* (New York: Harper & Brothers, 1955), 158–62.

41. American Law Institute, *Restatement of the Law of Property,* vol. 4 (St. Paul, Minn.: American Law Institute Publishers,1944): ch. 30, sec. 406, at 2411–2412 (ch. 30, sec. 406, comments (l.) and (m.)
42. Sugrue, "Crabgrass-Roots Politics," 564.

6. The Emergence of the Norm Breakers

1. For increased minority housing costs and relationship to collective white segregation efforts, see David M. Cutler, Edward L. Glaeser, and Jacob Vigdor, "The Rise and Decline of the American Ghetto," *Journal of Political Economy* 107 (1999):455–506, 457, 476, 479–80, 487.
2. St. Clair Drake and Horace R. Cayton, *Black Metropolis: A Study of Negro Life in a Northern City* (New York: Harcourt, Brace & Co. 1945), 199–200. For the collective action problems in breaking widespread norms, see Robert Sugden, "Contractarianism and Norms," 100 *Ethics* (1990): 768–786, 778–83.
3. The NAACP set up a separate Legal Defense and Education Fund, Inc., commonly known as the "Inc. Fund," in 1938. Although Thurgood Marshall was the sole national legal staff member at the outset, the staff expanded in the early 1940s. See Marc V. Tushnet, *Making Civil Rights Law: Thurgood Marshall and the Supreme Court, 1936–1961* (New York: Oxford University Press, 1994), 26–37.
4. Robert C. Weaver, *The Negro Ghetto* (New York: Russell & Russell, 1948), 214, named Chicago, Detroit, Washington, D.C., Los Angeles, and also Columbus, Ohio, as cities with high percentages of covenanted areas; see also 246–47, noting that St. Louis covenants were strategically located near areas of potential black expansion, and that Detroit was a rapidly expanding latecomer to covenants. A widely cited though perhaps overstated figure for Chicago's percentage of covenanted housing was 80 percent, apparently based on an estimate by Chicago Housing Authority vice-chairman Robert Taylor that was then noted in an article in the NAACP journal: "The Iron Ring in Housing," *The Crisis,* July 1940, 205; see Wendy Plotkin, " 'Hemmed In': The Struggle Against Racial Restrictive Covenants and Deed Restrictions in Chicago," *Journal of the Illinois State Historical Society* 94 (2001): 39–69, 44–45. New York on the other hand had relatively few covenants; Weaver, *Negro Ghetto,* 121.
5. Robert J. Blakely, *Earl B. Dickerson: A Voice for Freedom and Equality* (Evanston, Ill.: Northwestern University Press, 2006), 50–52, 65; see also the review of this book by Jay Tidmarsh and Stephen Robinson, " 'The Dean of Chicago's Black Lawyers' ": Earl Dickerson and Civil Rights Lawyering in the Years Before Brown," *Virginia Law Review* 93(2007): 1335–1387, 1359–68.
6. Hansberry v. Lee, 311 U.S. 32 (1940), reversing Lee v. Hansberry, 24 N.E. 2d 37 (Ill. 1939); Blakely, *Dickerson,* 95–100. For background and discussions focusing

on the case's procedural importance, see also Jay Tidmarsh, "The Story of Hansberry: The Rise of the Modern Class Action," in *Civil Procedure Stories*, ed. Kevin Clermont (2d edition; New York: Foundation Press, 2006), 233–294, and Allen R. Kamp, "The History Behind *Hansberry v. Lee*," *University of California, Davis, Law Review* 20 (1987), 481–499 (1987). More details are available in the excellent doctoral dissertation by Wendy Plotkin, "Deeds of Mistrust: Race, Housing, and Restrictive Covenants in Chicago, 1900–1953" (Ph.D. diss., University of Illinois at Chicago, 1999).

7. For early twentieth-century migration, see Allan H. Spear, *Black Chicago: The Making of a Negro Ghetto, 1890–1920* (Chicago: University of Chicago Press, 1967), pp. 7, 11–19, 129–33; Louise Venable Kennedy, *The Negro Peasant Turns Cityward: Effects of Recent Migrations to Northern Centers* (New York: AMS Press, 1930), pp. 46–47.
8. For growth related to WWI, Drake and Cayton, *Black Metropolis*, 8–9; after 1920, the African American population more than doubled again by 1930, to just under 234,000, roughly 7 percent of the city's population. See also Thomas Lee Philpott, *The Slum and the Ghetto: Neighborhood Deterioration and Middle-Class Reform* (New York: Oxford University Press, 1978), 116, 119–20, 134
9. Spear, *Black Chicago*, 18–21, 26–27, 111–130, 167; see also Kennedy, *Negro Peasant*, 143–44; Philpott, *The Slum and the Ghetto*, pp. 119–120.
10. Spear, *Black Chicago*, 122–24, 187–91; Drake and Cayton, *Black Metropolis*, 108–111.
11. Spear, *Black Chicago*, pp. 129, 134–37, 168–69,184–92; see also Kennedy, *Negro Peasant*, 53; see also the numerous references to the *Defender* in the biographical accounts in Isabel Wilkerson, *The Warmth of Other Suns: The Epic Story of America's Great Migration* (New York: Random House, 2010).
12. Spear, *Black Chicago*, at 20, 150, 208; see also Drake and Cayton, *Black Metropolis*, pp. 61–64; Kennedy, *Negro Peasant*, at 147.
13. Philpott, *The Slum and the Ghetto*, 154–56, 177–80; Spear, *Black Chicago*, 22–23; Drake and Cayton, *Black Metropolis*, 182–184; Plotkin, "Deeds of Mistrust," 32, 57–64.
14. For the Chicago Real Estate Board's 1917 zoning proposal, Philpott, *The Slum and the Ghetto*, 162–63. For covenant activity, Plotkin, "Deeds of Mistrust," 15, 66–68; Plotkin, " 'Hemmed In," 41–42; Richard Sterner, *The Negro's Share A Study of Income, Consumption, Housing and Public Assistance* (New York, London: Harper & Brothers, 1943), 207, note 33 citing the 80 percent residential coverage figure that had appeared in the July 1940 issue of the NAACP's *The Crisis*. Arnold R. Hirsch, *Making the Second Ghetto: Race and Housing in Chicago, 1940–1960* (Cambridge: Cambridge University Press, 1983), 17–24, describes the dearth of new housing in Depression and WWII years, along with the severe black housing shortage then and later.

15. Chicago Commission on Race Relations, *The Negro in Chicago: A Study of Race Relations and a Race Riot* (Chicago: University of Chicago Press, 1922), 1–48; Spear, *Black Chicago,* 214–17.
16. For the renewed zoning proposal, Drake and Cayton, *Black Metropolis,* 69–70; Spear, *Black Chicago,* pp 216–17, 219; Philpott, *The Slum and the Ghetto,* 177, see also 219. The renewed racial zoning proposal, unlike that in *Buchanan,* would have set aside specific areas classified by race.
17. Philpott, *The Slum and the Ghetto,* 220–28; Stephen Grant Meyer, *As Long As They Don't Move Next Door: Segregation and Racial Conflict in American Neighborhoods* (Lanham, Md.; Oxford: Rowman & Littlefield, 2000), 35–36.
18. Spear, *Black Chicago,* 125–26, 221–22. The quotation is from Drake & Cayton, *Black Metropolis,* 201.
19. For MacChesney, Philpott, *The Slum and the Ghetto,* 189–93; Plotkin, "Deeds of Mistrust," 45–46. For the state licensing statute and its dampening effect on racial mixing in housing, Herman H. Long and Charles S. Johnson, *People vs. Property: Race Restrictive Covenants in Housing* (Nashville, Tenn.: Fisk University Press, 1947), 66–67; Morton Keller, *Regulating a New Economy: Public Policy and Economic Change in America 1900–1933* (Cambridge, Mass., and London: Harvard University Press, 1990), 92–93.
20. Philpott, *The Slum and the Ghetto,* 190–92; Rose Helper, *Racial Policies and Practices of Real Estate Brokers* (Minneapolis: University of Minneapolis Press, 1969), 229. The model covenant is reprinted in Philpott, *The Slum and the Ghetto,* 407–410; the *Corrigan* covenant is reprinted in Mara Cherkasky, "'For Sale to Colored': Racial Change on S Street, N.W.," *Washington History* 8 (1996/97): 40–57, 47. For the significance of *Corrigan* as a model, Tidmarsh, "Story of Hansberry," 237. In MacChesney's 1927 book on real estate practice in 1927, he also made light of constitutional doubts about racial covenants. See Chapter 3. For the pamphlet and neighborhood drives, Plotkin, "Deeds of Mistrust," 47–48.
21. Plotkin, "Deeds of Mistrust," 48, 70–71.
22. Helper, *Racial Policies,* 358, 360, footnote 47 (quoting 1955 interview with Broker N). For the new subdivisions and their racial restrictions, see the samples in Philpott, *The Slum and the Ghetto,* 189, and Appendix B, 411–412.
23. Plotkin, "Deeds of Mistrust," 73; Philpott, *The Slum and the Ghetto,* 192, and 374, note 24.
24. Plotkin, "Deeds of Mistrust," at 71–78; Philpott, *The Slum and the Ghetto,* 192–193, 196–97.
25. Plotkin, "Deeds of Mistrust," 101–102; Tidmarsh, *Story of Hansberry,* 240–241. In general, however, banks refused to give mortgages to black buyers in all-white areas. See Hirsch, *Making the Second Ghetto,* 30.

26. See, e.g., Helper, *Racial Policies,* 358, 360, footnote 47 (interview with real estate official, describing active participation in neighborhood covenant drive). For an extensive discussion of the neighborhood improvement associations, see Long and Johnson, *People vs. Property,* 39–55. For institutional and business support for covenants, Philpott, *Slum and Ghetto,* 192–93, 196; and Plotkin, "Deeds of Mistrust," 75, 117. Robert Hutchins, then president of the University of Chicago, rejected Earl Dickerson's request that the university not support the white neighborhood association defending covenants in Hansberry v. Lee; see Blakely, *Dickerson,* 97–98. Tidmarsh, "Story of Hansberry," 238, describes the university as turning away from the covenant supporters somewhat later. For the Oakland neighborhood and more general infiltration patterns, Plotkin, "Deeds of Mistrust," 100–106.
27. Plotkin, "Deeds of Mistrust," 165–166, 180–181, 234.
28. For Back of the Yards' political and "physical" power, Helper, *Racial Policies,* 74. Proponents of racial covenants, on the other hand, stressed that these devices were peaceful and nonagressive; see Philpott, *The Slum and the Ghetto,* 191.
29. Drake and Cayton, *Black Metropolis,* pp. 182–190, also describing the covenant breachers as well-to-do.
30. Blakeley, *Dickerson,* 95–96, describes the discussions between Hansberry and Dickerson; Tidmarsh, "Story of Hansbury," 248–55, lays out the complicated positions of the University of Chicago as well as the somewhat murky transactions leading to sales to Pace and Hansberry.
31. Tidmarsh, "Story of Hansberry," p. 248.
32. Lorraine Hansberry, *To Be Young, Gifted, and Black* (Englewood Cliffs, N.J.: Prentice-Hall, 1969) 20–21 (from letter to *New York Times,* April 23, 1964); Tidmarsh, "Story of Hansberry," 255.
33. Plotkin, "Deeds of Mistrust," 146–47.
34. See generally Plotkin, "Deeds of Mistrust," 148–50, 166–171; see also Tidmarsh, "Story of Hansberry," 238, 250–252 (Pace background), 257 (conspiracy theory), 279 (accusation that Pace later passed for white); Blakeley, *Dickerson,* 96. For the *Defender* stories, see for example "Building Ghettos," *Chicago Defender,* October 2, 1937, 16; "U. of C. Head Criticized on Segregation," *Chicago Defender,* November 6, 1937, 1–2; "Debate Stand of University on Housing," *Chicago Defender,* December 4, 1937, 22.
35. Kamp, "History behind Hansberry," 486–487; Tidmarsh, "Story of Hansberry," at 240–41, 247–255. Harold I. Kahen, "Validity of Anti-Negro Restrictive Covenants: A Reconsideration of the Problem," *University of Chicago Law Review* 12 (1945): 198–213, 204, note 30, stated that white owners who had signed covenants in the *Hansberry* neighborhood were effectively caught: the covenants had been held valid but no white purchasers would buy.

36. Tidmarsh, "Story of Hansberry," 262–64; Plotkin, "Deeds of Mistrust," 152, 172–74. The earlier case was Burke v. Kleiman, 277 Ill. App. 519 (1934)
37. Lee v. Hansberry, 24 N.E. 2d 27 (Ill. 1939); see also Tidmarsh, "Story of Hansberry," 270–71. For the trial judge's view of Burke, Plotkin, "Deeds of Mistrust," 173.
38. Hansberry v. Lee, 311 U.S. 31 (1940). For later events, Tidmarsh, "Story of Hansberry," 277; Plotkin, "Deeds of Mistrust," 175, 179–80.
39. For the NAACP's longstanding concentration on covenants, see for example "Resolutions Adopted at NAACP Confab," Chicago Defender, July 17, 1937, 7, listing "Property Covenants" as subject of one resolution of the annual NAACP conference. For opinions that the organization should have been diversifying away from covenants, Plotkin, "Deeds of Mistrust,"178–79. For the Chicago conference, Clement E. Vose, *Caucasians Only: The Supreme Court, the NAACP, and the Restrictive Covenant Cases* (Berkeley and Los Angeles: University of California Press, 1959), 57–64. Tushnet, *Making Civil Rights Law,* 87, points out that the national NAACP organization had observed but not participated in the *Hansberry* case, but now joined the issue.
40. The *Tovey* case, outrun by the *Shelley* litigation, was ultimately decided in favor of the African American defendants on the basis of *Shelley.* Tovey v. Levy, 82 N.E. 2d 441 (Ill. 1948). However, the *Tovey* litigation generated a considerable body of information on covenants in Chicago, reflecting the NAACP's emerging litigation strategy of highlighting sociological data. For more on *Tovey,* as well as Marshall's wariness and Vaughn's moves and other cities' cases, Vose, *Caucasions Only,* 63, 151–158; see also Tushnet, *Making Civil Rights Law,* 87–91. A 2012 doctoral dissertation promises to become a definitive background history to the *Shelley* litigation: Jeffrey David Gonda, "Home Front: The Restrictive Covenant Cases and the Making of the Civil Rights Movement" (Ph.D. diss, Yale University, 2012)
41. For the significance of *Hansberry,* Tidmarsh, "Story of Hansberry," 234, 260–61; see generally Kenneth W. Mack, "Rethinking Civil Rights Lawyering and Politics in the Era Before *Brown,*" *Yale Law Journal* 115 (2005) 256–354, 266–67.
42. Notes and Comments (Scovel Richardson), "Some of the Defenses Available in Restrictive Covenant Suits Against Colored American Citizens in St. Louis," *Natonal Bar Journal* 3 (1945): 50–56. For more on Richardson's covenant case, see Colin Gordon, *Mapping Decline: St Louis and the Fate of the American City* (Philadelphia: University of Pennsylvania Press, 2008), 80–81. See also "Note, Challenges to Racial Restrictive Covenants," *Chicago Law Review* 15 (1947) 193–202, describing the flurry of challenges to racial restrictions in the then-recent past.
43. Plessy v. Ferguson, 163 U.S. 537, 538 (1896).

44. Vose, *Caucasians Only* 60–61, 84–87, 126–31. For Houston's central role in the black civil rights bar, see also Mack, "Rethinking Civil Rights Lawyering."

45. Sipes v. McGhee, 25 N.W. 2d 638, 641 (Mich. 1947), reversed in Shelley v. Kraemer, McGhee v. Sipes, 334 U.S. 1 (1948); for the McGhees' experiences as well as Graves' and Dent's tactics, see Gonda, "Home Front," 54–55, 73–74, 104–113, 117. The meaning of race has attracted considerable attention among legal scholars in the last two decades. For a recent exploration of the fragility of racial categories, see the beautifully written and poignant book by Daniel J. Sharfstein, *The Invisible Line* (New York: Penguin Press, 2010). For some other modern scholarship on racial categories, see Ian Haney-Lopez, *White By Law: The Legal Construction of Race* (New York: New York University Press, 1996); Ariela Gross, "Litigating Whiteness: Trials of Racial Determination in the Nineteenth Century South," *Yale Law Journal* 108 (1998): 109–188; Cheryl I. Harris, "Whiteness as Property," *Harvard Law Review* 106 (1993): 1709–1791.

46. Sipes v. McGhee, 641. For the circuit court and the McGhee's self-identification on their marriage documents, Vose, *Caucasions Only,* 132–133.

47. Hirsch, *Making the Second Ghetto,* 17–37; Robert C. Weaver, *The Negro Ghetto* (New York: Russell & Russell, 1948), 82–86, 90–94; Alfred McClung Lee and Norman D. Humphrey, *Race Riot (Detroit, 1943)* (New York: Octagon Books, 1968), 20–71 (1943 riots), 92–94 (population, housing). For an extensive treatment of the background to the Sojourner Truth riots, Dominic J. Capeci, Jr., *Race Relations in Wartime Detroit: The Sojourner Truth Housing Controversy of 1942* (Philadelphia: Temple University Press, 1984); Capeci gives population statistics from several slightly different perspectives, 9, 28–29, and passim.

48. See Hundley v. Gorewitz, 132 F.2d 23, 24–25 (1942), describing the white seller's difficulty in finding a white purchaser for covenanted property, and an African American's higher bid. See also Weaver, *Negro Ghetto,* 266–68. For a discussion of several changed conditions cases in this era, particularly in Washington, D.C., see David Delaney, *Race, Place and the Law 1836–1948* (Austin: University of Texas Press, 1998), 156–180. For white efforts to remove covenants, "Even Whites Now Object to Restrictive Covenants," *Chicago Defender,* September 21, 1940, 3; some of the remarks of the complaining "Small Property Owners Associated, Inc." show that the members were landlords rather than homeowners.

49. Gilbert Osofsky, *Harlem: The Making of a Ghetto* (2d ed.; New York: Harper & Row, 1971), 108–110; for Binga, Spear, *Black Chicago,* 112–13, 211, 219–20;

50. Hirsch, *Making the Second Ghetto,* 34–36.

51. Gonda, "Home Front," 58–59; Vose, *Caucasians Only,* 80. Urciolo was himself an unusual man who richly deserves a full biography. According to the *Washington Post's* obituary (Oct. 7, 1994, D4), he emigrated at an early age from Italy and became a linguist who held, among others, degrees in philology from the University of Maryland and the University of Rome. He also had a

law degree. He spoke nine languages and, aside from his real estate business, taught French, German, and business, and authored a scholarly treatise on the origins of Sardian words as well as a dictionary of Haitian French creole.

52. Vose, *Caucasians Only,* 58–59, 80. Urciolo represented himself in *Hurd,* while Houston represented the other defendants.
53. Gunnar Myrdal, *An American Dilemma* (New York, London: Harper & Bros. 1944); see also Rawn James, Jr., *Root and Branch: Charles Hamilton Houston, Thurgood Marshall, and the Struggle to End Segregation* (New York; Berlin; London: Bloomsbury Press, 2010), 188–189, describing Houston's speeches comparing segregation to Nazi practices.
54. Fairchild v. Raines, 151 P. 2d 260 (Cal. 1944).
55. Mays v. Burgess, 147 F.2d 869, 873 (1945).
56. The Sugar Hill case was reported as "Victory on Sugar Hill," *Time Magazine,* December 17, 1945, 24. For the Bronx case, Kemp v. Rubin, 69 N.Y.S.2d 680 (1947); the quotation was from Justice Murphy's concurrence in Hirabayashi v. United States, 320 U.S. 81 (1943), the case upholding a wartime curfews on an American citizen of Japanese ancestry. For more on Loren Miller and the Sugar Hill case, Gonda, "Home Front," 124–128; for some of Miller's earlier covenant practice, see Kenneth W. Mack, *Representing the Race: The Creations of the Civil Rights Lawyer* (Cambridge, Mass.: Harvard University Press, 2012), 200–204. Miller participated in an amicus brief in the *Fairchild* case. The Ontario case was Re Drummond Wren, (1945) O.R. 778 (1945); the NAACP lawyers brought it up to the Michigan Supreme Court in Sipes v. McGhee, the companion case to *Shelley,* where the United Nations Charter was cited but treated as a "plea for justice" rather than a legal rule; 25 N.W.2d 638, 644 (Mich. 1947). The Justice Department and the American Civil Liberties Union's briefs in *Shelley* also cited the case and the UN Charter. See Bert B. Lockwood, Jr., "The United Nations Charter and United States Civil Rights Litigation," *Iowa Law Review* 61 (1984): 901–955, 932–937. For *Shelley*'s place in international citation practice in the U.S. Supreme Court, see Judith Resnik, "Law's Migration: American Exceptionalism, Silent Dialogues, and Federalism's Multiple Ports of Entry," *Yale Law Journal* 115 (2008): 1564–1670, 1579, 1601–1603.
57. *To Secure These Rights: The Report of the President's Committee on Civil Rights* (Washington, D.C.: U.S. Government Printing Office, 1947), 91, 100, 146–48, 169; see also Mary L. Dudziak, "Desegregation as a Cold War Imperative," *Stanford Law Review* 41 (1988) 61–120, 100–101,describing State and Justice Department actions in connection with the *Shelley* case.
58. Brief for the United States as Amicus Curiae, at 19–20. For this and the other amicus briefs, see Vose, *Caucasians Only,* 163–64, 169–70, noting the NAACP's concern that too many briefs might be filed.

59. Barbara M. Kelly, *Expanding the American Dream: Building and Rebuilding Levittown* 3–33 (Albany: State University of New York Press, 1993); Federal Housing Administration, *Underwriting Manual* (National Housing Agency: Federal Housing Administration, Washington D.C. Revised January 1, 1947), par. 1320.

7. The Great Dilemma for Legal Norms

1. Colin Gordon, *Mapping Decline: St. Louis and the Fate of the American City* (Philadelphia: University of Pennsylvania Press, 2008), 83–89, describes the St. Louis Real Estate Exchange's role in maintaining segregation, and in the *Shelley* case in particular, including picking the Kraemers as plaintiffs. For the assistance to both parties, see Leland B, Ware, "Invisible Walls: An Examination of the Legal Strategy of the Restrictive Covenant Cases," *Washington University Law Quarterly* 67 (1989): 737–772, 752. For the role of the black real estate brokers in particular, Jeffrey David Gonda, "Home Front: The Restrictive Covenant Cases and the Making of the Civil Rights Movement" (Ph.D. diss., Yale University, 2012), 74–75, 84–90.
2. Gonda, "Home Front," 54–55, 62–64, 73–74, 193–196; Clement E. Vose, *Caucasians Only: The Supreme Court, the NAACP, and the Restrictive Covenant Cases* (Berkeley and Los Angeles: University of California Press, 1959), 125–126, 157.
3. Sipes v. McGhee, 25 N.W.2d 638 (Mi. 1947); Kraemer v. Shelley, 198 SW2d 679 (Mo. 1946)
4. Shelley v. Kraemer, 334 U.S. 1 (1948). The amici curiae briefs opposing racial covenants very much outnumbered the briefs supporting them, perhaps reflecting misplaced confidence on the part of established real estate interests. See also William H. Ming, Jr., "Racial Restrictions and the Fourteenth Amendment: The Restrictive Covenants Cases," *University of Chicago Law Review* 16 (1949): 203–238, noting the unusual interest in the case.
5. Hurd v. Hodge, Urciolo v Hodge, 334 U.S. 24, 34–35 (1948). An alternative ground was the Civil Rights Act of 1866, discussed as applicable in the federal District of Columbia; ibid., 33.
6. See particularly Brown v. Board of Education of Topeka, 347 U.S. 483 (1954). The use of social science data in this pivotal school desegregation case generated much discussion, some very critical. See Geoffrey R. Stone, Louis M. Seidman, Cass R. Sunstein, and Mark V. Tushnet, *Constitutional Law* (4th ed.; Gaithersburg, Md., New York: Aspen Publishers, 2001), 450–451.
7. Corrigan v. Buckley, 271 U.S. 323 (1926) (holding that racial covenants presented no federal question for jurisdiction); see also the citations to *Corrigan* in Mays v. Burgess, 147 F.2d 869, 870–71 (D.C. Cir. 1945), cert. denied 325

U.S. 868 (1945) (citing *Corrigan* and more recent cases); Kraemer v. Shelley, 198 S.W.2d 679, 683 (Mo. 1946) (same) Sipes v. McGhee, 25 N.W. 2d 638, 643–44 (Mich. 1947) (citing *Corrigan* and noting that the court knew of no court of last resort overturning private racial covenants on constitutional grounds).

8. See Chapter 3 for precedents. See also the very sharp critique by Richard C. Baker, "Restrictive Covenant Cases Reviewed," *South Carolina Law Quarterly* 3 (1951), 351–365, 351–356, describing a broad array of prior legal support for racial covenants, including state antidiscrimination legislation that exempted these covenants. For the view that housing discrimination would collapse without covenants, at least in the North, see, e.g., Gunnar Myrdahl, *An American Dilemma: The Negro Problem and Modern Democracy* (New York, London: Harper & Bros. 1944), 624.
9. More precisely, the NAACP legal team argued the *Sipes* companion case to *Shelley.* Since at the Supreme Court level, both cases are commonly referred to by the *Shelley* name, we shall use that name for both.
10. Mark V. Tushnet, *Making Civil Rights Law: Thurgood Marshall and the Supreme Court, 1936–1961* (New York: Oxford University Press, 1994), 86, is one of many commentators noting that judicial enforcement as state action would collapse the entire distinction between state and private. For the Court's backtrack, see, e.g., Peterson v. Greenville, 373 U.S. 244 (1963) (reversing a trespass conviction in an antisegregation sit-in case, but on the ground that official state policy supported segregation); see also Moose Lodge No. 107 v. Irvis, 407 U.S. 163 (1972) (racially-motivated refusal of service in private club not state action, even though club had a state liquor license). See also Mark D. Rosen, "Was Shelley v. Kraemer Incorrectly Decided? Some New Answers," *California Law Review* 95 (2007) 451–512, 458–470, detailing a number of cases rejecting or limiting *Shelley*'s state action doctrine.
11. The 1960s civil rights laws were based on the commerce clause as well as the Fourteenth Amendment, which meant that they only applied after some minimal commercial threshold had been passed; e.g., in the case of housing, advertising an apartment in a newspaper or listing it with a broker.
12. For several others that have appeared subsequently, see Rosen, "Was Shelley Incorrectly Decided?", 470–483.
13. Vose, *Caucasions Only,* 160. The frictions between the national NAACP legal team and Vaughn are extensively described in Gonda, "Home Front," 182–206; see also Ware, "Invisible Walls," 756–757.
14. See also the discussion of the state action issue in Chapter 3. Rosen, "Was Shelley Incorrectly Decided?" does not mention Vaughn, but he has revived Vaughn's argument for deciding the case under the 1866 Civil Rights Act, predicated on Thirteenth Amendment justification.

15. Risa L. Goluboff, "The Thirteenth Amendment and the Lost Origins of Civil Rights," *Duke Law Journal* 50 (2001) 1609–1685; Risa L. Goluboff, *The Lost Promise of Civil Rights* (Cambridge, Mass.: Harvard University Press, 2007), 110–173.
16. John Locke, "Second Treatise," *Two Treatise of Government,* ed. Peter Laslett (Cambridge: Cambridge University Press, 1963 [1698]) par. 85, 365–366. For the economics of the phenomenon of self-purchase, see Yoram Barzel, "An Economic Analysis of Slavery," *Journal of Law and Economics* 20 (1977): 87–110, 99–100.
17. Jones v. Alfred H. Mayer Co., 392 U.S. 409 (1968) (upholding 1866 Civil Rights Act under the Thirteenth Amendment).
18. Goluboff, "Thirteenth Amendment," 1680–1685. In her more recent book, Goluboff sharply criticizes the NAACP lawyers for jettisoning the labor and economic issues of earlier Thirteenth Amendment cases, as well as for failing to exploit *Shelley* itself as a case that could have weakened the state action doctrine's public versus private divide. See her *Lost Promise of Civil Rights,* 250–252, 259–263.
19. Kraemer v. Shelley, 689; Shelley v. Kraemer, 5–6.
20. Kraemer v. Shelley, 819; Shelley v. Kraemer, 5, note 1; Vose, *Caucasians Only,* 111; Gonda, "Home Front," 52–53.
21. Ware, "Invisible Walls," 751–752; Vose, *Caucasians Only,* 111; Gonda, "Home Front," 50–52.
22. Herman H. Long and Charles S. Johnson, *People vs. Property: Race Restrictive Covenants in Housing* (Nashville, Tenn.: Fisk University Press, 1947), 29–31, describe the pattern of buffering; see also their maps at pages 24 and 28, showing, respectively, the areas of racial covenants (1945) and African American residence (1940) in St. Louis. The Labadie Avenue house is located between Cora and Taylor, which was then the northwestern corner of the black concentration; this area was heavily covered by covenants but with some "openings." For the "ring of steel," see Gordon, *Mapping Decline,* 80, attributing the phrase to St. Louis attorney and activist Scovel Richardson.
23. Kraemer v. Shelley, 683.
24. Ibid., 681–682.
25. For example, the California cases by this time were treating issues of the original covenantors' intent as questions of fact and thus generally deferring to trial courts' findings; see, e.g., Stone v. Jones, 152 P. 2d 19, 22–23 (Cal. App. 1944).
26. Francis A. Allen, "Remembering Shelley v. Kraemer: Of Public and Private Worlds," *Washington University Law Quarterly* 67 (1989): 709–735, 722, 729–32. As Allen noted, the Justice Department's long brief also suggested this kind of judicial policy making; see Brief for the United States as Amicus Curiae,

Shelley v. Kraemer, at 107–108, 114. For "mere spoilation," Corrigan v. Buckley, 271 US 323, 331–32 (1926).

27. For a case raising but not settling this question, see Stop the Beach Renourishment v. Florida Department of Environmental Protection, 130 Sup. Ct. 592 (2010). See also, e.g., E. Brantley Webb, "How to Review State Court Determinations of State Law Antecedent to Federal Rights," *Yale Law Journal* 120 (2011): 1192–1249 (2011); Barton H. Thompson, Jr., "Judicial Takings," *Virginia Law Review* 76 (1990): 1449–1544.
28. Gonda, "Home Front," 183–194; Ware, "Invisible Walls," 753–758; Vose, *Caucasians Only*, 157, 159–60; Tushnet, *Making Civil Rights Law*, 90–91.
29. Smith v. Allwright, 321 U.S. 649 (1944); see also Terry v. Adams, 345 U.S. 461 (1953), holding another ostensibly private political association to be a delegated arm of the state. Another important contemporary case finding state action in what appeared to be a private entity was Louisville & Nashville Railway Co., 323 U.S. 192 (1944) (railroad union could not discriminate on basis of race). NAACP lawyer Thurgood Marshall argued the *Smith* case, while Charles Houston argued the *L&R Railway* case. Still another was Marsh v. Alabama, 326 U.S. 501 (1946), discussed below.
30. Vose, *Caucasians Only*, at 151–152; for one of the explicit references to *Smith*, see Shelley v. Kraemer, Brief for the American Civil Liberties Union, Dec. 9, 1947, 17–20. For the revival of the argument that covenants were zoning in disguise, see, for example, Note, Current Legal Attacks on Racial Restrictive Covenants, *University of Chicago Law Review* 15 (1947): 193–202, 201 (1947). For the NAACP lawyers' intense interest in deploying social science data in the restrictive covenant cases, see Gonda, "Home Front," 206–229.
31. Meade v. Dennistone, 333 A. 330, 333 (Md. 1938); Brief for the United States, 45–46, 62–69, 78–85.
32. "The Iron Ring in Housing," *The Crisis*, July 1940, 205; for St. Louis and Richardson, Gordon, *Mapping Decline*, 78–80; Long and Johnson, *People vs. Property*, 12–31, 69. For Vaughn's conspiracy argument, Kraemer v. Shelley, 679.
33. Marsh v. Alabama, 326 U.S. 501 (1946).
34. After the *Shelley* decision, one article raised the possibility that housing discrimination violated the antitrust laws: Philip Marcus, "Civil Rights and the Anti-Trust Laws," *University of Chicago Law Review* 18 (1951):171–217, 208–241. Compare Richard A. Epstein, "Lest We Forget: Buchanan v. Warley and the Constitutional Jurisprudence of the Progressive Era," *Vanderbilt Law Review* 51 (1998): 787–796, 789 fn. 9, arguing that monopoly power could have been an issue for racial covenants, though rejecting a state action analysis. For the *Restatement of Property*, see Chapter 5; D. O. McGovney, "Racial Residential Segregation by State Court Enforcement of Restrictive Agreements, Covenants

or Conditions is Unconstitutional," *California Law Review* 33 (1945): 5–39, 7–15; Brief for the United States as Amicus Curiae, Dec. 7, 1947, 108–110.

35. As noted in Chapter 3, the phrase originated with Gary S. Becker, *The Economics of Discrimination* (2d ed.; Chicago: University of Chicago Press, 1971 [1st ed. 1962]), 14.
36. Civil Rights Cases, U.S. 3, 17–18 (1883).
37. For many of these and other incidents of violence associated with African American moves to white neighborhoods, see, e.g., Charles Abrams, *Forbidden Neighbors: A Study of Prejudice in Housing* (New York: Harper & Brothers, 1955), 85–94.
38. See for example Abrams, *Forbidden Neighbors*, 73, citing the original 1948 article by sociologist Robert K. Merton.
39. For a contract example, see Walnut Creek Pipe Distributors, Inc., v. Gates Rubber Co. Sales Division, 39 Cal. Rptr. 767, 771 (Cal. App. 1964) ("The courts cannot make better agreements for the parties than they themselves have been satisfied to enter into. . . ."). By comparison, the first racial restriction case in a high state court, Queensborough Land Co. v. Cazeaux, 67 So. 641, 643 (La. 1915) noted that a condition on alienability was only valid if based on a "substantial reason" and not merely "caprice." Helen Monchow's mid-1920s survey of subdivision restrictions of all kinds also noted that covenants had to have value; see her book, *The Use of Deed Restrictions in Subdivision Development* (Chicago: Institute for Research in Land Economics and Public Utilities, 1928), 17.
40. Shelley v. Kraemer, 8–9; Hurd v. Hodge, 29–30.
41. Brief for ACLU, Amicus Curiae, 24; Brief for Petitioners, McGhee v. Sipes, 9.
42. See, Kraemer v. Shelley, 198 S.W.2d at 683 (describing parties rights under covenants as matter of "contract"); Sipes v. McGhee, 25 N.W.2d at 643 (same); Hurd v. Hodge, 162 F.2d at 234 (same); see also, e.g., Mays v. Burgess, 147 F.2d 869, 871 (1945) (same); Burkhardt v. Lofton, 146 P. 2d 720, 724 (Cal. App. 1944) (same); but see *Mays*, at 875–76 (Edgerton, diss) (noting difference between contract and covenants).
43. For the power of informal norms, see Robert C. Ellickson, *Order Without Law: How Neighbors Settle Disputes* (Cambridge, Mass.: Harvard University Press, 1991), 52–62; for informal norms' passage to legal norms, see for example Ghen v. Rich, 8 F. 159 (D.C., Mass. 1881) (adopting whalers' norms on ownership of animals despite deviance from common law rule).

8. After *Shelley*

1. Among the most influential was senior scholar D. O. McGovney's "Racial Segregation by State Court Enforcement of Restrictive Agreements, Covenants or Conditions in Deeds is Unconstitutional," *California Law Review* 33 (1945):

5–39. Also important, though shorter, was Harold I. Kahen, "Validity of Anti-Negro Restrictive Covenants: A Reconsideration of the Problem" *University of Chicago Law Review* 15 (1945) 198–213. For some others, see Comment (Isaac N. Groner and David M. Helfeld), "Race Discrimination in Housing," *Yale Law Journal* 57 (1948): 426–458; Note, "The Disintegration of a Concept—State Action under the 14th and 15th Amendment," *University of Pennsylvania Law Review* 96 (1948) 402–414. For the NAACP's role and an extensive list of similar articles and books, see Leland B. Ware, "Invisible Walls: An Examination of the Legal Strategy of the Restrictive Covenant Cases," *Washington University Law Quarterly* 67 (1989): 737–772, 760–61, note 105

2. Comment (Clare B. McDermott, Jr.), "The Effects of the Rule in the Modern Shelley's Case," *University of Pittsburgh Law Review* 13 (1952): 647–665, 647, note 2, lists many post-*Shelley* comments. For a few examples of favorable commentary, see William H. Ming, Jr., "Racial Restrictions and the Fourteenth Amendment: The Restrictive Covenants Cases," *University of Chicago Law Review* 16 (1949): 203–238, 205; Note, "State Action Reconsidered in the Light of Shelley v. Kraemer," *Columbia Law Review* 48 (1948): 1241–1245; Comment (Harry L. Gershon), "Restrictive Covenants and Equal Protection—The New Rule in Shelley's Case," *Southern California Law Review* 21(1948): 358–373.
3. R. Gordon Lowe, "Racial Restrictive Covenants," *Alabama Law Review* 1(1948): 15–39, 27–28, 39.
4. Richard C. Baker, "Restrictive Covenant Cases Reviewed," *South Carolina Law Quarterly* 3 (1951) 351–65; for other crtics, see, among others, James A. Crooks, "Racial Covenant Cases," *Georgetown Law Journal* 37 (1949): 514–525; Comment, "Unenforceability of Racial Restrictive Covenants," *Maryland Law Review* 10 (1949) 263–271.
5. See, e.g., Ming, "Racial Restrictions," 216–224; McDermott, "Rule in Modern Shelley's Case," 648–649; Note, "Constitutional Law: Circumvention of the Rule Against Enforcement of Racially Restrictive Covenants," *California Law Review* 37 (1949): 493–498; Comment, "Practical Effects in Tennessee of the Non-Enforceability of Restrictive Racial Covenants," *Tennesee Law Review* 20 (1949): 679–684; B. T. McGraw & George B. Nesbitt, "Aftermath of Shelley v. Kraemer on Residential Restriction by Race," *Land Economics* 29 (1953): 280–287, 286.
6. "Mutual Faith Covenant Here Names Negroes," *Washington Post*, June 6, 1948, M1. See also "Other Devices Being Studied as Substitutes for Covenants," *Washington Post*, May 5, 1948, 11.
7. Philip Marcus, "Civil Rights and the Anti-Trust Laws," *University of Chicago Law Review* 18 (1951): 171–217, 210, note 214 (quoting extensively from newsletter).
8. *Federal Housing Administration Underwriting Manual* (Washington, D.C.:

National Housing Agency, 1947), sections 1320 (1)–(2). For the letter to Marshall, Charles Abrams, *Forbidden Neighbors: A Study of Prejudice in Housing* (New York: Harper & Bros., 1955), 233. See also Clement E. Vose, *Caucasians Only: The Supreme Court, the NAACP, and the Restrictive Covenant Cases* (Berkeley and Los Angeles: University of California Press, 1959), 225–227; David M.P. Freund, *Colored Property: State Policy and White Racial Politics in Suburban America* (Chicago and London: University of Chicago Press, 2007), 206–213; Evan McKenzie, *Privatopia: Homeowners Associations and the Rise of Private Government* (New Haven: Yale University Press, 1994), 66; Leonard S. Rubinowitz and Elizabeth Trosman, "Affirmative Action and the American Dream: Implementing Fair Housing Policies in Federal Homeownership Programs," *Northwestern University Law Review* 74 (1979): 491–616, 514–519; John Kimble, "Insuring Inequality: The Role of the Federal Housing Authority in the Urban Ghettoization of African Americans," *Law and Social Inquiry* 32 (2007): 399–434, 417–21.

9. FHA *Underwriting Manual* (rev. ed. 1947), secs 1320 (1) & (2); Abrams, *Forbidden Neighbors*, 232; Davis McEntire, *Residence and Race: Final and Comprehensive Report to the Commission on Race and Housing* (Berkeley and Los Angeles: University of California Press 1960) 74, 160; Kimble, "Insuring Inequality," 423–424. For the 1952 revision, FHA *Underwriting Manual* (rev. ed. 1952), at sec. 1309(2), cited in Rose Helper, *Racial Policies and Practices of Real Estate Brokers* (Minneapolis: University of Minneapolis Press, 1969), 205. For the FHA's continued sluggishness, see U.S. Commission on Civil Rights, *Civil Rights U.S.A.: Housing in Washington, D.C.* (Washington, D.C.: Government Printing Office, 1962), 14; Rubinowitz and Trosman, "Affirmative Action and the American Dream," 515–520; Adam Gordon, "'The Creation of Homeownership: How New Deal Changes in Banking Regulation Simultaneously Made Homeownership Accessible to White and Out of Reach for Blacks," *Yale Law Journal* 115 (2005): 186–226, 216–18; Freund, *Colored Property*, 208-210.

10. For the Virginia meeting, Vose, *Caucasians Only*, 284, note 107; for Los Angeles, McKenzie, *Privatopia*, 73; Stephen Grant Meyer, *As Long As They Don't Move Next Door: Segregation and Racial Conflict in American Neighborhoods* (Lanham, Md. and Oxford: Rowman & Littlefield, 2000), 95.

11. Belsheim and the form book are discussed in Gabriel J. Chin, "Jim Crow's Long Goodbye," *Constitutional Commentary* 21 (1940): 107–132, 124–25 (2004).

12. Phyllis Palmer, *Living as Equals* (Nashville: Vanderbilt University Press, 2008), 108.

13. On skepticism and the self-recusing justices, Francis A. Allen, "Remembering Shelley v. Kraemer: Of Public and Private Worlds," *Washington University Law Quarterly* 67 (1989) 709–735 (1989), 721; see also Marcus, "Civil Rights and the

Anti-Trust Laws," 210, n. 214; Dillard Stokes, "Three Justices Retire from Racial Case," *Washington Post,* January 16, 1948, 1. For brokers' hope that buyers would not know of the legal change, see Note, "Practical Effects in Tennessee," 681; Chin, "Jim Crow's Long Goodbye," 125. After banking regulations changed, conventional loans could still not match the FHA's low down payment and long payoff times, but they could come closer. See Gordon, "Creation of Homeownership," 194–206.

14. 334 U.S. 24, 36 (Frankfurter concurrence); 162 F.2d 233, 240, n. 22 (D.C. Cir. 1947) (Edgerton dissent). Justice Vinson may also have been influenced by Judge Edgerton's view in his own dissent in the later Barrows v. Jackson case, discussed below. See Allen, "Remembering Shelley," 723, note 58. For various legal uncertainties after *Shelley,* including the law/equity distinction, see Harry E. Groves, "Judicial Interpretation of the Holdings of the United States Supreme Court in the Restrictive Covenant Cases," *Illinois Law Review* 45 (1950): 614–631.
15. Vose, *Caucasians Only,* 230–31; see Roberts v. Curtis, 93 F. Supp. 604 (D.C. D.C. 1950) (deny action for damages); Phillips v. Naff, 52 N.W.2d 158 (Mich. 1952) (same); Barrows v. Jackson 247 P. 2d (Cal. App. 1952) (same). On the other side were Weiss v. Leaon, 225 S.W.2d 127 (Mo.1949) (permit action for damages); Correll v. Earley, 237 P. 2d 1017 (Okla. 1951) (same).
16. Barrows v. Jackson, 346 U.S.249 (1953).
17. See, for example, "Recent Decisions: Real Property," *Georgetown Law Journal* 42 (1954): 323–26; "Recent Decisions: Constitutional Law," *Michigan Law Review* 52: (1953): 293–295; "Recent Decisions: Constitutional Law—Equal Protection," *Minnesota Law Review* 37 (1952–1953): 65–66; "Recent Decisions: Constitutional Law," 102 *University of Pennsylvania Law Review* 102 (1953–1954): 134–36; "Supreme Court, 1952 Term—Damages for Breach of Restrictive Covenants," *Harvard Law Review* 67 (1953): 105–107 (1953). For the Mississippi comment, "Recent Decisions: Constitutional Law—Restrictive Covenants," *Mississippi Law Journal* 25 (1954): 169–171 (1954).
18. Barrows v. Jackson, 268.
19. Vose, *Caucasians Only,* 243–44.
20. See, for example, Vogeler et al. v. Alwyn Improvement Corp., 159 N.E. 886 (N.Y. 1928); Neponsit Property Owners' Assn. v. Emigrant Industrial Savings Bank, 278 N.Y. 248 (1938) (relaxing real estate covenant rules for the benefit of successor owners, but in equity). Third-party beneficiary doctrine in American contract law began as a quasi-equitable doctrine, and its extension derives largely from the efforts of contracts scholar Arthur Corbin; see Anthony Jon Waters, "The Property in the Promise: A Study of the Third Party Beneficiary Rule," *Harvard Law Review* 98 (1985): 1109–1210. For the preference for property law in real estate matters, see Charles Edward Clark, *Real Covenants and*

Other Interests Which "Run With Land" (2d ed; Chicago: Callaghan, 1947), 171, note 4.

21. Scovel Richardson, "Notes and Comments: Some of the Defenses Available in Restrictive Covenant Suits Against Colored American Citizens in St. Louis," *National Bar Journal* 3 (1945): 50–56.
22. For considerations of public policy in contracts, see the classic case of Williams v. Walker-Thomas Furniture Co., 122 U.S.App. D.C. 315 (D.C. Cir. 1965), invalidating a consumer contract on grounds of unconscionability.
23. For these various evasion ideas, see Comment (Roger B. Leland), "Equal Protection—Enforcement of Racial Covenants," *Kentucky Law Journal* 43 (1954): 151–162, 159–62; Vose, *Caucasians Only,* 230; McDermott, "Rule in the Modern Shelley's Case," 662–64; McGraw & Nesbitt, "Aftermath of Shelley," 286; Comment, "Practical Effects in Tennessee," 682; Note, "Circumvention of the Rule Against Enforcement," 495; Comment (Arthur N Greenberg and Robert Franklin), "Discrimination in Ownership and Occupancy of Property since Shelley v. Kraemer," *UCLA Intrmural Law Review* 1 (1952): 14–22, 117.
24. See Rosemarie Maldonado and Robert D. Rose, "The Application of Civil Rights Laws to Housing Cooperatives: Are Co-ops Bastions of Discriminatory Exclusion or Self-Selecting Models of Community-Based Living?" *Fordham Urban Law Journal* 23 (1996): 1245–1282; Comment (Sabrina Malpeli), "Cracking Down on Cooperative Board Decisions that Reject Applicants Based on Race: Broome v. Biondi," *St. John's Law Review* 73 (1999): 313–324 (1999). For a leading case, see Robinson v. 12 Lofts Realty, Inc, 610 F.2d 1032 (2d Cir., 1979). For the Dakota, see Peter Lattman and Christine Haughney, "Man at the Center of a Bitter Dispute at the Dakota," *New York Times,* February 26, 2011, A15, reporting on the suit by Alphonse Fletcher Jr., a wealthy African American financier, who already owned four Dakota apartments and wanted another; Fletcher noted that the co-op board had rejected an acting couple believed to be Melanie Griffith and Antonio Banderas (Banderas is Latino); the board gave as a reason the wish to avoid celebrity residents. For financing issues with co-op ownership, see Note, "Legal Characterization of the Individual's Interest in a Cooperative Apartment: Realty or Personalty?" *Columbia Law Review* 73 (1973): 250–288, 272–79.
25. Charles Abrams, "Race Bias in Housing I: The Great Hypocrisy," *The Nation,* July 19, 1947, 67–69, 68 (quoting Ecker); Dorsey v. Stuyvesant Town, 87 N.E.2d 541 (NY 1949), certiori denied, 339 U.S 981 (1950) (rejecting claim that Stuyvesant Town resulted from state action under U.S. Constitution).
26. Among others debating whether *Shelley* applied to reversionary interests, McDermott, "Rule in the Modern Shelley's Case," 648, 657–661; Lowe, "Racial Restrictive Covenants," 32–34; and Comment (Greenberg and Franklin), "Discrimination in Ownership and Occupancy Since Shelley," 17–18. For more

on these types of "estates," technically called "possibilities of reverter" since they may never occur, see the discussion in Chapter 4.

27. Charlotte Park and Recreation Commission v. Barringer, 88 S.E.2d 114 (N.C. 1955), certiorari denied, Leeper v. Charlotte Park and Recreation Commission, 350 U.S. 983 (1956). For a critical view, see Notes, "Consititutional Law—Equal Protection—Determinable Fee as Devise to Impose Racial Covenants," *Michigan Law Review* 54 (1956): 698–701.

28. After a fifteen year lapse, this view was reinforced in a trust case, Evans v. Abney, 396 U.S. 435 (1970), involving a property that had been given in trust to Macon, Georgia, for a park for whites only. The U.S. Supreme Court's original ruling on the property was that a newly appointed private trustee could not operate the park for whites only because of the city's pervasive involvement, Evans v. Newton, 382 U.S. 296 (1965). The Georgia courts subsequently ruled that the purpose of the trust had failed because of desegregation, and that the property reverted to the estate of the donor. In response to a new challenge, the U.S. Supreme Court held that the reversion implicated no state action by the court, but simply the normal construction of the state's law of decedents' estates. Evans v. Abney, 439–447.

29. For a case treating a reversionary interest as equivalent to an unenforceable racial covenant, Capitol Savings & Loan Assn. v. Smith, 316 P. 2d 252, 254 (Colo. 1957); a similar case decided just after *Shelley* was Clifton v. Puente, 218 S.W.2d 272 (Tex. Civ. App. San Antonio 1948), involving a condition against sale to "persons of Mexican descent." For the mortgage finance problems that could be raised by the reversionary form, see Comment (Greenberg and Franklin), "Discrimination in Ownership and Occupancy Since Shelley," 17–18; and see generally Jonathan Entin, "Defeasible Fees, State Action, and the Legacy of Massive Resistance," *William and Mary Law Review* 34 (1993): 769–800.

30. 407 U.S. 163 (1972).

31. Lior Jacob Strahilevitz, "Exclusionary Amenities in Residential Communities," *Virginia Law Review* 92 (2006): 437–499.

32. For Spring Valley and its covenants, Benefsheh D. Verell, "Spring Valley, Washington DC: Changing Land Use and Demographics 1900–2000," *Geographical Bulletin* 49 (2008): 103–119, 105, 113; Diane Shaw Wasch, "Models of Beauty and Predictability: The Creation of Wesley Heights and Spring Valley," *Washington History* 1 (1989): 58–76. Spring Valley got something of a jolt in the 1990s; prior to the Miller Brothers' development, the cite had been used for military testing, and by the end of the twentieth century, the residues had turned into an environmental problem.

33. For the State Department concerns, U.S. Commission on Civil Rights, *Hearings*

Before the United States Commission on Civil Rights: Housing in Washington. Hearings held in Washington, D.C., April 12–13, 1962, testimony of David A. Sawyer, 81–82; for specific restrictions, ibid., 58–60 (testimony of Irving Engel, quoting Spring Valley covenants).

34. "Nixon Home's Racial Provision Cited in Paper," *Washington Post,* October 4, 1952, 2; "Rusk Rejects Racial Barriers in Buying House," *Washington Post,* February 19, 1961, 17.
35. For finance, see U.S. Commission on Civil Rights, *Hearings, Housing in Washington,* 343 (testimony of Harry P. Bergman, vice president, Riggs National Bank), testifying that Riggs had a very close relationship with the Miller firm, and that it had financed every house in Spring Valley.
36. Conventional loans were coming closer to FHA terms in this era; see Gordon, "Creation of Homeownership," 194–206. Even if lower-end conventional financing was available for a given purchaser, however, developers and first purchasers might still wish to ensure that the property was FHA-eligible so as to enhance resale opportunity to future purchasers.
37. "Realty Covenants Still Barring Minority Groups in US Cities," *Washington Post,* Jan. 17, 1949, 1.
38. Palmer, *Living as Equals,* 108.
39. Helper, *Racial Policies,* 82–95. See also U.S. Commission on Civil Rights, *Hearings, Housing in Washington,* 19–20 (testimony of sociologist George Grier), 86–87 (testimony of George DeFranceiux, president, Washington Board of Realtors)
40. McGraw & Nesbitt, "Aftermath of Shelley," 285.
41. For brokers' explanation of their ethics, Helper, *Racial Policies,* 117–120; for continued steering practices in St. Louis, Clarence Lang, *Grassroots at the Gateway: Class Politics and Black Freedom Struggle in St. Louis, 1936–75* (Ann Arbor: University of Michigan Press, 2009), 142; for Caplan's remark, U.S. Commission on Civil Rights, *Hearings, Housing in Washington,* 416.
42. For interview, Craig Thompson, "Growing Pains of a Brand-New City," *Saturday Evening Post,* Aug. 7, 1954, 26, 72; for later statement, U.S. Commission on Civil Rights, *Hearings, Housing in Washington,* 244 (letter of Ira Goldberg, Vice-President and General Counsel, Levitt and Sons).
43. Arnold R. Hirsch, *Making the Second Ghetto: Race and Housing in Chicago, 1940–1960* (Cambridge: Cambridge University Press, 1983), 30–31; Richard R. W. Brooks, "Covenants without Courts: Enforcing Residential Segregation with Legally Unenforceable Agreements," *American Economic Review: Papers and Proceedings* 101 (2011): 360–365; Yana Kucheva and Richard Sander, "The Misunderstood Consequences of *Shelley v. Kraemer,*" April 5, 2010, draft on

file with the authors. See also David M. Cutler, Edward L. Glaeser, and Jacob Vigdor, "The Rise and Decline of the American Ghetto," *Journal of Political Economy* 107 (1999): 455–506, 487, concluding, from a study of minority housing cost prices over time, that coordinated collective action, including racial covenants, had effectively ghettoized minorities during the pre-*Shelley* period.

44. Helper, *Racial Policies,* 360–361, note 47.

9. Changing Games in the Twilight of Covenants

1. Rose Helper, *Racial Policies and Practices of Real Estate Brokers* (Minneapolis: University of Minneapolis Press, 1969) 90, 117–120; on the reluctance of "pioneers," see also U.S. Commission on Civil Rights, *Civil Rights U.S.A.: Housing in Washington, D.C.* (Washington, D.C.: Govt. Printing Office, 1962), 9–10 (testimony of sociologist George Grier); Stephen Grant Meyer, *As Long as They Don't Move Next Door: Segregation and Racial Conflict in American Neighborhoods* (Lanham, Md. and Oxford: Rowman and Littlefield, 2000), 221.
2. Amanda Irene Seligman, "'Apologies to Dracula, Werewolf, Frankenstein': White Homeowners and Blockbusters in Postwar Chicago," *Journal of the Illinois State Historical Society* 94 (2001): 70–95, 90, note 2, dates the first uses of "blockbusting" in the real estate context at 1954 and 1959, though the practices were much older; she dates the synonym "panic peddlar" to 1959. Ibid., 76, 91, and note 28.
3. Helper, *Racial Policies,* 127–128, 173, 177–178, 183, 256. See also Seligman, "'Apologies to Dracula,'" 75–77 on neighborhood hostility. Seligman also notes that Chicago's large apartment buildings were increasingly owned non-locally in the postwar period, making the owners less susceptible to neighborhood pressure.
4. Helper, *Racial Policies,* 90. One unconventional financing method was the installment land contract, which later became the subject of a mid-1960s lawsuit, described at length in Beryl Satter, *Family Properties: Race, Real Estate, and the Exploitation of Black Urban America* (New York: Henry Holt & Co., 2009).
5. Abraham Bell and Gideeon Parchomovsky, "The Integration Game," *Columbia Law Review* 100 (2000):1965–2029, 1991–1994.
6. Helper, *Racial Policies,* 175; Chester Rapkin & William Grigsby, *The Demand for Housing in Racially Mixed Areas: A Study of the Nature of Neighborhood Change.* (Berkeley and Los Angeles: University of California Press, 1960), 106–110. Henry Clark, *The Church and Residential Desegregation: A Case Study of an Open Housing Covenant* (New Haven, Conn.: College and University Press, 1965), 20–21, noted that white residents sometimes told fair housing

groups that "I couldn't do that to my neighbors." For the views about Jews, Satter, *Family Properties*, 71–72; see also Helper, *Racial Policies*, 173.

7. Bell and Parchomovsky, "Integration Game," 1991–1994. In addition to the "Resegregation Game" as the white neighbors' response to the entry of a minority neighbor, the authors also describe an Assurance Game and an Integration Game, in which the parties may remain (assurance) or definitely will stay (integration). They observe that falling property values may turn the Integration Game into the Resegregation Game, but they only very briefly allude to any possible role for covenants in any of these games. Id., 2004, 2024.
8. Helper, *Racial Policies*, 38, 360 (Broker N).
9. Ibid., 360.
10. Ibid., 98; compare Bell and Parchomovsky, "Integration Games," 1994–1995, arguing that changes in property values at least in theory should not affect Assurance Games. Actual experience appears to have differed, perhaps because of the destabilizing effects of larger numbers of players, differing individual preferences, and mixed strategies, discussed below.
11. Arnold R. Hirsch, *Making the Second Ghetto: Race and Housing in Chicago, 1940–1960* (Cambridge, Mass.: Cambridge University Press, 1983), 30–31
12. See Henry E. Smith, "The Language of Property: Form, Context, and Audience," *Stanford Law Review* 55 (2003): 1105–1191; for the inverse relationship between message intensity and size of audience, 1107–1108.
13. For signs, see Seligman, "'Apologies to Dracula,'" 73–74, 84; see also U.S. Commission on Civil Rights, *Hearings, Housing in Washington*, 397–398, testimony of Marvin Caplan about the effort of one Washington neighborhood to halt posting of Sold signs. For more on the possible use of Assurance Games to counter racial tipping, see Bell and Parchomovsky, "Integration Games," 1992 and passim.
14. Victor S. Navasky, "The Benevolent Quota," *Howard Law Journal* 6 (1960), 30–69, 35–36.
15. Morton Grodzins, *The Metropolitan Area as a Racial Problem* (Pittsburgh: University of Pittsburgh Press 1958), 6.
16. Thomas C. Schelling, *Micromotives and Macrobehavior* 140–55 (1978). Schelling also explored patterns of segregation that emerged when the populations were of different sizes and/or had differing preferences for like-race neighbors.
17. For Broker N, Helper, *Racial Policies* 360. For signers' percentages, Herman H. Long & Charles S. Johnson, *People vs. Property* (Nashville: Fisk University Press, 1947), 17–21; Wendy Plotkin, "Deeds of Mistrust: Race, Housing, and Restrictive Covenants" (Ph.D. diss., University of Illinois at Chicago, 1999), 19, 49; Wendy Plotkin, " 'Hemmed In:' The Struggle Against Racial Restrictive Covenants and Deed Restrictions in Post WWII Chicago," *Journal of the Illinois State Historican Society* 94 (2001): 39–69, 41.

18. Amanda I. Seligman, *Block by Block: Neighborhoods and Public Policy on Chicago's West Side* (Chicago and London: University of Chicago Press 2005), 154–159; Thomas J. Sugrue, "Crabgrass-Roots Politics: Race, Rights, and the Reaction against Liberalism in the Urban North, 1940–1964," *Journal of American History* 82 (1995) 551–576, 560; Douglas S. Massey and Nancy A. Denton, *American Apartheid: Segregation and the Making of the Underclass* (Cambridge:, Mass. Harvard University Press, 1993), 38. For similar tactics early in the twentieth century, see Thomas Lee Philpott, *The Slum and the Ghetto: Middle-Class Reform, Chicago, 1880–1930* (New York: Oxford University Press, 1978), 150.
19. Gerald Korngold, "The Emergence of Private Land Use Controls in Large-Scale Subdivisions: The Companion Story to *Village of Euclid v. Ambler Realty Co.*," *Case Western Law Review* 51 (2001): 617–644, 621, 638–39
20. Linmark Associates, Inc. v. Township of Willingboro, 431 U.S. 85 (1977), Brief of Amici Curiae The Cities of Shaker Heights, Ohio, and Cleveland Heights, Ohio, 3; see also Seligman, *Block by Block,* 204–205, noting that the prevalence of For Sale signs in a Chicago neighborhood was seen as a problem as early as 1960, and the subject of a campaign against them in the region a few years later.
21. Linmark Associates v. Willingboro, City of Oak Park Michigan Ordinance No. 0-73-24, in Brief of Amicus Curiae City of Oak Park Michigan, Appendix A, 27.
22. Linmark Associates v. Willingboro, 87; Brief for Respondents in Opposition, 2; see also Brief for the Petitioners, 4–5.
23. Linmark Associates v. Willingboro, 85; Brief for the Petitioners, 5, citing U.S.C.A. Joint Appendix at 179a–182a)
24. Linmark Associates v. Willingboro, Brief for the N.A.A.C.P. Legal Defense and Education Fund, Inc. As Amicus Curiae 2, 9 (emphasis in the original).
25. Justice Rehnquist did not participate in the case or the decision.
26. Linmark Associates v. Willingboro, 97.
27. Helper, *Racial Policies,* 298.
28. Linmark Associates v. Willingboro, 96–97.
29. Rapkin and Grigsby, *Demand for Housing in Racially Mixed Areas,* 54–55. The greater tolerance of renters is also noted in St. Clair Drake and Horace R. Cayton, *Black Metropolis: A Study of Negro Life in a Northern City* (New York: Harcourt, Brace & Co. 1945), 185.
30. See, e.g., Rapkin and Grigsby, *Demand for Housing in Racially Mixed Areas,* 70, note 6 (citing two studies of self-fulfilling prophecies).
31. Phyllis Palmer, *Living as Equals* (Nashville: Vanderbilt University Press, 2008), 96. Another area that attempted to remain stably integrated, in the face of

blockbuster pressure, was the Austin area in west Chicago. See Seligman, *Block by Block,* 183–207.

32. Palmer, *Living As Equals,* 118.
33. Ibid.,137–39.
34. Grodzins, *Metropolitan Area as a Racial Problem,* 7, 17. See also United States v. Starrett City Associates, 660 F. Supp. 668, 673–675 (E.D. N.Y.,1987), where expert witnesses noted estimates of tipping as low as 1 percent minority to as high as 60 percent, with typical tipping percentages estimated at 20 to 40 percent.
35. Helper, *Racial Policies,* 296–98, quoting James C. Downs, chairman of the Real Estate Research Corporation in Chicago.
36. See, e.g., Navasky, "Benevolent Quota," 30–69; Note (William F. Parker), "The Integration Ordinance: Honi Soit Qui Mal y Pense," *Stanford Law Review* 17 (1965):280–298; Alexander Bickel, *The Least Dangerous Branch: The Supreme Court at the Bar of Politics* (Indianapolis: Bobbs-Merrill, 1962), 64–65, 71.
37. U.S. v. Starrett City, 840 F.2d 1096 (2d Cir., 1988), certiorari denied 488 US 946 (1988). For further details about Starrett City, see the federal district court opinion, 660 F. Supp. 668, 670–677.
38. Brown v. Board of Education of Topeka, Shawnee County, Kan., 347 US 483 (1954).
39. Richard C. Baker, "Restrictive Covenant Cases Reviewed," *South Carolina Law Quarterly* 3 (1951) 351–65.
40. Reitman v. Mulkey, 387 U.S. 369 (1967), affirming Mulkey v. Reitman, 413 P. 2d 825 (1966), For a review of the two acts, see, e.g., Comment (Andrew DeMarco and Alan R. Freeman), "The Rumford Fair Housing Act Reviewed," *Southern California Law Review* 37 (1964): 427–451; for prominent contemporary commentary on the California and U.S. Supreme Court decisions, see Kenneth L. Karst and Harold W. Horowitz, "Reitman v. Mulkey, A Telophase of Substantive Due Process," 1967 *Supreme Court Review* 39–80; Charles L. Black, "The Supreme Court–Foreword," *Harvard Law Review* 81 (1967):69–109.
41. Fair Housing Act, 42 U.S.C. Secs 3601–3619. Later amendments added protections for the disabled. For the sections concerning discrimination, steering, and references to discrimination, Secs. 3604(a)–(d).
42. Jones v. Alfred H. Mayer Co., 392 U.S. 409 (1968). Joseph Lee Jones's suit against the real estate firm predated the Fair Housing Act and hence relied chiefly on the 1866 act. The plaintiff's lawyers in *Jones* also argued that discrimination in a large housing complex was state action, under the Fourteenth Amendment, a claim similar to the public takeover argument discussed in Chapter 7; 392 U.S. 449, note 1 (Harlan, dissenting), but the *Jones* Court did not address this issue. One interesting note: the arguments before the U.S. Supreme Court

occurred on April Fools' Day 1968. Later cases, relying on *Jones,* cited the Thirteenth Amendment as constitutional support for the Fair Housing Act; see, e.g., U.S. v. Bob Lawrence Realty, Inc., 474 F.2d 115, 120–121 (5th Cir. 1973), cert. denied 414 U.S. 826 (1973).

43. Sec. 3603(b). Sec. 3607 also created an exemption for religious organizations and private clubs in noncommercial transactions.
44. Fair Housing Act, Sec. 3604(e). The exact language now makes it unlawful "For profit, to induce or attempt to induce any person to sell or rent any dwelling by representations regarding the entry or prospective entry into the neighborhood of a person or persons of a particular race, color, religion, sex, handicap, familial status, or national origin."
45. Seligman, *Block by Block,* 162; Vernon Jarrett, "New Realty Law Has Hidden Intent," *Chicago Tribune,* Oct. 28, 1973, A3.
46. See Sheryl Cashin, *The Failures of Integration: How Race and Class are Undermining the American Dream* (New York: Public Affairs, 2004), 32–38 (giving recent examples of steering). For the expansion of African American housing, though still largely segregated, see Richard H. Sander, "Housing Segregation and Housing Integration: The Diverging Paths of Urban America," *University of Miami Law Review* 52 (1997): 977–1010, 977–979; Wendell E. Pritchett, "Where Shall We Live? Class and the Limitations of the Fair Housing Law," *Urban Lawyer* 35 (2003):399–470, 466–470; Massey & Denton, *American Apartheid,* 186–216.
47. For changes in stated preferences for integration, Cashin, *Failures of Integration,* 11–12.

10. Conclusion

1. For the breach-in-the-dike effect, Colin Gordon, *Mapping Decline: St. Louis and the Fate of the American City* (Philadelphia: University of Pennsylvania Press, 2008), 73; Robert C. Weaver, *The Negro Ghetto* (New York: Russell & Russell, 1948), 234–235.
2. United States v. Starrett City Assn., 840 F.2d 1096 (2d Cir., 1988); certiorari denied 488 US 946 (1988).
3. As we noted in the last chapter, cooperative housing is organized formally on a landlord-tenant model, with the entire association as landlord; this effectively operates on a neighbor consent-model, but as landlords, cooperative housing boards are also subject to the Fair Housing Act's prohibition of racial discrimination.
4. "The American Council Blunders," *Chicago Defender,* December 8, 1945, 14. For another and slightly earlier version of Weaver's idea, see S. I. Hayakawa's column. "Second Thoughts," *Chicago Defender,* July 14, 1945, 13. Hayakawa

proposed covenants against liquor establishments and property deterioration, as well as "covenants that would protect a community from ill-mannered and noisy and irresponsible people of all races." For Oakland/Kenwood "conservation agreements," Arnold R. Hirsch, *Making the Second Ghetto: Race and Housing in Chicago, 1940–1960* (Cambridge: Cambridge University Press, 1983), 38–39.

5. Probably the most cited and most discussed case on exclusionary zoning is Southern Burlington NAACP v. Township of Mount Laurel, 336 A.2d 713 (N.J. 1975), appeal dismissed and certiori denied, 423 U.S, 808 (1975).
6. See, e.g., Robert C. Ellickson, "New Institutions for Old Neighborhoods," *Duke Law Journal* 48 (1998): 75–110 (1998).
7. Sam Roberts, "Metro Matters: Public Housing Finds a Friend in a Safeguard," *New York Times,* Sept. 12, 1988, B1.
8. R. Bruce Dold and Thomas M. Burton, "Thompson Signs Home Equity Bill; Groups Prepare Petition Push for Referendum," *Chicago Tribune,* July 14, 1988, 1 (Illinois bill, opposition); Dirk Johnson, "Plan to Insure Home Value Brings Chicago Racial Rift," *New York Times,* Feb. 9, 1988, A18 ("black insurance"). For other jurisdictions, Roberts, "Metro Matters"; Kate Coscarelli, "Diversity is Aim of Land Plan; Two Essex Towns May Assure Equity," Newark (New Jersey) *Star-Ledger,* Feb. 16, 1999, 1. For academic interest in Oak Park's plan, Lee Anne Fennell and Julie Roin, "Controlling Residential Stakes," *University of Chicago Law Review* 77 (2010): 143–176, 156–57 and authorities cited therein; Abraham Bell and Gideon Parchomowvski, "The Integration Game," *Columbia Law Review* 100 (2000): 1965–2029, 2005–2009; William A. Fischel, "Voting, Risk Aversion, and the Nimby Syndrome: A Comment on Robert Nelson's 'Privatizing the Neighborhood,'" *George Mason Law Review* 7 (1999): 881–903, 886–89.
9. Sheryll Cashin, *The Failures of Integration: How Race and Class Are Undermining the American Dream* (New York: Public Affairs, 2004), 43–57.
10. For various suggestions about lowering homeowner stakes, see A. Mechele Dickerson, "The Myth of Home Ownership and Why Home Ownership is Not Always a Good Thing," *Indiana Law Journal* 84: (2009) 189–237; Lee Anne Fennell, *The Unbounded Home: Property Values Beyond Property Lines* (New Haven: Yale University Press, 2009). See also Stephanie M. Stern, "Reassessing the Citizen Virtues of Homeownership," *Columbia Law Review* 111: (2011) 890–938, 905–906, 931–32 citing the "dark side" of homeownership commitment and questioning the social value of homeowner assistance programs.
11. See, e.g., Susan Welch, Lee Sigelman, Timothy Bledsoe, and Michael Combs, *Race and Place: Race Relations in and American City* (Cambridge, New York: Cambridge University Press, 2001), 159–160, noting "softening" of Detroit whites' attitudes about residential integration and preference of both whites

and nonwhites for integrated neighborhoods—though with quite different views of what integration means.

12. For one such assertion that recording deeds is state action, Milton L. McGhee and Ann Fagan Ginger, "The House I Live In: A Study of Housing for Minorities," *Cornell Law Quarterly* 46 (1960–61): 194–257, 242.
13. For postwar violence and its impact, Stephen Grant Meyer, *As Long As They Don't Move Next Door: Segregation and Racial Conflict in American Neighborhoods* (Lanham, Md., Oxford: Rowman & Littlefield, 2000), 80, 116–129, 220–229; Leonard S. Rubinowitz and Imani Perry, "Crimes Without Punishment: White Neighbors' Resistance to Black Entry," *Journal of Criminal Law and Criminology* 92 (2002): 335–428. For stink bombs among other forms of harassment and violence, Herman H. Long & Charles S. Johnson, *People vs. Property* (Nashville: Fisk University Press 1947), 73–85.
14. 42 U.S.C. sec 3604 (c). Later amendments added familial status and handicap to the protected categories.
15. Mayers v. Ridley, 465 F.2d 630 (D.C. Cir. 1972), reversing Mayers v. Ridley, 330 F. Supp., 447 (D.C. D.C. 1971). For the cited deed restrictions, 465 F.2d 631, note 2. For reference to brokers and title insurers, Mayers v. Ridley, 330 F. Supp. 449.
16. The opinion by Judge Wright (speaking for four judges) viewed the recorder's acts as a violation not only of the Fair Housing Act but also as unconstitutional state action. Judge Wilkey's opinion (speaking for three judges) agreed on the statutory basis but found it unnecessary to reach the constitutional question. Judge Tamm's dissent (agreed to by all three dissenters) inserted his earlier opinion, in which he had upheld the trial court's ruling against the plaintiffs on both statutory and constitutional grounds. Judge McKinnon filed an additional dissent.
17. 465 F.2d 640 (Wright), 653 (Wilkie).
18. Woodward v. Bowers, 630 F.Supp 1205 (E.D. Pa. 1986). In *Mayers*, the dissenting opinion by Judge McKinnon had pointed out that some racial covenants were obvious whereas others were much more obscure, and thus burdensome for the recorder to interpret; he may have been thinking of deed clauses that referred to other recorded encumbrances without repeating their language. 645 F.2d 661. The Woodward covenant was of this type—the recorded deed did not include racial restrictions on its face, but it referred to some 1924 subdivision restrictions that included a prohibition on sales to African Americans.
19. Thomas Schelling, *The Strategy of Conflict* (Oxford, New York: Oxford University Press, 1963), 144; Chicago Lawyers' Committee for Civil Rights Under Law v. Craigslist, Inc., 519 F.3d 666 (7th Cir. 2008).

20. Mayers v Ridley, 465 F.2d 642, note 14 (Wright opinion); 646 (Wilkey opinion) (references to Justice Department pressure); Letter of Assistant Attorney Jerris Leonard, Civil Rights Division, Department of Justice, to the president of The Title Guaranty Company, Nov. 29, 1969.
21. Bradley v. City of Richmond, 338 F. Supp. 67, at 73 (D.C. Va., 1972) referring to the Lawyers Title Insurance Company's practice of including racial covenants in Richmond title abstracts. The Justice Department's letter noted above had referred to that firm, and to its assent to the request to remove offending language. For the Milwaukee area, telephone interview by Richard Brooks and Carol Rose of Leonard Rubinowitz, November 1, 2011. For Seattle, Lornet Turnbull, "Homeowners Find Records Still Hold Blot of Racism," *Seattle Times,* June 3, 2005, A1 (quoting homeowners' association lawyer Peter Eglick).
22. Telephone interview by Richard Brooks with Marvin C. Bowling, retired attorney and past president of the Lawyers Title Company, Sept. 1, 2010.
23. Brooks interview with Bowling. Readers may wish to note these interests are technically "possibilities of reverters." See Chapter 4.
24. Ibid. (practice of dropping reference to or flagging reversions as illegal); Capitol Savings & Loan Assn. v. Smith, 316 P. 2d 252, 254 (Colo. 1957) (Colorado case treating racial reversions as ordinary covenants); for another case where a lower court ignored the covenant/reversion distinction, Clifton v. Puente, 218 S.W.2d 272 (Tex. Civ. App. 1949). The *Clifton* case involved a covenant against Mexican Americans.
25. For Florida, see *Florida Statutes Annotated,* sec. 689.18; Biltmore Village v. Royal, 71 So. 2d 727 (Fla. 1954); J. C. Vereen & Sons, Inc., v. City of Miami, 397 So.2d 979 (Fla. 3d DCA 1981). For other states, see William F. Fratcher, "A Modest Proposal for Trimming the Claws of Legal Future Interests, *Duke Law Journal* 1972: 517–555, 527–531; Ronald C. Link and Kimberly A. Licata, "Perpetuities Reform in North Carolina: The Uniform Statutory Rule Against Perpetuities, Nondonative Transfers, and Honorary Trusts," *North Carolina Law Review* 74 (1996): 1783–1841, 1802.
26. Jonathan Entin, "Defeasible Fees, State Action, and the Legacy of Massive Resistance," *William and Mary Law Review* 34 (1993) 769–800, 791.
27. 330 F. Supp. 448.
28. Cal. Gov't Code sec. 12596.2.
29. For an example of difficult requirements for amending CC&Rs, see U.S. v. University Oaks Civic Club, 653 F. Supp. 1469, 1472–73 (S.D. Tex 1987).
30. Cal. Civ. Code sec. 1352.5 (homeowners' associations' duties to remove discriminatory provisions from documents). For other states, Wash. Rev. Code Ann. 49.60.227 Colo. Rev. Stat. Ann. 38-30-169-170. Mo. Ann. Stat. sec 213.041;

neighboring Kansas has similar legislation: Kan. Stat. Ann. sec 44 1017a (b)–(c). Ohio puts the burden of eradication on the recorder's office: Ohio Rev. Code Ann. 5309.281, 5309.33.

31. 330 F.Supp. 448.
32. Julian Walker, "$4,500 Awarded in Bias Lawsuit; Chesterfield Man Refused to Sell His Home to Black Woman," *Richmond Times-Dispatch,* Dec. 9, 2005, Area/State section. The defendant was also required to pay $7,500 to the equal housing organization that had worked with the plaintiff.

Acknowledgments

We have many debts to many people for their assistance on this book and on the scholarly articles that preceded it. Some parts of this book rely on previously published articles and book chapters, and we are grateful to the publishers for permission to use them here. Those are Carol M. Rose's "Shelley v. Kraemer," in *Property Stories,* ed. Gerald Korngold and Andrew P. Morriss (2d ed., New York: Foundation Press, 2009), in Chapters 2–7; Richard R. W. Brooks's "Incorporating Race," *Columbia Law Review* 106 (2006): 2023–2094, in Chapter 3; and Richard R. W. Brooks's "Covenants without Courts: Enforcing Residential Segregation with Legally Unenforceable Agreements," *American Economic Review: Papers and Proceedings* 101 (2011): 360–365, in Chapter 8.

We have also received generous grant support for this work, principally from the Yale Law School and the University of Arizona Rogers College of Law, but also from the Straus Institute for the Advanced Study of Law and Justice at New York University. Research librarians have played a major role too: John Nann, Margaret Chisholm, and Ryan Harrington at Yale; Maureen Garmon and Cindy Hirsch at the University of Arizona; and Marcia Lehr at Northwestern University

We seem to have talked and workshopped and given speeches about various parts of this opus all over creation, and we have received vast numbers of useful suggestions and critiques at all of them: at our home bases at Yale Law School and the University of Arizona Law College, of course, but also (in alphabetical order) the annual meetings of the American Economic Association, the American Law and Economics Association, and the American Society for Legal History; the Arizona State University Law School, Columbia Law School, Duke Law School, George Mason University Law School, Harvard Law School, Lewis and Clark Law School, Loyola of Los Angeles Law School, New York University Law School,

Princeton Program on Law and Public Affairs, Stanford Law School, the Straus Institute at New York University, the University of Auckland Law School, UC Berkeley Law School, UCLA Law School, the University of Colorado, the University of Hawai'i, the University of North Carolina Law School, and the University of Virginia Law School.

There are of course individuals at these and other institutions who have been especially generous with their comments, suggestions, and references to other work: Bruce Ackerman, Margo Bagley, Michael Blumm, Marvin C. Bowling, Al Brophy, Ed Brunet, Grainne de Burca, Bo Burt, Jack Chin, Albert Choi, Ronald Coase, William Collins, Meier Dan-Cohen, Adrienne Davis, Drew Days, John Donohue, Robert Ellickson, Lee Fennell, Price Fishback, Janice Fridie, Clayton Gillette, Vick Goldberg, Risa Goluboff, Daniel Hulsebosch, Douglas Kysar, Daryl Levinson, Steve Levitt, Toni Massaro, Bill McAuliffe, Tracy Meares, Tom Merrill, Barak Orbach, John Parry, Claire Priest, Andrzej Rapaczynski, Judith Resnik, George Rutherglen, Richard Sander, Richard Schragger, Peter Schuck, Alan Schwartz, Daniel Sharfstein, Reva Siegel, Fred Smith, Henry Smith, Avi Soifer, Jeremy Waldron, Joseph Weiler, Jay Weiser, Kenji Yoshino, and Eric Zoltz. Our wonderful Harvard University Press editor, Elizabeth Knoll, guided us past many confusions and graciously egged us on. We owe particular thanks to four people for sharing their own research with us: Phyllis Palmer, Jeffrey Gonda, Len Rubinowitz, and most especially Wendy Plotkin, whose terrific book on Chicago's racially restrictive covenants we hope to see in print.

We have had wonderful research assistants too, and among those who were particularly helpful on this project we would like to mention Elizabeth Black, Ida Araya Brumskine, Hal Frampton, Valerie Jaffee, Nicole Beeskow Johnson, Adam Kirschner, Craig J. Konnoth, Jake Lillywhite, Levi Pinsky, Michael Soules, Chris Stevens, and for his assistance on the index, Travers Brooks. On a more personal front, we have to acknowledge the enormous patience and encouragement of Sylvia Tesh and Heidi Brooks.

This is by no means an exclusive list, and we have undoubtedly neglected to mention some of the very large number of people who assisted us on this project. We profoundly hope that they will attribute this lapse to our dizziness at getting the parts of this project together, because we do sincerely appreciate all the many contributions of friends and colleagues along the way.

Index